Business
Vocabulary in Use

Advanced

Bill Mascull

CAMBRIDGE UNIVERSITY PRESS
Cambridge, New York, Melbourne, Madrid, Cape Town,
Singapore, São Paulo, Delhi, Mexico City

Cambridge University Press
The Edinburgh Building, Cambridge CB2 8RU, UK

www.cambridge.org
Information on this title: www.cambridge.org/9780521749404

First published 2010
5th printing 2013

Printed in Poland by Opolgraf

A catalogue record for this book is available from the British Library

ISBN 978-0-521-749404 Edition with answers and CD-ROM
ISBN 978-0-521-128292 Edition with answers

Contents

INTRODUCTION   8

THE HUMAN DIMENSION

1 Job satisfaction   10

A My work is so rewarding
B I like the teamwork
C I like the perks

2 Management styles 1   12

A Motivation 1
B Motivation 2
C Theory X and Theory Y

3 Management styles 2   14

A Hygiene factors
B Motivator factors
C Empowerment

4 Employment and employability   16

A Outsourcing
B Employability
C Freelancers and portfolio workers

5 Flexibility and inflexibility   18

A Ways of working
B Job flexibility
C Job protection

6 Work–life balance   20

A Stress
B The causes of stress
C Quality of life

7 Managing talent 1   22

A Talent
B Recruiting talent
C Managing talent

8 Managing talent 2   24

A Talent management 1
B Talent management 2
C Mentoring and coaching

9 Team building   26

A Teams
B Team players
C Stages of team life

10 The right skills   28

A Hard and soft skills
B Emotional intelligence 1
C Emotional intelligence 2

11 Equality and diversity   30

A Equality
B Diversity
C Word combinations with 'diversity'

QUALITY

12 What is quality?   32

A Quality in manufacturing
B Quality in services
C Widening the definition of quality

13 Quality standards   34

A Standards and certification
B ISO 9000 and others

14 Quality and people   36

A Investors in People
B The EFQM Excellence Model

15 Striving for perfection   38

A Benchmarking and best practice
B Six Sigma quality

COMPETITIVE STRATEGY

16 Strategic thinking   40
A Strategy
B Word combinations with 'strategic'
C Companies and markets

17 Competition   42
A Competition
B 'Competing' and 'competitive'

18 Companies and their industries   44
A Competitive forces
B SWOT analysis
C Be good at something

19 Key strategic issues   46
A Industries and their players
B Mergers and acquisitions (M&A)
C Make or buy?

20 Innovation   48
A Innovation and the development process
B Pioneers and followers
C Shakeout and consolidation

21 Preparing for the future   50
A Scenario planning
B Futurology
C Risk management

MARKETING

22 The four Ps and beyond   52
A The four Ps
B Three more Ps

23 Customer satisfaction   54
A The four Cs
B Customer expectations
C Customer dissatisfaction

24 Knowing your customers 1   56
A Market intelligence and market research
B Research stages
C Marketing plans

25 Knowing your customers 2   58
A Segmentation
B Customer groups
C New technologies, new concerns

26 Knowing your customers 3   60
A Data and databases
B Customer relationship management

27 Brands and branding   62
A Brand equity
B Brand positioning and differentiation
C Brand stretching

28 Global brands   64
A Steps abroad 1
B Steps abroad 2
C Think global, act local?

LOGISTICS

29 Supply chain management   66
A Manufacturing
B Vertical integration
C Retailing

30 Logistics   68
A Logistics
B Word combinations with 'logistical'
C Reverse logistics

31 Outsourcing and offshoring   70
A Outsourcing
B Business process outsourcing
C Offshoring

THE INTERNET AND ITS USES

32 The evolving Web 1   72
  A Broadband Internet
  B Mobile Internet
  C Moore's law

33 The evolving Web 2   74
  A Web 2.0
  B Keeping in touch
  C Website attractiveness

34 Knowledge and the Internet   76
  A Knowledge creation
  B Intranets
  C Global communities

35 Internet security   78
  A Attack and defence
  B Cybercrime
  C Privacy and confidentiality

36 Internet selling   80
  A E-commerce
  B B2C
  C B2B

37 Intellectual property   82
  A Downloading
  B Copyright infringement
  C Digital rights management

COMPANY FINANCE

38 Financial performance   84
  A Finance
  B Financial reporting
  C The financial year
  D Shareholders, bondholders and lenders

39 Profit and loss account   86
  A Accruals accounting
  B Profit and loss
  C Earnings

40 Balance sheet 1   88
  A Assets
  B Depreciation

41 Balance sheet 2   90
  A Liabilities
  B Shareholders' equity

42 Cashflow statement   92
  A Cash inflows and outflows
  B Types of cashflow

43 Comparing performance   94
  A Profit and profitability
  B Investment ratios
  C Return on equity
  D Leverage

44 Shareholder value   96
  A Yield
  B Price–earnings ratio
  C Maximizing shareholder value

45 Accounting standards   98
  A Audits and their transparency
  B International standards

BOOM AND BUST

46 The business cycle   100
  A Key indicators
  B The business cycle
  C Boom and bust

47 Bursting bubbles   102
  A Bubbles
  B The credit crunch
  C The real economy

CORPORATE RESPONSIBILITY

48 Corporate social
responsibility   104
- A Ethics
- B Accountability and transparency
- C Corporate social responsibility

49 Social reporting   106
- A Social reporting
- B Word combinations with 'social'
- C Labour standards

50 Green issues   108
- A Environmental damage
- B Eco-friendly products
- C Recycling

51 Climate change   110
- A Global warming
- B Carbon management
- C Carbon trading
- D Carbon capture

52 Corporate governance   112
- A Board organization
- B Separation of roles
- C Rewards for success (and failure)

53 Ethical investment   114
- A Activist shareholders
- B Controversial products
- C Socially responsible investment

THE GLOBAL ECONOMY

54 Globalization   116
- A Paths to prosperity
- B GDP and GNI
- C Globalizing trends

55 Investment and debt   118
- A Direct investment
- B Borrowing
- C Word combinations with 'debt'

56 Trade   120
- A Dismantling the barriers
- B Protected industries
- C Fair trade

57 The BRIC economies   122
- A Emerging economies
- B Similarities
- C Differences

58 International aid   124
- A Humanitarian aid
- B Development aid
- C The aims of aid

59 Sustainable development   126
- A Sustainability
- B New technologies
- C The triple bottom line

INTERCULTURAL ISSUES

60 Intercultural teams   128

  A   Cultural issues
  B   International teams

61 Intercultural meetings   130

  A   Meeting preparation
  B   Cultural preparation
  C   Running the meeting

62 Intercultural networking   132

  A   The right attitude
  B   Good etiquette
  C   Business cards

WRITING

63 Business writing 1   134

  A   CVs
  B   Job enquiry

64 Business writing 2   136

  A   Invitation
  B   Acknowledgement

65 Business writing 3   138

  A   Outlines
  B   Openings and introductions
  C   Describing visuals

66 Business writing 4   140

  A   Linking ideas
  B   Forecasts

Answer key   142

Index   161

Introduction

Who is this book for?

Business Vocabulary in Use Advanced builds on the success of *Business Vocabulary in Use Intermediate*. It is designed to help advanced learners of business English to improve their business vocabulary. It is for people studying English before they start work and for those already working who need English in their job.

The emphasis is on language related to today's important, and sometimes controversial, business issues.

You can use the book on your own for self-study, or with a teacher in the classroom, one-to-one or in groups.

How is the book organized?

The book has 66 two-page units. The first 59 of these are **thematic** and look at the vocabulary of business areas such as human resources, quality, strategy, logistics, IT, marketing, finance, corporate responsibility and the global economy.

There are then three units which focus on the language of the **skills** needed for doing business across cultures. The final four units develop business writing skills.

The left-hand page of each unit explains new words and expressions, and the right-hand page allows you to check and develop your understanding of the words and expressions, and how they are used through a series of exercises.

There is **cross-referencing** between units to show connections between the same word or similar words used in different contexts.

There is an **Answer key** at the back of the book. Most of the exercises have questions with only one correct answer. But some of the exercises, including the **Over to you** activities at the end of each unit (see below), are designed for writing and/or discussion about yourself and your own organization or one that you know.

There is also an **Index**. This lists all the new words and phrases which are introduced in the book and gives the unit numbers where the words and phrases appear. The Index also tells you how the words and expressions are pronounced.

The left-hand page

This page introduces new vocabulary and expressions for each thematic or skills area. The presentation is divided into a number of sections indicated by letters: A, B, C, etc., with simple, clear titles.

⊙ In this second edition of *Business Vocabulary in Use Advanced*, explicit reference is made to the business material in the **Cambridge International Corpus (CIC)** – business pages of newspapers, business textbooks, and business meetings and discussions. The texts are stored in a database, which is searchable in various ways to reveal the patterns of business usage. The database has been exploited to identify typical word combinations found in the data, and there are notes about their relative frequency.

As well as explanations of vocabulary, there is information about typical word combinations. Again, the CIC has been a prime source of information about these.

There are notes on the relative frequency of different words, for example:

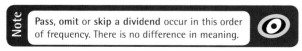

Note | **Pass, omit** or **skip a dividend** occur in this order of frequency. There is no difference in meaning. ⊙

There are notes about differences between British and American English, for example:

> **Note**
> BrE: labour; AmE: labor
> BrE: trade unions; AmE: labor unions

The right-hand page

The exercises on the right-hand page give practice in using the new vocabulary and expressions presented on the left-hand page. In gap-filling exercises, four-centimetre writing lines indicate that more than one word is needed to complete at least one of the gaps in the exercise; two-centimetre writing lines indicate that one word only is needed in each gap. Some units contain diagrams to complete or crosswords.

'Over to you' sections

An important feature of *Business Vocabulary in Use Advanced* is the **Over to you** section at the end of each unit. There are sometimes alternative **Over to you** sections for learners who are in work and for those who are studying pre-work. The **Over to you** sections give you the chance to put into practice the words and expressions in the unit in relation to your own professional situation, studies or opinions.

Self-study learners can do the section as a written activity.

In the classroom, the **Over to you** sections can be used as the basis for discussion with the whole class, or in small groups with a spokesperson for each summarizing the discussion and its outcome for the class. The teacher can then get students to look again at exercises relating to points that have caused difficulty. Students can follow up by using the **Over to you** section as a written activity, for example as homework.

The Answer key now contains sample answers for the **Over to you** questions.

How to use the book for self-study

Find the topic you are looking for by using the Contents page or the Index. Read through the explanations on the left-hand page of the unit. Do the exercises on the right-hand page. Check your answers in the Answer key. If you have made some mistakes, go back and look at the explanations and the exercise again. Note down important words and expressions in your notebook.

How to use the book in the classroom

Teachers can choose units that relate to their students' particular needs and interests, for example areas they have covered in coursebooks, or that have come up in other activities. Alternatively, lessons can contain a regular vocabulary slot, where students look systematically at the vocabulary of particular thematic or skills areas.

Students can work on the units in pairs, with the teacher going round the class assisting and advising. Teachers should get students to think about the logical process of the exercises, pointing out why one answer is possible and the others are not (where this is the case).

CD-ROM

This second edition of *Business Vocabulary in Use Advanced* is available in two versions. You can either use the book on its own or with the CD-ROM, a major innovation. This includes an audio file for every key word and expression in the book, with its pronunciation and an example sentence. In addition, there are two extra exercises for each unit of the book, thirteen summary tests so you can check your progress, and even some vocabulary games.

We hope you enjoy using *Business Vocabulary in Use Advanced*.

1 Job satisfaction

A My work is so rewarding

'I work in advertising. I love my work! It's really **rewarding** and **stimulating** – satisfying and interesting. **Originality** and **creativity** are very important in this industry, of course; we have to **come up with** – produce – lots of new ideas.

'**No two days are the same.** I could be contacting film companies for new advertising campaigns one day and giving client presentations the next. I like the **client contact** and I am very much **hands-on** – involved with the productive work of the agency rather than managing it.

'When I joined the agency, I **hit it off with** my colleagues immediately. I still **get on well with** them and there's a very good **rapport** between us. This is all part of my **job satisfaction**.'

B I like the teamwork

'I'm an aircraft engineer. I work on research and development of new aircraft. I love **putting ideas into practice.** I like **working on my own,** but it's also great being part of a team. I like the **teamwork** (see Unit 9) and the **sense of achievement** when we do something new. And of course, the planes we produce are very beautiful.

'Is there anything I don't like? I dislike days when I'm **chained to a desk**. I don't like **admin** and **paperwork.** Sometimes I feel I'm **snowed under** – there's so much to do I don't know how to deal with it. And in a large organization like ours, there can be a lot of **bureaucracy** or **red tape** – rigid procedures – that can slow things down.'

C I like the perks

'I'm in luxury goods sales. I have some nice **perks,** like a company car. I have to meet demanding sales targets every month, so the work can be very **stressful** (see Unit 6). But I enjoy the **flexibility** that I have in working when I want to without **someone breathing down my neck** all the time. Unlike my husband, who has to travel into London every day, I don't have to **commute** to an office – I'm out seeing clients most of the time. My boss allows me to **telecommute** – I can **work from home** when I'm not seeing clients. I only get two weeks a year **vacation time**. If there's a family emergency, I can take **time off** without having to ask my boss. I work quite **long hours** – about 60 hours a week – but I enjoy my job.'

Note

BrE: holiday
AmE: vacation

1.1 Complete the sentences with expressions from A opposite.

1 Work that is satisfying and interesting is .... and
....

2 If you spend time with customers, you have ....

3 If you have a good working relationship with your colleagues, you ....
them.

4 If you do the actual work of the organization rather than being a manager, you are
....

5 If you want to say that work is not repetitious, you can say '..'.

6 .... and .... are when you have new and
effective ideas that people have not had before.

1.2 The aircraft engineer talks about his work. Complete his statements with expressions from B opposite.

1 I don't always like working with other people. I like ....

2 It's great to see what I learnt during my engineering course at university being applied in
actual designs. I like ....

3 I hate it when there is a big stack of documents and letters on my desk that I have to deal
with. I don't like .... and ....

4 I love the .... when we all work together to create something new.

5 It's rare, but sometimes when I come into the office and see a huge pile of work waiting for
me, I feel ....

6 When we see a new plane fly for the first time, we all feel a great ....

7 I get frustrated when you have to get permission to spend anything over £50. I don't like
.... and ....

1.3 Look at C opposite. Put four of the headings in the correct places in this article.

Commuting	Hours worked	Stress	Telecommuting	Time off	Vacation time

Most satisfied employees work longer

People who are satisfied on the job have the best perks in areas you might expect, but they actually put in longer hours than less satisfied employees, according to a new survey. Workers who expressed satisfaction at work had substantially better conditions across the board, with easier unscheduled time off and better telecommuting options.

Satisfaction vs. (1) ....

There are a lot of workers who are both stressed and extremely satisfied. Forty per cent of respondents in the most satisfied category said they were above the average in feeling stress, according to the study. But that number jumped to over half of respondents in less satisfied categories.

(2) ....

The distance people travelled to work wasn't as correlated to stress and satisfaction as most other categories. The most satisfied workers did have the shortest journeys – 85 per cent reported under an hour. But that category had almost as many journeys of over two hours as others.

(3) ....

The hours category showed a real shocker – that extremely satisfied employees are putting in a lot more time at work than others. They worked 56 hours a week on average – 11 hours more than the least satisfied group.

(4) ....

Overall, 16 per cent of respondents said they could work from home any time they pleased, 28 per cent could do so with their manager's approval and 55 per cent were not allowed to. Satisfied workers had more work-from-home options than other respondents, with only 38 per cent saying that this was never an option.

Over to you

Talk about your own job, or one you would like to have, in relation to the headings in the article above.

2 Management styles 1

A Motivation 1

Yolanda is a senior manager of a car rental firm:

'I believe that all our employees can find **satisfaction** in what they do. We give them **responsibility** – the idea that the decisions they take have a direct impact on our success – and encourage them to **use their initiative** – they don't have to ask me about every decision they make. My style of management is **participative** – employees take part in the **decision-making process**. They are given a sense of **empowerment** (see Unit 3).

'We hope this feeling of empowerment gives employees the feeling that they are **valued** – with management knowing the effort they make. We believe that all this leads to a higher sense of **motivation** – interest, enthusiasm and energy – among employees. When everyone feels motivated, **morale** is good and there is a general feeling of **well-being** in the organization. This leads to improved **job satisfaction**.'

B Motivation 2

Xavier is a factory manager:

'I don't believe in all this talk about motivation. My **subordinates** – the people **working under me** – are basically lazy. They need constant **supervision** – we have to check what they are doing all the time. Some people think this is **authoritarian**, but I think it's the only way of managing. There have to be clear rules of **discipline** – you have to be able to tell subordinates what is right and wrong, with a consistent set of **disciplinary procedures**.

'Decisions must be **imposed** from above without **consultation** – we don't discuss decisions with workers, we just tell them what to do.'

> **Note** **Subordinate** is very formal and can be negative. It is much less frequent than **employee**.

C Theory X and Theory Y

Xavier believes in what the US management thinker Douglas McGregor in *The Human Side of Enterprise* called **Theory X** – the idea that people dislike work and will do everything they can to avoid it.

Yolanda believes in **Theory Y** – the more advanced view that, given the right conditions, everyone has the potential to find satisfaction in work.

2.1 Yolanda's employees are talking about her management style (see A opposite). Replace each underlined item with an expression from A, keeping the rest of the sentence as it is. Pay attention to the grammatical context. The first one has been done as an example.

1 She knows exactly what's involved in our jobs. She makes us feel <u>she understands the effort we make</u>. *valued*
2 She encourages us to <u>do things without asking her first</u>.
3 <u>The feeling among employees</u> here is very good. We feel really <u>involved and want</u> to work towards the company's goals.
4 We have a real sense of <u>the idea that our efforts are important for the success of the company</u>.
5 We have a real sense of <u>liking what we do and feeling good when we achieve specific goals</u> in our work.

2.2 Look at B and C opposite. Read the text and answer the questions.

> McGregor's ideas about managerial behaviour had a profound effect on management thinking and practice. His ideas give a frame of reference for managerial practice. His Theory Y principles influenced the design and implementation of personnel policies and practices. Today they continue to influence participative styles of management and the continued practice of staff performance appraisal – the evaluation of employees' work.
>
> McGregor defined theories that he felt underpinned the practices and attitudes of managers in relation to employees. These were evident from their conversations and actions. The two sets of ideas were called Theories X and Y. McGregor was saying that what managers said or exhibited in their behaviour revealed their theories-in-use. These led managers to pursue particular kinds of policies and relationships with employees. Regrettably, McGregor's Theory Y was interpreted and promoted as a 'one-best-way', i.e. Y is the best! Managers or aspects of their behaviour became labelled as Theory X, the bad stereotype, and Theory Y, the good. McGregor's ideas were much informed by Abraham Maslow's model of motivation. People's needs provide the driving force which motivates behaviour. Maslow's ideas suggested that worker dissatisfaction with work was due not to something intrinsic to workers but to poor job design, managerial behaviour and too few opportunities for job satisfaction.

1 What have the long-term effects of McGregor's thinking been, according to the article?
2 Which factors reveal whether a manager believes more in Theory X or Theory Y?
3 Name two things that result from these factors.
4 Did McGregor think that Theory X or Theory Y represented the best way of doing things?
5 Who influenced McGregor's thinking? What did this thinker believe to be the main factor in determining people's behaviour?
6 Is employee dissatisfaction due to something within employees themselves, according to this thinker? Why? / Why not?

Over to you

Write a memo to the head of your organization or one you would like to work for, suggesting ways to encourage initiative among employees.

3 Management styles 2

Hygiene factors

Yolanda, the car rental manager we met in the previous unit, went on a management course. She looked at the work of Frederick Herzberg*, who studied what motivates employees. Here are the notes she took:

> Some aspects of work can lead to **dissatisfaction** if they are not at a high enough standard. These are what Herzberg calls the **hygiene factors**:
>
> **supervision** – the way employees are managed
>
> **policy** – the overall purpose and goals of the organization
>
> **working conditions** – the place where you work, hours worked, etc.
>
> **salary**
>
> **peer relationships** – how you relate to and work with others on the same level of the organization
>
> **security** – level of confidence about the future of your job

B Motivator factors

> Other aspects of work can give positive satisfaction. These are the **motivator factors**:
>
> **achievement** – the feeling that you have been successful in reaching your goals
>
> **recognition** – the feeling that your employers understand and value what you do by giving **positive feedback**, which means telling you what a good job you are doing
>
> **the work itself** – the nature and interest of the job
>
> **responsibility** – when you are in charge of something and its success or failure
>
> **advancement** – how far you will be promoted in the organization and/or how far you will go up the **career ladder**
>
> **personal growth** – how you develop personally in your work, and your opportunities to do this

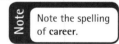

Note | Note the spelling of **career**.

C Empowerment

Now look at the more recent idea of **empowerment** (see Unit 2).

> **Empowerment** is the idea that decisions, where possible, should be made by employees who are close to the issues or problems to be solved, without having to **consult** their managers further up the **hierarchy**. In other words, managers have to **delegate** as much as possible. **Delegation** is one of the keys to employees being **empowered** in this way. Also, organizations become less **hierarchical**, with fewer management levels.

*Work and the Nature of Man, 'One More Time: How Do You Motivate Employees?' Harvard Business Review, 2008.

3.1 Look at this job advertisement. Match the underlined items (1–6) with the hygiene factors in A opposite.

Duval and Smith

Legal Translator English–French

Paris (1) €50,000

Large Anglo–French law firm seeks legal translator to translate and correct French and English legal documents. Legal qualifications and experience essential.

Based in the firm's busy translation department, you will work **(2)** under the head of translation **(3)** as part of a team of five translators **(4)** in line with the overall policies of the firm.

You will work **(5)** a 35-hour week, with a **(6)** one-year contract in the first instance.

Email CV to jmartin@duvalandsmith.fr

3.2 Vanessa Holt got the job in the advertisement in 3.1 above. Three months later, she writes an email to a friend. Complete the gaps in the email using expressions from B opposite.

From: vanessaholt@aol.com
Subject: Back to the UK?
Date: 14 November
To: jane.rourke@hotmail.com

Hi Jane, How are you? I've been at Duval and Smith, an Anglo–French law firm in Paris, for three months now. I've had experience of translating a lot of different documents, so (1) .... is interesting enough, but I don't get any (2) .... for the work I do – my boss never says anything. He never gives us any (3) .... – for example, he never lets us deal with clients directly. I never get a sense of (4) .... – my boss takes all the credit for the work we do.

There are quite good opportunities for promotion and (5) .... at Duval and Smith, but I'm not sure I want to stay. I think there must be better opportunities elsewhere for me to develop, and as (6) .... is important to me, I've decided to move back to the UK and look for a job there.

So hope to see you in London soon – I'll give you a call.

All the best

3.3 Complete this table with words from C opposite.

Verb	Noun	Adjective
empower		empowered
	consultation	consulted
–		hierarchical
		delegated

4 Employment and employability

A Outsourcing

Nigel, a 30-year-old information technology (IT) specialist, talks about his career so far:

'I used to work in the IT department of a bank. All the IT work was done **in-house**. I thought I had a **job for life**. But then one day the work was **outsourced** to a specialized IT company called IT Services (ITS), based in India. Outsourcing abroad like this is **offshoring** and involves the use of **offshore companies** (see Unit 31). The bank saw outsourcing as a way of saving money and keeping its **competitive edge** – advantage. They said that it would be more **cost-effective** – would cost less – to concentrate on their **core activities** – most important ones.

'Luckily, the bank didn't **make me redundant** – I didn't lose my job – and I started working for ITS instead. At first I didn't know what to expect, but now I am very happy. We work with a lot of different clients. I work for ITS as a **contractor** and I give clients advice.'

B Employability

'ITS put a lot of emphasis on **professional development**. We often go on training courses so that we can keep up with **current trends** – the way things are changing in the industry.

'ITS tell us that we may not have a job for life with the company, but that our up-to-date skills will mean that we will always be **employable**. Companies and governments talk about the importance of **lifelong learning** – continuing to develop our knowledge by going on courses, reading, etc.

'In the next year or two, I may make a **career move** and join another company.'

C Freelancers and portfolio workers

'When I'm about 40, I want to **set up on my own** as a **freelancer** offering **consultancy services** to different companies. The idea of working **freelance** on different projects for different clients attracts me.'

The management thinker Charles Handy calls freelancers **portfolio workers** because they have a **portfolio** – range of different clients. Some experts say that increasing numbers of people will work this way in the future, as companies outsource more and more of their work because they want to concentrate on their core activities.

> **Note**
> You can say **freelancers** or **freelances**. The corresponding adjective is **freelance**, as in **freelance work**.

4.1 Complete the article with expressions from A opposite.

Outsourcing to India

David Galbenski's firm Contract Counsel's **(1)** .... had always been its low price. Clients call them when dealing with complicated merger-and-acquisition deals, which can require as many as 100 lawyers to manage the related documents. Contract Counsel's temps cost about $75 an hour, roughly half of what a law firm would charge, which allowed the company to be competitive despite its relatively small size.

To continue to be **(2)** .... , Galbenski started to think about the use of **(3)** .... employees in other countries. India seemed like the best bet. With more than 500 law schools and about 200,000 law students graduating each year, it had no shortage of attorneys. What amazed Galbenski, however, was that thanks to the Web, lawyers in India had access to the same research tools and case summaries as any associate in the US. Sure, they didn't speak American English. "But they were highly motivated and highly intelligent," he says. "They were also eager to tackle the kinds of tasks that most new associates at law firms look down upon" – such as analyzing thousands of documents in advance of a trial. In other words, they were perfect for the kind of document-review work he had in mind.

After a visit to India, Galbenski signed a contract with two legal services companies: QuisLex in Hyderabad and Manthan Services in Bangalore. Using their lawyers, Galbenski figured he could cut his document-review rates to $50 an hour. He has also **(4)** .... the maintenance of the database used to store the contact information for his thousands of **(5)** ....

4.2 Answer the questions about the text in 4.1 above.

1 What area of law does Contract Counsel work in?
2 What is the cost of its temporary workers? How does this relate to the firm's aims?
3 Which country was most attractive for offshoring? Why?
4 With how many firms in India does Contract Counsel work?
5 Which activities did Contract Counsel outsource?

4.3 Complete the sentences with correct forms of expressions from A, B and C opposite.

1 There's a lot to be said for .... It would encourage more working men and women to refresh their skills on university short courses tailored to their needs. That way they can keep up with .... – the latest thinking in their area.
2 I love my new job. This is definitely the best .... I could have made.
3 The new chief executive fired 11,000 employees and sold several business units. Non-core .... were outsourced.
4 Some former advertising executives offer .... for ad agencies, bringing expertise the agencies do not have themselves.
5 Some 'creative' businesses, like design services, are kept going by work done by .... and have hardly any permanent staff.
6 Of course, there are advantages to doing some things .... You don't have to explain to outsiders what you want them to do.

Over to you

- Would it be possible to do your job as a freelancer? Why? / Why not?
- What are the advantages and disadvantages of being a freelancer?

5 Flexibility and inflexibility

Ways of working

The US is often described as having a **flexible job market** with **flexible working**. For example:

- **temporary workers** who only work for short periods when they are needed, either on a **temporary contract** with a company or through a **temp agency**
- **part-time workers** who work less than the maximum number of hours each week
- **job sharing** where two people share a particular job, each of them working part-time

B Job flexibility

Another aspect of **job flexibility** in the US is that companies can **hire and fire** employees easily. When **letting people go** – telling employees that they are no longer required – companies only have to **give** them very short **notice** – warning – and relatively small **redundancy payments** – money to compensate for losing their job.

Unemployment benefits – the money paid to people without jobs – are very low. It is said that all these measures make for a **flexible job market** and encourage **job creation**. Critics say that this approach leads to **job insecurity**, with employers able to get rid of employees too easily.

C Job protection

France is a country with a very different approach. Companies in trouble are only allowed to **make employees redundant** after a long period of **consultation**. If employees are made redundant, they receive generous redundancy payments and then unemployment benefits. The government says people need this sort of **job protection**, and **trade unions** – organizations that protect the interests of workers – are fighting hard to keep it.

Payments to employees such as **sick pay** and **parental leave** – when they have time off following the birth of children – are also very generous. Mothers get long paid **maternity leave**. But the **social charges** which employers and employees have to pay the government are very high.

Critics say that these policies contribute to a **rigid labour market** – one with too much job protection. They say that this sort of **inflexibility** discourages job creation and leads in the long run to higher **unemployment** and slower **economic growth**. As a consequence, companies may look abroad for cheaper bases and workforces.

> **Note**
> BrE: labour; AmE: labor
> BrE: trade unions; AmE: labor unions

5.1 Which type of work or workers in A opposite is each of these people referring to?

1 'I work at the local council for two days a week, and my friend works in the same job on the other three days.'
2 'I work in a petrol station 20 hours a week.'
3 'I'm on a job at Clarkson's until the end of next week. Then I'll try and find something else.'

5.2 Two American managers working in France, Melinda and Nat, are talking about the issues in B and C opposite. Replace the underlined expressions with items from those sections. Pay attention to the grammatical context.

Melinda: It's ridiculous! We can't **(1)** get rid of people without a lot of **(2)** meetings and discussion with **(3)** employee organizations, government officials, and so on. We have to keep even the laziest, most incompetent people.

Nat: I know what you mean. I don't have the opportunity to **(4)** recruit and get rid of people as I want! This sort of **(5)** rigidity must be bad for the job market. **(6)** The number of people without jobs in this country is very high.

Melinda: It's a nightmare! If you do want to get rid of people, you have to **(7)** tell them three months in advance.

Nat: Yes, and you should see the **(8)** amount of tax I have to pay for each of my employees just so they can get **(9)** money when they fall ill, and so on.

Melinda: We should move back to the US. There the job market is **(10)** one that gives employers a lot of freedom. When the economy is going well, the level of **(11)** new jobs that can be created there is incredible.

5.3 Look at the expressions in B and C opposite. Say if these statements are true or false.

1 When companies talk about letting employees go, they make them redundant.
2 One person's job flexibility might be another's job insecurity.
3 In flexible job markets, hiring and firing is complex.
4 Employee benefits are paid for through social charges.
5 Rigidity is another word for inflexibility.
6 When fathers take parental leave, this is called maternity leave.
7 The cost of job protection might be higher unemployment.

Over to you

- Is your country more like the US or France in its ways of working?
- Think of one advantage and one disadvantage of flexible working from the point of view of employers.

6 Work–life balance

Stress

People talk about being **under (a lot of) stress** or **pressure.** They say their work is **stressful** (see Unit 1) and that they feel **stressed** or **stressed out.** They want to find ways to **de-stress.** They may complain that they have a **stress-related illness.** Some people may suffer **burn-out** or a complete **(nervous) breakdown,** which means they are no longer able to work.

Here are some frequent combinations with 'stress':

stress		
	counsellor	someone who advises stress sufferers
	factor	something that causes stress
	symptom	a sign that someone is under stress
	management	ways of dealing with stress
	industry	used by critics who say that stress problems are overestimated and to refer to the unnecessary (in their view) counselling, research, etc. done in relation to stress

B

The causes of stress

The most common causes of stress are:

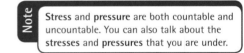

Note

Stress and **pressure** are both countable and uncountable. You can also talk about the **stresses** and **pressures** that you are under.

- **heavy workloads** – you try to do too much and you're **overworked**
- **office politics** – problems with colleagues who want to advance their own position, etc. These people like **playing politics.**
- **role ambiguity** – responsibilities are unclear
- **lack of management support** – managers do not provide the necessary help and resources
- **effort–reward imbalance** – not getting sufficient recognition or pay
- **home–work imbalance** – not enough time for family, personal interests, etc.

C

Quality of life

Some people are **workaholics** – they think about very little except work. Others are increasingly looking for a better **quality of life:** less **commuting,** more time with their families, etc. Journalists write about people **downshifting** or **rebalancing** their lives – getting a better balance between work, family life, etc. They may work part-time, work from home, move to the country, and so on.

In a recent survey:

a Ninety-five per cent of **homeworkers** said that they have a better **work–life balance** or **home–work balance** than when they were in-company because they can spend more time with their families, on leisure activities, etc.

b Eighty-two per cent said that they have more **autonomy** and **independence** – they are able to organize their work and their time how they want.

But also:

c Seventy-three per cent of homeworkers said that there is no **boundary** between work on the one hand and personal life on the other – the two **overlap.**

d Fifty-seven per cent said that they feel lonely and **isolated** – out of contact with others because they don't have colleagues around them.

6.1 Match the two parts of the extracts containing expressions from A opposite.

1 Having so many streams of instant communication leads to information overload.
2 Many companies are reacting to the problems of their staff experiencing stress by throwing training courses at them
3 Those working in the stress industry are mostly genuine, well-meaning people.
4 It's important to treat damaging stress symptoms
5 Our stress counsellors are fully qualified to deal with the

a on stress management without addressing the underlying organizational causes.
b Such demands are becoming a major stress factor at work.
c before they affect your physical or mental health.
d effects of losing your job.
e But some of them use methods which are clearly not working.

6.2 Which of the causes of stress in B opposite are each of these people (1–6) referring to?

1 Managers just don't seem to care about the stress we are under.

2 I thought I was in charge of this, but Leila thinks she's responsible.

3 I left the office at eleven o'clock last night and I was back here at eight this morning – I can't go on like this.

4 It's not so much the work hours – it's the intensity of the work and the pressure we are all under.

5 He's not interested in finding the best solution to problems – he's just interested in scoring points.

6 No one appreciates the work that we do.

6.3 Look at C opposite. Match these answers (1–4) with the findings in the survey (a–d).

1 'Sometimes I wish I was working every day as part of a team in an office.'
2 'Yes, I see much more of my children.'
3 'Yes, my boss isn't breathing down my neck the whole time.'
4 'I work in the living room, and the work is always there, waiting. I can't get away from it.'

Over to you
• Name three jobs that you think are stressful.
• What is the main cause of stress in your job? How do you combat stress?

7 Managing talent 1

A Talent

People with special skills and abilities have **talent** (uncountable) or particular **talents** (countable). You can also refer to the people themselves as **talents**. They are **talented**. Companies talk about managing and developing their **talent pool** – the talent that they have available in the organization.

B Recruiting talent

Preston Bottger and Jean-Louis Barsoux* put the management of a company's talent under these headings:

a **Spot** and **recruit the raw talent** – find and employ untrained people. This requires identifying **candidates** – possible recruits – who match the needs of the business system and selecting those who are most likely to fit with the firm's **culture** – the way it does things.

b **Induction** The recruits then need to be educated on the key success factors of the business system and their role within it.

c **Training and development** After the induction to the firm and its culture, training and development ensure that the employee has the **capabilities** – skills – necessary to get the job done.

C Managing talent

d **Performance assessment** – evaluation – (see Unit 8) is a seemingly simple concept, but it is difficult to carry out without tremendous effort and expense. Managers need a high degree of training in order to standardize the approach so that all managers use the same **criteria** – ways of judging their employees.

e **Performance improvement interventions** The purpose of these is to provide experiences to help the person increase their capabilities. Such experiences include:

- **job rotation** where employees do different jobs
- **executive education** – management training
- **360-degree analysis** where managers assess employees and employees assess their managers, and this is followed up with **coaching** – individual training (see Unit 8)

f **Culture** or **Fit interventions** are aimed at those who cannot or will not adapt to the company's culture. People are given early and forceful **feedback** – information on how they are doing.

g **Succession planning** The chief human resources officer (CHRO) needs to plan the future **staffing** needs of the organization in relation to its objectives. Specifically, the CHRO must identify and provide the managers who will take over and continue to put into practice the firm's **business model** – the ways it makes money.

h **Compensation for contribution** Each employee has a 'deal' with the company: the performance of tasks in exchange for **rewards** – salary, increased responsibilities, etc. The CHRO oversees this deal and ensures that it works. Firms expect a lot from their employees, in terms of performance, **commitment** – belief in and support for the firm – and **mobility** – moving to different jobs in the company.

*'Leading within and across the functions' in *Leading in the Top Team: The CXO Challenge*, edited by Preston Bottger, CUP, 2008.

7.1 Look at A opposite. Which of these uses of 'talent' is uncountable and which countable?

1 I believe we have the talent available to grow and become a better business.
2 Young talents have started to question old assumptions about how work is done.
3 In markets where top talent is regarded as the determining factor, firms battle furiously for the top-quality workers.
4 An organization must make maximum use of the talent available in the labor pool.
5 She has a talent for identifying potential problems and offering solutions to customers.

7.2 Match the examples (1–8) with the topics (a–h) in B and C opposite.

1 So the CHRO must also be able to explain to people, 'Here's what's in it for you.' The CHRO must be the best salesperson for the idea of the exchange between the person and the firm.

2 Workers are told what their job entails, what is expected from them and how it fits in with what the company is doing.

3 It requires managers to identify, for example, their bottom 10 per cent and top 20 per cent of performers.

4 The private banking division of a global financial services organization discovered that it lacked succession candidates to meet the needs of its growth strategy, based on a new business model for private banking for very rich people. Thus it selected, based on specific leadership and performance criteria, a pool of high-potential managers.

5 The method must reliably assess past short-term performance, the individual's agility to rotate to new assignments, and medium-term capacity and calibre to take on wider and higher levels of responsibility.

6 In an international airline, the quality of customer care was found to be directly influenced by the technical knowledge and pleasant attitudes of front-line employees. This in turn was influenced by the quality of supervision. As a result, all supervisors were systematically trained in an in-house programme designed to improve their employee management skills.

7 A pharmaceutical company observed that one division was growing only at market average, despite product quality superior to competitors. All sales leaders and candidates for sales leadership positions around the world were put through a programme involving assessment centres, 360-degree feedback and leadership training. The results were evaluated and used to reorganize and focus the sales leader on key tasks. Subsequently sales/market share rose by 20 per cent.

8 A low-cost airline has a team-based culture, which is fundamental to the success of its business model. The leaders and key professionals in this company take care of business by taking care of relationships. People need to help at all levels to solve problems when they arise. The company carefully selects new individuals to fit this culture.

Over to you

What arrangements are there for performance assessment in your organization or one you would like to work for?

8 Managing talent 2

A Talent management 1

An expert in management trends says:

'More and more organizations put effort into identifying the **key people** – the specially talented people – in their **talent pool**. Some experts call these **super-talents** or **core competents**. (Compare this with a company's **core competences** – see Unit 18.) One study found that a computer company had identified 100 core competents out of its staff of 16,000; these were people who were **mission-critical** – essential to the firm's success.

'This relates to the **ABC approach**, practised in organizations like Microsoft and McKinsey. In **performance assessment** (see Unit 7), managers identify three groups: the As are the **top performers** – the core competents, the best 10 or 20 per cent; the Bs are the middle group who perform well; and the Cs are the bottom 10 per cent, who are encouraged to improve or leave the organization. Executives making judgements like this are **talent managers**.'

> **Note**
> The people in an organization who are seen to have the potential to become part of its senior management may be referred to, slightly informally, as **high fliers**.

B Talent management 2

The expert continues:

'And in some businesses, there is a clear division between **creatives** – the people with ideas – and their managers. For example, in advertising the creatives are the people who devise the campaigns and the **suits** are those who manage them.

'In some industries, people come together for a particular project and then **disband**. For example, in software development, managers and programmers may come together to contribute to a particular project and then leave to work on others. Such workers are part of a **virtual organization**.'

> **Note**
> **Suits** is mostly used in the plural and is quite informal.

C Mentoring and coaching

Mentoring is when a **mentor** – a more senior manager – gives advice to a **mentee** – a younger colleague – on their career, how to improve their job performance, etc. **Reverse mentoring** is when a younger employee mentors an older manager, for example to inform them about new technology, social trends, etc. These are two forms of **mentoring** or **mentorship**.

Mentoring is related to **coaching** (see Unit 7), where the **coach** – the senior person – gives personal, one-to-one training to a **coachee** – an employee.

8.1 Look at A opposite. Then complete the article with these expressions. You can use some expressions more than once.

| ABC approach | super-talent | talent manager |
| core competents | talent management | talent pool |

If the talent manager makes sure it is operated in a way that is consistent with motivation, the ABC approach seems to offer a way to discriminate within the pool of talented people those with (1) .... : the (2) .... It might well be useful for the (3) .... periodically to review the talent pool and decide who are the core competents and who, perhaps, should not really be in the (4) .... On the other hand, the ABC approach seems less generally useful as a way of identifying the broader talent.

(5) .... is essentially about identifying talented people, finding out what they want and being prepared to give it to them. The idea of identifying the 10 or 20 per cent of (6) .... suffers from the immediate problem of deciding 10 or 20 per cent of what? Clearly, not the entire organization or we would be comparing the receptionist with the finance director. So it has to be a percentage of the managerial or professional staff. For some organizations, it might make sense to say that about 10 to 20 per cent of managerial-grade staff are potential future leaders and therefore the (7) .... For other organizations, such as professional service firms, one would imagine that a far greater percentage are to be managed as 'the talent', albeit perhaps with a small number identified as future key executives. So the (8) .... does not seem generally applicable as a way of defining the talent pool.

8.2 Look at B opposite. On the staff of a magazine, are the following people 'creatives' or 'suits'?

1 the finance director
2 the journalists
3 the photographers
4 the editor-in-chief
5 the head of HR
6 the designers

8.3 Complete the sentences with correct forms of expressions from C opposite. You can use some expressions more than once.

1 Harriet Green, president of the Contract Manufacturing Services Group, has regular breakfasts with her .... She also has a marker in her diary that alerts her when she hasn't heard from her .... in a long time, in which case she contacts them.
2 Well-designed .... programs have been found to produce three times more behavioral changes than traditional training approaches.
3 In this innovative .... scheme, the leaders of a global firm engage with younger diverse talented individuals who lead the .... relationship, providing unique insight for the chief executive and top team into how things really are lower down the firm.
4 To establish some degree of trust, many firms find it necessary to create conditions of confidentiality. The .... can speak with the .... , of course, but not with the coachee's boss.
5 Ernst & Young uses the system of professional .... in order to transmit the firm's values. The .... follows the professional development of the new employees and transmits the company's values to them.

Over to you

Is there a formal or informal mentoring system in your school or organization? If so, how does it work?

9 Team building

A Teams

In some (but not all) situations, tasks can be achieved more easily by **teams** with a **common purpose** rather than by **individuals**. Of course, it's important to develop **teamwork** through **team building** so as to get the best from the team. The level of **engagement** and **commitment** is the degree to which team members feel involved with the team.

Here are some frequent combinations with 'team':

team	leader	the person in charge of the team
	effort	the work done together by the team
	performance	the results that the team produces
	dynamics	the way the team works together
	effectiveness	the degree to which the team produces results
	learning	when people learn in teams rather than individually

B Team players

Meredith Belbin* has identified these types of team members or **team players**:

a The **Implementer** converts the team's plan into something achievable.
b The **Coordinator** is a confident member who sets objectives and defines team members' roles.
c The **Shaper** defines issues, shapes ideas and leads the action.
d The **Plant** is a creative and imaginative person who supplies original ideas and solves problems.
e The **Resource investigator** communicates with the outside world and explores opportunities.
f The **Monitor–Evaluator** sees all the possibilities, evaluates situations objectively and sees what is realistically achievable.
g The **Team worker** builds the team, supports others and reduces conflict.
h The **Completer** meets deadlines, corrects mistakes and makes sure nothing is forgotten.

C Stages of team life

The typical team goes through a series of stages:

a **Forming** The group is anxious and feels dependent on a leader. The group tries to discover how it is going to operate and what the 'normal' ways of working will be.
b **Storming** The atmosphere may be one of conflict between members, who may resist control from any one person. There may be the feeling that the task cannot be achieved.
c **Norming** At this stage, members of the group feel closer together and the conflicts are forgotten. Members of the group will start to support each other. There is increasingly the feeling that it is possible to achieve the task.
d **Performing** The group is carrying out the task for which it was formed. Members feel safe enough to express differences of opinion in relation to others.
e **Mourning** The group's work is finished, and its members begin to have pleasant memories of their activities and achievements.

*Management Teams: Why They Succeed or Fail, Butterworth–Heinemann, 1996.

9.1 Look at A opposite. Then read the article and answer the questions.

In many manufacturing industries, a daily meeting is used to keep the plant running smoothly; but this level of daily communication is seldom employed in knowledge work or administration. Sarah manages a team of nurses. Sitting together in the morning and building positive emotion, energy, and shared tasks for the day helps build their focus on the work of the whole unit. Shared knowledge helps limit mistakes and keep people engaged in learning. And knowing who may need help distributes the work of the unit across the formal team structures. The practice of daily meeting and discussion of tasks is another crucial way in which Sarah builds engagement.

Sarah's transparency in terms of performance requirements is another leadership practice that reinforces engagement. Once a month, Sarah shares information with the group that shows the unit's overall productivity numbers and their clinic-by-clinic performance. This monthly meeting, to discuss the unit's performance and the breakdown of each team's performance, creates performance pressure for all members of the team.

1 What is Sarah's job?
2 Two types of meeting are mentioned. How often does each of them happen?
3 How are knowledge work and administration different from manufacturing?
4 What are the advantages of regular meetings?
5 What negative things can regular meetings prevent?
6 What is the advantage of the monthly meetings?

9.2 Look at the types of team members in B opposite and say if these statements are true or false.

1 Implementers are not interested in final results.
2 Coordinators tend to take a leading, organizing role.
3 Shapers tend to follow what other people say.
4 Plants can be useful in providing new ideas when the team has run out of steam.
5 Some Resource investigators might love using the Internet.
6 Monitor–evaluators are not good at seeing all sides of a problem.
7 Team workers may help to defuse arguments between members.
8 Completers are bad at finishing things on time.

9.3 Members of a team brought together to work on a design project said the following things. Match what they said (1–5) with the stages (a–e) in C opposite.

1 We had such a great time working together.

2 We need to appoint a leader.

3 We're beginning to get to know each other better.

4 Who does Jane think she is, taking over and behaving like she's in charge?

5 We're really making progress now and we get on so well together.

Over to you
- What teams have you worked in or are you working in?
- Do you recognize the types in B opposite in your team?
- What role do you usually play?

10 The right skills

A Hard and soft skills

For a long time, **hard skills** – for example, skills in technical subjects – were considered the most important thing in business. But more and more, people are realising the importance of **soft skills** – the skills you need to work with other people, and in the case of managers, to manage people in **tactful** and **non-authoritarian, non-dictatorial** ways. These are some of the **emotional competencies** that are becoming important.

B Emotional intelligence 1

The ideas behind **emotional intelligence** (**EI**) were first put forward in the 1980s[1], and later developed by Daniel Goleman[2]. He says that EI is made up of:

a **self-awareness** – examining how your emotions affect your performance: being **self-confident** about your capabilities, values and goals; using your values to guide decision making

b **self-regulation** – the ability to control yourself and to think before you act: controlling your temper and handling **impulses** – sudden desires to do things you may later regret

c **motivation** – ability to take the **initiative** – do things without being told to: enjoying challenge and **stimulation**; the drive to work and succeed (see Unit 2); optimism

d **empathy** – avoiding the tendency to **stereotype** others – have unfair ideas about them not based on facts: being aware of **cultural differences** (see Units 60–62)

e **social skills** – the ability to communicate and to relate to others: the use of influencing skills such as persuasion; **cooperation** – working well with others; **dispute resolution** – the ability to solve arguments; good communication with others, including employees; listening skills; negotiation

A measure of someone's intelligence is their **intelligence quotient** (**IQ**). Similarly, a measure of someone's emotional awareness and self-awareness is their **emotional quotient** (**EQ**).

C Emotional intelligence 2

Other researchers[3] have identified three main areas of emotional intelligence, containing seven **traits** – characteristics – in these categories:

- **drivers** – traits that make people do things: **motivation** and **decisiveness** – the ability to take decisions when necessary

- **constrainers** – traits that control in a good way what people do: **conscientiousness** – putting a lot of effort into your work and doing everything to the best of your ability; and **integrity** – honesty

- **enablers** – traits that help people to perform and succeed: **sensitivity** – knowing how others feel; **influence** and **self-awareness**

[1] John D. Mayer and Peter Salovey: *Emotional Intelligence: Key Readings*, National Professional Resources, 2004.
[2] Daniel Goleman: *Emotional Intelligence: Why it can matter more than IQ*, Bloomsbury, 1996.
[3] Malcolm Higgs and Victor Dulewicz: *Making Sense of Emotional Intelligence*, NFR Nelson, 1999.

10.1 Look at A opposite. Were hard skills or soft skills mainly required at each of the following stages of a project to design insurance products?

The project manager:

1 employed someone with a doctorate in mathematics to work on risk probabilities
2 gave three days off to a team member who said they had family problems at home
3 analyzed her own feelings of frustration that the project was going too slowly
4 dealt politely but firmly with a request by her boss to finish the project a month early
5 did market testing of the product with a number of potential consumers of the product and analyzed the results on computer
6 did careful research on the Internet to find the best advertising agency to launch the product

10.2 Look at B opposite. To which category (a–e) do each of these aspects of emotional intelligence (1–10) belong?

1 ability to deal with others' emotions, especially group emotions
2 behaving openly and honestly with others
3 being guided by personal preferences in choosing goals and seeking out achievement
4 capacity to start and manage change among people
5 commitment
6 controlling your stress by being more positive
7 learning from your experiences
8 retaining the ability to think clearly even when under pressure
9 the ability to see other people's points of view and opinions
10 understanding yourself, your strengths and weaknesses, and how you appear to others

10.3 People in a company are talking about their colleagues and managers. Complete what they say with expressions from C opposite.

1 A: Annabelle really knows what her own strengths and weaknesses are.
   B: Yes, she's got great ....
2 A: Ben doesn't work particularly hard and he doesn't pay attention to detail.
   B: His problem is that he lacks ....
3 A: Caroline never does anything to upset anybody.
   B: I know. She has great ....
4 A: When Dan speaks, people listen.
   B: Yes, he has a lot of .... round here.
5 A: Ella has never done anything dishonest.
   B: You're right. She has a high level of ....
6 A: Frank never puts off making decisions.
   B: That's true. He always acts with great ....
7 A: Georgina really puts everything into her work – her job is the only thing that drives her.
   B: I wish I had her .... !

Over to you
Write a description of the soft skills required for your job or one you would like.

11 Equality and diversity

A Equality

If people are treated differently from each other in an unfair way, they are **discriminated against**. **Discriminatory** practices might be based on someone's:

- race
- gender
- geographic origin
- **sexual orientation** – heterosexual, homosexual, etc.
- **family status** – married, single, etc.
- **social background** – someone's social class

- age
- education
- disability

For example, if a woman is unfairly treated just because she is a woman, she is a victim of **sexism** at work, **sexist attitudes** or **sex discrimination**. In many organizations, women complain about the **glass ceiling** that allows them to get to a particular level but no further.

Stereotypical – fixed and unjustified – ideas about what men and women can do, and about the **roles** – jobs and activities – that they can have, constitute **gender stereotyping**.

If someone is treated unfairly because of their **race** or **ethnicity**, they are a victim of **racial discrimination** or **racism**. Offensive remarks about someone's race are **racist** and the person making them is **a racist**.

Older people discriminated against because of their age are victims of **ageism** and **ageist attitudes**.

In the US, **affirmative action** is when help is given in education and employment to groups who were previously discriminated against. In Britain, affirmative action is known as **equal opportunities**. These actions are also called **positive discrimination** in both countries.

Some companies have an **equal opportunities policy** or **dignity at work policy** covering all the issues above, which is designed to increase **equality** – treating people fairly and in the same way.

B Diversity

Many organizations now aim for **diversity** in the workforce, with policies that encourage **inclusion** – employees from as many different **backgrounds** as possible. This goes beyond equal opportunities, and enables an organization to keep up with **social** and **demographic** changes – changes in the make-up of society and the population as a whole. Examples of such changes include increases in the number of women, older workers, **ethnic minorities** – people from particular countries and racial groups. Organizations are looking for a **diverse workforce**. (See Unit 49 for the importance of diversity in **social reporting**.)

C Word combinations with 'diversity'

diversity	**training**	teaching employees about the importance of diversity
	initiative	an action designed to increase diversity
	statement	a company's communication about their attitude to diversity
	strategy	a long-term plan for putting diversity into action
	management	how diversity is managed in a company or companies in general
	programme	a series of actions designed to put diversity into practice

Note: BrE: **programme**; AmE: **program**
In connection with computers, **program** is always used.

11.1 Complete the table with words from A and B opposite.

Noun	Adjective	Related noun
age		
	racist	
sex		
stereotype		
	diverse	–
discrimination		–
	equal	–
	ethnic	–

11.2 Complete these sentences with correct forms of expressions from the table in 11.1 above.

1 When we first joined the company, our roles were .... : he was the marketing risk-taker and I was the conventional accountant.

2 .... housing policies confined Blacks and Latinos to neighborhoods close to industrial zones.

3 'Hispanic' refers to people whose .... stems from a variety of Spanish-speaking cultures throughout Latin America and the Caribbean.

4 They accused lenders in Los Angeles of 'systematic ....', saying that blacks were 30 per cent more likely to pay higher interest rates than whites.

5 The notoriously .... computer industry rarely puts 50-somethings on permanent employment contracts.

6 The issues that Jennifer raised about .... in the military can affect women after they get out of the military as well.

7 The bank has struck a blow for .... by appointing the first woman executive director to its male-dominated board.

8 Allowing employees to take unpaid leave to observe a religious or cultural holiday is one policy used to show that an organization encourages ....

11.3 Match the two parts of these sentences containing expressions from C opposite.

1 People with stronger ethnic identities were more attracted to organizations that described a diversity

2 One way to assess the potential effectiveness of diversity

3 About 250 state employees attended the diversity

4 The company makes its diversity

5 Affirmative action statements signal an organization's attention to race and gender, but diversity

a programs is to ask how likely they are to change employee attitudes.

b statements might signal an organization's concerns about a broader range of differences.

c strategy transparent by having a section on equality and diversity in its annual report.

d initiative in their recruiting materials than to organizations that did not describe a diversity initiative.

e training seminar, titled 'How to Work Effectively with Indian Nations and Tribal Members'.

Over to you

Give an example of what organizations can do to encourage diversity and inclusion.

12 What is quality?

A Quality in manufacturing

Gordon Greer is head of quality at a car component company:

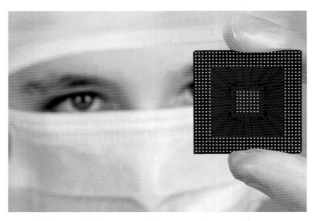

'From the point of view of producers, quality can be seen in terms of **conformity** or **conformance to specification**, which means that the **components** – parts – and the product as a whole are made exactly as designed. In other words, there is **consistency** and **elimination of variation** – no variations – resulting in **zero defects** – no mistakes at all in the manufacturing process.

Everything must be done **right first time** to avoid the need for **reworking** – working again on – components in order to correct **faults** and **defects** – mistakes.

'The design for each component embodies the intentions of its designer. So conformity to specification means putting these intentions into practice when we make the components. Put another way, this is elimination of variation.

'We are also inspired by ideas of **employee involvement** – quality should be the concern of everyone in the company.

'Like many ideas in relation to quality, these ideas were first developed in Japan as part of **Total Quality Management** (**TQM**), but they have been copied all over the world.'

B Quality in services

Serena Togliatti is customer relations manager at a large bank:

'In services, there is a parallel situation to the one in manufacturing. But quality can also be seen from the point of view of customers. The service must **satisfy customer needs**. The service received by the customer must be exactly what is planned and intended; mistakes in their accounts, for example, make customers extremely annoyed.

'Quality could be defined in terms of **customer approval** – recognition that we are satisfying customer needs and **customer expectations**. And if we **exceed** – go beyond – those **expectations**, there may even be **customer delight** – extreme satisfaction (see Unit 23).'

C Widening the definition of quality

However, as Andy Neely points out*, quality can be seen in wider terms:

a **performance** – how well the product performs its main function
b **features** – additional parts or characteristics that the product offers
c **reliability** – how well the product continues to perform without **breakdowns**
d **technical durability** – how long the product lasts before becoming technically **obsolete** – out of date
e **serviceability** – how easy the product is to **service** – maintain and repair
f **aesthetics** – the **look and feel** of the product
g **perceived quality** – the customer's judgement of the product's level of quality
h **value for money** – what the product does in relation to the price paid for it

* *Business Performance Measurement*, CUP, 2004.

12.1 Read the article and answer the questions with expressions from A opposite.

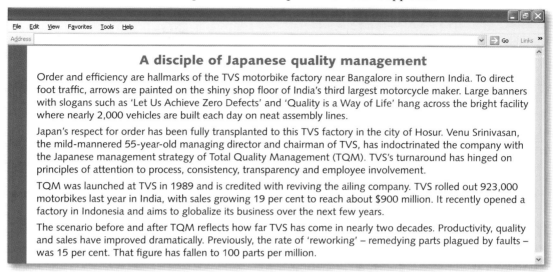

A disciple of Japanese quality management

Order and efficiency are hallmarks of the TVS motorbike factory near Bangalore in southern India. To direct foot traffic, arrows are painted on the shiny shop floor of India's third largest motorcycle maker. Large banners with slogans such as 'Let Us Achieve Zero Defects' and 'Quality is a Way of Life' hang across the bright facility where nearly 2,000 vehicles are built each day on neat assembly lines.

Japan's respect for order has been fully transplanted to this TVS factory in the city of Hosur. Venu Srinivasan, the mild-mannered 55-year-old managing director and chairman of TVS, has indoctrinated the company with the Japanese management strategy of Total Quality Management (TQM). TVS's turnaround has hinged on principles of attention to process, consistency, transparency and employee involvement.

TQM was launched at TVS in 1989 and is credited with reviving the ailing company. TVS rolled out 923,000 motorbikes last year in India, with sales growing 19 per cent to reach about $900 million. It recently opened a factory in Indonesia and aims to globalize its business over the next few years.

The scenario before and after TQM reflects how far TVS has come in nearly two decades. Productivity, quality and sales have improved dramatically. Previously, the rate of 'reworking' – remedying parts plagued by faults – was 15 per cent. That figure has fallen to 100 parts per million.

1 Which expression refers to a Japanese approach to quality? What is the abbreviation?
2 Which two aspects of quality are mentioned along with attention to process and transparency?
3 Which two words are used for 'mistakes in manufacturing'?
4 What is one of the aims of TVS in relation to these mistakes?
5 What problem in the manufacturing process now affects 100 parts per million rather than 150,000 as before?

12.2 Use correct forms of expressions from A and B opposite to complete this memo.

CLUB SOLEIL

Memo   From: Jacqueline Toubon   To: All hotel managers

Of course, buying a family holiday is a big investment for a lot of people, both financially and emotionally. We don't just want to satisfy customer needs. We want **(1)** them to be extremely happy.

We want to avoid the situation where things are not what customers were expecting; we want **(2)** standards to be exactly as described. When the hotel does not come up to the description in the brochure, our clients are extremely angry. This means **(3)** avoiding changes or differences in relation to what we promise.

Things may be better than customers thought they would get. For example, the food may be better. This may be a way of going beyond **(4)** what customers were hoping for, but you must keep control of costs.

12.3 Match the sentences (1–8) with the points in C opposite (a–h).

1 We guarantee five years or 100,000 kilometres of trouble-free motoring.
2 No other brand gives better performance in this price category.
3 It only requires servicing every 25,000 kilometres.
4 It has beautiful lines.
5 It has heated seats for the driver and the passenger.
6 It has the latest engine technology.
7 It goes from zero to 100 kilometres per hour in four seconds.
8 Customer surveys give us top marks for quality compared to other leading car makes.

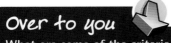

Over to you
What are some of the criteria for quality in your organization (school, company, etc.)?

13 Quality standards

A Standards and certification

The **International Organization for Standardization** is based in Geneva. It is a network of national **standards institutes** in over 145 countries working in partnership with international organizations, governments, industry, business and consumer representatives.

ISO has developed more than 14,000 **International Standards**, which it says are 'documented agreements containing **technical specifications** or other precise **criteria** and guidelines to ensure that materials, products, processes and services are **fit** – suitable – **for purpose**'.

There are two series of standards for management systems:

- the ISO 9000 series on **quality management**, which 'gives the requirements for **quality management systems** … the standard for providing assurance about the ability to satisfy quality requirements and to enhance **customer satisfaction** in **supplier–customer relationships**'.

- the ISO 14000 series on **environmental management** 'for organizations wishing to operate in an **environmentally sustainable** manner' (see Unit 50).

Organizations can **apply for certification** to ISO 9001:2008 and ISO 14001:2004. These are **generic standards** that can be applied to any industry.

There are also specific standards for particular industries, for example ISO 90003 for computing and telecommunications.

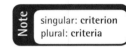

Note
singular: **criterion**
plural: **criteria**

B ISO 9000 and others

The most recent (2008) version of the ISO 9000 standards puts particular importance on:

a the role of **top management** in setting policies for quality – top managers have to be seen to be involved in quality issues, not leaving this to middle management

b **statutory** and **regulatory requirements** – for example, the car industry has to pay particular attention to safety and environmental laws, and standards in relation to the components that it uses

c **measurable objectives** – we have to be able to measure quality and by how much it is improving

d **resource management** – how you manage the **inputs** to your products, for example in **human resources** and **materials**

e monitoring **customer satisfaction** – customers are the ultimate judges of quality and we have to constantly check and improve the 'score' that they give us

f **training effectiveness** – the training of our staff is an investment and we have to measure how effective it is in terms of our future profitability

g **continual improvement** – 100 per cent quality is never achieved and there is always room for improvement (this is what the Japanese call **kaizen**)

13.1 Look at the expressions in A opposite and complete the table.

	Verb	Noun(s)	Adjective
1		application	applied
2	certify	certificate, ...	certified
3	standardize	.... , ...	standardized

13.2 Complete each sentence using the correct form of the word from the line with the same number in the table in 13.1 above.

1 They told us to bring in ISO-approved consultants to check our operations and make our .... through them.

2 The .... process was very long and we had to provide vast amounts of documentation before we could be ....

3 Now we can put the ISO 9000 logo on all our literature. We've .... all our documentation so that it's clearly visible. Our clients feel reassured – in fact, they love it!

13.3 Here are some examples of work on quality at a company producing car components. Match each one with an aspect of quality in B opposite.

1 All the people in the call centre were sent on a course to develop their sense of teamwork, and this increased sales by 15 per cent.

2 The senior managers invited a quality expert to do a consultancy project on production quality.

3 The production manager looked at the latest regulations on car safety on a government Ministry of Transport website.

4 Employees are always paid bonuses for suggesting improvements, however small.

5 The company developed new software to analyze quality data more closely.

6 They have checked the quality procedures in place for the components used at all of their suppliers.

7 The car firms who buy the company's components are totally satisfied.

Over to you

Find out about an organization (perhaps your own, or one of its suppliers) that has adopted standards such as ISO 9000. Identify one of the ways in which this has changed the way that the company works.

14 Quality and people

A Investors in People

There are **models** and **frameworks** that emphasize the human dimension in improving quality.

Investors in People is a framework developed in the UK. It sets a level of **good practice** for training and development of people to achieve business goals. It is used by more than 37,000 organizations in the UK and elsewhere.

The **Investors in People Standard** is based on four key principles:

a **Commitment** to invest in people to achieve business goals.
b **Planning** how skills, individuals and teams are to be developed to achieve these goals.
c **Action** to develop and use necessary skills in a well defined and continuing programme directly tied to business objectives.
d **Evaluating outcomes** – the results of training and development for individuals' progress towards goals, the value achieved and future needs.

B The EFQM Excellence Model

The **EFQM Excellence Model** was developed by EFQM, a non-profit organization set up by leading European companies to 'help European businesses make better products and deliver improved services through the effective use of leading edge management practices'.

In the EFQM model, people are very much part of the wider quality picture. The model refers to company **stakeholders** – not only its employees, shareholders and customers, but the community as a whole. The model refers to:

- **Resources** – the materials, skills and knowledge used by the firm
- **Policy & Strategy** – the firm's **strategies** (see Unit 16) and **policies** – actions to carry out those strategies
- **People management** – the way that employees are managed
- **Leadership** – the way the organization is led
- **Processes** – how all the above are combined and exploited

The five factors above that contribute to quality are **enablers**.

Results are the outcome of the factors above. They can be measured in terms of:

- **Business results** – the final outcome, i.e. the profits made by the firm
- **Customer satisfaction** – the way customers feel about the firm
- **Impact on society** – the effect of the firm's products and activities on society
- **People satisfaction** – the way managers, employees, shareholders and other stakeholders feel about the firm

14.1 A firm decided to introduce Investors in People principles. Look at the reports from the management and match them with the four principles in A opposite. There are two statements relating to each principle.

1 We have a committee of managers to work on the planning of skills development for individuals and teams in their departments.

5 We asked groups of employees to contribute ideas on ways of improving their skills.

2 We've announced in the internal company newspaper that we are going to apply the principles.

6 I've asked all our managers to report verbally on the progress of their employees in working towards the goals.

3 We've asked an external consultant to quantify financially the effectiveness of the actions that we have undertaken.

7 I was sent on a training course with the other managers. We learned how to improve our management techniques.

4 We sent all employees on a three-day quality training course.

8 We've announced on our customer website that we're going to apply the Investors in People principles.

14.2 Complete the model, using the factors in B opposite.

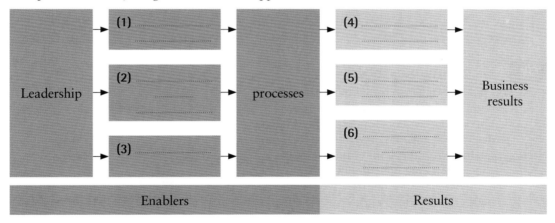

Over to you

Describe your own organization, or one you know, in terms of the EQFM model.

15 Striving for perfection

A Benchmarking and best practice

Benchmarking is when a firm finds out which company performs a particular task best and models its **performance** on this **best practice** – ways of doing things that have produced the best results elsewhere and can be adapted to a new situation. Companies talk about carrying out a **benchmarking exercise**. To do this, they **benchmark themselves against** other companies.

Large companies can measure the performance of different departments in relation to each other in an **internal benchmarking** exercise.

Competitive benchmarking involves looking outside the company at how other companies in the same industry do things.

Functional benchmarking looks at how the same function such as manufacturing or personnel recruitment is done by non-competitors. Companies can learn a lot from firms who are not their direct competitors. For example, a train company can learn how to clean its trains in a better way by looking at how an airline organizes the cleaning of its planes.

One way of seeing how a competitor's product is made is by **reverse engineering** – taking the product apart to see how it is made. The same principle can also be applied to services. This technique can also be used in benchmarking.

> **Note**
> **Best practice** is usually uncountable, but you can also talk about **the best practices** in a particular area.

B Six Sigma quality

Quality can be measured in terms of the number of **defects per million** parts, operations, etc. For example, with 45,000 defects per million parts, this is **Two Sigma quality**. With this level of quality, the chances of a manufactured product such as a mobile phone being defective are quite high.

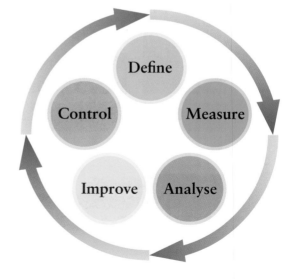

Motorola was the first company to aim for **Six Sigma quality**. In manufacturing, Six Sigma quality is when there is less than one defect in 300,000 components. Motorola saved $15 billion over an 11-year period with Six Sigma.

This idea can also be applied in areas outside manufacturing. In invoicing, for example, it means fewer than three or four mistakes per million transactions.

Six Sigma quality has been taken up by several other companies.

And the ultimate goal is **zero defects** – no defects at all.

15.1 Complete the sentences with appropriate forms of expressions from A opposite.

1 The manufacturers' association wants to help companies improve manufacturing
.... , so it's offering a new service designed to help companies
.... themselves against the best in their industries.

2 Engineers made replacement parts for the cars by copying the shape and dimensions of the
original parts, a process known as ....

3 Internal .... looks for internal .... and tries to
establish them throughout the organization.

4 We use .... to evaluate the effectiveness of our website against those
of our competitors.

5 Look outside your industry! .... can teach you a lot – as the firms
you are asking for advice are not your competitors, they may be more willing to help.

15.2 Look at B opposite. Then read this article and answer the questions.

What is Six Sigma?

Globalization and instant access to information, products and services continue to change the way our customers conduct business.

Today's competitive environment leaves no room for error. We must delight our customers and relentlessly look for new ways to exceed their expectations. This is why Six Sigma quality has become a part of our culture.

What is Six Sigma? First, what it is not. It is not a secret society, a slogan or a cliché. Six Sigma is a highly disciplined process that helps us focus on developing and delivering near-perfect products and services.

Why 'Sigma'? The word is a statistical term that measures how far a given process deviates from perfection. The central idea behind Six Sigma is that if you can measure how many 'defects' you have in a process, you can systematically figure out how to eliminate them and get as close to 'zero defects' as possible. To achieve Six Sigma quality, a process must produce no more than 3.4 defects per million opportunities. An 'opportunity' is defined as a chance for non-conformance, or not meeting the required specifications. This means we need to be nearly flawless in executing our key processes.

Key Concepts of Six Sigma

At its core, Six Sigma revolves around a few key concepts:

- Critical to quality: Attributes – characteristics – most important to the customer
- Defect: Failing to deliver what the customer wants
- Process capability: What your process can deliver
- Variation: What the customer sees and feels
- Stable operations: Ensuring consistent, predictable processes to improve what the customer sees and feels
- Design for Six Sigma: Designing to meet manufacturing capability

1 What is the central idea behind Six Sigma?
2 What is an 'opportunity' in this context?
3 What word is used to describe something without faults?
4 How is 'defect' defined here?
5 What word is used to describe something without unwanted variations?
6 What word is used to describe something where you know what you're going to get?

Over to you

Think about your company or one you would like to work for. Then think about one of its competitors. Is it useful to know how effective they are in different areas?

16 Strategic thinking

A Strategy

A **strategy** (countable) is a plan or series of plans for achieving success. **Strategy** (uncountable) is the study of the skills, knowledge, etc. required to make such plans. **Strategic success** in a commercial organization is often measured in terms of **profitability** – the amount of money it makes in relation to the amount invested.

An important part of **planning** is **resource allocation**. This is the way that **resources** such as finance, people and **assets** – equipment, buildings, know-how, etc. – are used to achieve a particular **objective**.

A company's senior executives decide or **formulate strategy**. Many organizations state their main overall objective or **vision** in a **mission statement**.

A strategy requires **commitment**. Everyone in the organization must work towards the **implementation** of the strategy – putting it into practice – and its success.

B Word combinations with 'strategic'

Here are some frequent combinations with 'strategic':

strategic	**move**	an action with a particular purpose in relation to objectives
	partnership	when two companies work together towards a specific goal
	decision	when a company decides something important for its long-term future
	acquisition	when one company buys another for strategic purposes
	goal	an objective the company wants to reach
	vision	when someone has clear ideas about actions to take for future success

C Companies and markets

When a company:		
a **defends**	a market,	it tries to prevent competitors from being successful there.
b **attacks**		it starts selling there for the first time.
c **establishes a foothold/ toehold in**		it occupies a small part of the market in preparation for gaining a larger part.
d **invades**		it starts to be very successful there.
e **dominates**		it is the biggest competitor there.
f **withdraws from**		it stops selling there.

16.1 Here are some questions from shareholders at the annual meeting of a car company. Complete the chief executive's answers with appropriate forms of expressions from A opposite.

1 Q: Why has the company bought out one of its biggest rivals?
 A: This was part of our .... to broaden our customer base.
2 Q: Some of our plants have very low productivity. What are you doing about this?
 A: We have taken steps to ensure that our .... are used more effectively. This is an important part of our strategic .... process.
3 Q: Why are you closing one of the plants?
 A: This is an issue of .... We don't have infinite financial resources and we want to concentrate investment on the most profitable models.
4 Q: Where can we read about the company's goals and values?
 A: Our main objectives are in the company's ....

16.2 Match the two parts of these extracts containing expressions from B opposite.

1 As large retail chains such as J. C. Penney make strategic

2 Rockwell has direct ties to technical universities. Its strategic

3 The CEO of First Guaranty said, 'We intend to make other strategic

4 Japanese firms' R&D units have the strategic

5 In the 1990s, Nokia made a strategic

6 Howard Schultz, the founder and leader of Starbucks, had the strategic

a vision to build a national retail brand.

b moves to stand-alone stores, what are traditional shopping malls to do?

c objective of building close ties with local universities and research organizations.

d partnerships in the US include Case Western Reserve University and Cleveland State University.

e acquisitions as well as focus on our own organic growth.'

f decision to concentrate on telecommunications and become a leading supplier of mobile telephone technology and networks.

16.3 Rewrite this article, replacing the underlined phrases with appropriate forms of expressions from C opposite. You can use some expressions more than once.

McDonald's arrived in China quite early and **(1)** was the biggest competitor by the time Burger King decided to **(2)** open restaurants there. Burger King did not have the resources to **(3)** aggressively enter the market, so it **(4)** occupied a small part of the market by opening just a small restaurant in Shanghai in order to test it. This was successful, so Burger King decided to open restaurants in cities all over China. Five years later, McDonald's **(5)** was still the biggest company in the market, with a 20 per cent market share. Meanwhile, one of their competitors, Schlotzsky's Deli, had already given up and decided to **(6)** leave the market.

Over to you

Think about your organization or one you would like to work for. Look at its website and find its mission statement. If it doesn't have one, what would you suggest?

17 Competition

A Competition

Very strong **competition** in an industry can also be described as:

- **cut-throat**
- **ferocious**
- **intense**
- **fierce**
- **stiff**

Actions that increase competition are said to **encourage, intensify** or **sharpen** it. Actions that limit competition are said to **harm, inhibit** or **stifle** it.

The main **competitors** in a particular industry are its **key players** (see Unit 19). Smaller competitors may be referred to as **minor players**.

Situations where there is only one supplier and no competition are **monopolies**.

B 'Competing' and 'competitive'

Competing and **competitive** are adjectives related to 'competition'. Two companies may produce **competing products** – products that compete with each other. A **competitive product** is one that has real and specific benefits in relation to others of the same type.

Here are some frequent combinations with 'competing':

competing		
	bids	price offers for a company in a takeover
	offerings	products from different companies
	suppliers	companies offering similar products or services
	technologies	technical ways of doing something

Here are some frequent combinations with 'competitive':

competitive		
	position	where a company is in relation to its competitors in terms of size, growth, etc.
	pressure	the force that one competitor can bring to bear in relation to another
	price	one that is similar to or lower than those for similar products
	threat	something that one competitor may do to weaken another's position
	advantage / edge	superior products, performance, etc. that a competitor can offer in relation to others and which give it a lead over its rivals
	strategy	a plan or plans for success in relation to competitors, and the study of this in business schools

17.1 Complete the sentences with appropriate forms of the correct verb in brackets from A opposite.

1 In banking in the European Union, 25 separate national rules and all sorts of exceptions may result in .... (encourage / stifle) competition rather than .... (encourage / stifle) it.
2 Fast bullet trains have .... (intensify / harm) competition in South Korea's domestic travel market.
3 The Federal Trade Competition rejected the idea that the combined companies would .... (intensify / harm) competition, noting that the two parties weren't direct competitors.
4 International agreements regulating market access by airlines .... (sharpen / inhibit) competition and are bad for customers.
5 Consumers should welcome new entrants to the credit market, not just because it widens their choice, but because it could lower the cost of credit by .... (sharpen / inhibit) competition.

17.2 Look at B opposite. Match the two parts of these extracts containing expressions with 'competing'.

1 What is to stop supposedly competing

2 Commtouch can position itself in the middle of the competing

3 Diamond Fields Resources Inc was the target of competing

4 The software is 25 per cent cheaper than competing

a bids from mining giants Inco Ltd and Xstrata.

b suppliers from secretly agreeing to keep prices high?

c offerings, with prices ranging from $300 to $450.

d technologies by offering 'unified messaging solutions'.

17.3 Look at B opposite again. Complete the sentences with appropriate forms of words that can follow 'competitive'.

1 He was criticized for being too Eurocentric and failing to pay sufficient attention to the competitive .... from south-east Asia.
2 The trick is to find businesses that can sustain their performances over the long term and have some competitive .... (2 expressions) to keep them ahead of their rivals.
3 For the price-conscious consumer, alternative retail outlets can offer organic food at more competitive ....
4 BankOne will enhance its competitive .... and boost its financial growth through the transaction, which is expected to add to earnings immediately.
5 Mall stores are under the most competitive .... that they've been under in their 40-year history, with new discounters and superstores increasingly moving in alongside traditional malls.
6 Decades of management theorizing around the world have produced mountains of books, many of which promise to deliver the secrets of success. But there is no consensus on competitive ....

Over to you

Think about your organization or one you would like to work for. Who are its fiercest competitors? Why are they a threat?

18 Companies and their industries

A Competitive forces

An important strategic thinker is Michael Porter[1]. He defines the five **competitive forces** at work in any **industry**.

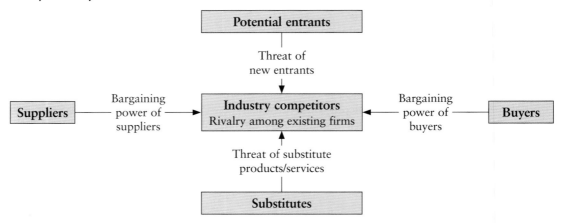

These are the factors that a firm needs to consider in developing its **competitive strategy** (see Unit 17). A successful firm has to **build** and **maintain** – keep – its **competitive advantage** in relation to these forces.

B SWOT analysis

SWOT stands for **strengths, weaknesses, opportunities, threats**.

In formulating strategy, a company should look at its strengths and weaknesses in relation to its competitors. For example, a good sales team is a strength, and poor internal communication is a weakness.

The company should also look at opportunities and threats in its **environment** – the strength of competitors, government regulation, the way that society is changing, etc. These are **external factors**. For example, a change in a country's legislation on broadcasting might represent an opportunity for a group that wants to buy a television company there. The change would probably also pose a threat to existing broadcasters.

The particular ways that a company organizes and combines its human resources, know-how, equipment and other assets are what Hamel and Prahalad[2] call its **core competencies**. These are **internal factors**.

C Be good at something

Porter says that competitive advantage can be based on:

- **cost leadership** – offering products or services at the lowest cost; this is one strategy to adopt in **volume industries** with competitors producing large numbers of similar products

- **differentiation** – offering products or services that give **added-value** in terms of quality or service compared to competitors

- **focus** – combining elements of the above two strategies to concentrate on a **niche** – a specific part of the market with particular needs

The danger, says Porter, is when a company does not follow any of these particular strategies and is **stuck in the middle**.

[1]*Competitive Strategy: Techniques for Analyzing Industries and Competitors*, Free Press, 2nd edition, 2004.
[2]*Competing for the Future*, Harvard Business School Press, 1996.

18.1 Look at A opposite and the examples (1–5) below of the expressions in the diagram boxes. Match each example with an appropriate form of one of the expressions.

1 Coca-Cola and Pepsi-Cola in soft drinks
2 a company that starts selling computer games when it has not sold them before
3 electrically powered cars in relation to petrol-driven cars
4 car manufacturers in relation to component manufacturers
5 component manufacturers in relation to car manufacturers

18.2 The head of a UK university is presenting a SWOT analysis of his institution in relation to its attractiveness to foreign students. Complete the table below with the expressions in italics in note form. The first one has been done as an example.

1 'We have some *very good lecturers*, especially in science and engineering.'
2 'There may be an *economic slowdown next year*, with fewer students able to afford to come here.'
3 'We are *situated in one of the UK's most attractive cities*.'
4 'We *need to improve our facilities* – students these days expect very high class accommodation, restaurants, etc.'
5 '*The English language* is a key asset. Everyone wants to study in English.'
6 'There are some *excellent universities in the US* that are also strong in the subjects that we teach. They may challenge our position.'
7 'In the long term, there are *potentially more and more students from abroad* looking to study in the UK.'

Strengths	Weaknesses	Opportunities	Threats
very good lecturers			

18.3 Look at the mission statements of these companies. Which strategy in C opposite does each correspond to?

1 'To make sports cars for discerning enthusiasts with high technical knowledge.'
2 'To sell clothing more cheaply than department stores.'
3 'To sell electrical goods with a high level of after-sales service.'

Over to you

Analyze your organization, or one you would like to work for, in relation to the industry it is in and to the forces in A opposite.

19 Key strategic issues

A Industries and their players

In some industries, like steel or tyres, there are few companies: these industries are **concentrated**. These are industries with just a few **key players** (see Unit 17). Other industries are **fragmented**; for example, there are millions of restaurants worldwide, and even the largest chain, McDonald's, only has a **market share** of less than 1 per cent in terms of all restaurant meals served worldwide.

Some industries have **low entry barriers** – anyone with a small amount of capital can open a restaurant.

If an industry has low entry barriers and is **attractive** because of its high potential **profitability**, there may be new **entrants**. This was the case for internet service providers a few years ago; a lot of companies offered this service at first.

Other industries, like steel, require massive investment in equipment, know-how, etc. Such investments are **high entry barriers**, and new entrants to the industry are rare.

B Mergers and acquisitions (M&A)

Some companies are very **acquisitive** – buying competitors in their industry or companies in other industries in a series of **acquisitions** or **takeovers**, which they may refer to as **strategic acquisitions**. Or a company may **merge** – combine as an equal – with another company of similar size.

A company may also own or buy its suppliers and customer companies in a situation or process of **vertical integration**.

The result of this may be an **unwieldy conglomerate** – a holding company with a large number of **subsidiaries** which may not be easy to manage profitably as a group.

C Make or buy?

Supporters of conglomerates pointed to **portfolio theory** – the idea that when demand for goods or services of one of the companies in the group was weak, it would be compensated by stronger demand for those of other companies in the group. This meant that overall profitability would be regular despite variations in profit from the different companies.

Recent strategic thinking, especially in the West, holds that conglomerates are not good. Many conglomerates have **disposed of** or **divested** their **non-core businesses**, selling them off in order to **concentrate on** their **core business**. This is related to the **make or buy decision** where companies decide whether to produce particular components or perform particular functions **in-house** or, on the other hand, to buy them in from an outside supplier (see Unit 31).

However, many conglomerates continue to exist. For example, in South Korea, there are **chaebols**. They were often started as **family(-owned) businesses**, where different members of the same family each owned and managed companies dealing with different parts of the industrial process in a situation of vertical integration (see above).

 Note The nouns relating to **dispose** and **divest** are **disposal** and **divestment**. They can be both countable and uncountable nouns. Compare **divestment** with **investment**.

19.1 Complete the crossword with the correct form of words from A, B and C opposite.

Across

8 and 5 Things that make it difficult to get into an industry (5,8)

9 A type of large Korean group of companies (7)

11 When a company sells a business activity (10)

13 See 12 down

15 If an industry is difficult to get into, entry barriers are .... (4)

17 A large group of different businesses (12)

Down

1 The idea used by believers in conglomerates (9,6)

2 A large industry with not many companies is .... (12)

3 When two companies join as equal partners, they .... (5)

4 A company's most important business activity: its .... business (4)

6 A company that buys lots of other companies is .... (11)

7 A large industry with lots of small competitors is .... (10)

10 A profitable industry that companies want to get into is .... (10)

12 and 13 across When a company owns or buys its suppliers or customers (8,11)

14 In a fragmented industry, each competitor only has a small market .... (5)

16 If an industry is easy to get into, entry barriers are .... (3)

19.2 An executive in a consumer goods company is talking. Complete what she says with expressions from A and B opposite.

'We make a wide range of consumer goods. Over the years we have made a number of **(1)** .... , buying companies that fit in with our long-term plan of being the number one consumer goods company in Europe. These **(2)** ....
(2 expressions) mean that we now own a large number of **(3)** .... , each with its own brands. We have become an **(4)** .... , and all this is very difficult to manage. So we are now reducing the number of brands from 300 to 100, and getting each unit of the company to concentrate on our long-term goal – increased **(5)** .... , which means better results for our shareholders. And our increased power will certainly dissuade new **(6)** .... from coming into the industry, so our position will be further strengthened.'

Over to you

Think of a recent merger or takeover. What benefits were claimed for it at the time? Have they materialized?

20 Innovation

A Innovation and the development process

Enrique Sanchez is head of new product development at a large consumer products company:

'We want to **foster creativity** and **innovation** – the development of new ideas. Ours is a large company, but we want to avoid becoming **bureaucratic**, with slow decision making.

'We encourage employees to be **creative** within the organization and to work on their own projects outside the usual frameworks; we allow them to spend 15 per cent of their time on this. We set up **skunk works** – a place away from the main company sites and outside the usual structures, to work on innovations. This is the way we do our **new product development**. The most famous example of this was IBM, when it developed its PC away from the company's main **research and development (R&D)** sites.

'We firmly believe that companies have only two basic functions: innovation and marketing. Our marketing people are heavily involved in new product development. They get the reactions of **focus groups** – groups of consumers who say what they think of the product – at a very early stage in the **development process**.'

B Pioneers and followers

'One problem is to know whether to introduce a product or service before anyone else or to wait for others to introduce similar products. Some say that if you **bring a product to market** first, you have **first mover advantage** – you can influence the way the market develops. These companies or their products are **trendsetters** or **innovators**. Others say that it's better to be **followers** and learn from the mistakes of the **pioneers**.'

Note
Pioneer is also a verb but is more frequent as a noun.

C Shakeout and consolidation

A new or **emerging industry**, perhaps one based on a new **technology**, can be **attractive**; the future **structure** of the industry is not yet **established** and there is room for many competitors. But as growth in the new market slows, smaller competitors with higher costs can no longer compete. They **drop out** or are bought by the larger companies in a process of **shakeout and consolidation**, leaving the larger companies with the resources to **dominate** the industry, which is now **mature**.

20.1 Look at A opposite. Then decide which category (a–f) these rules (1–14) used by Lockheed for skunk works projects to produce aircraft belong to.

> a budget and financing
> b dealings with contractors
> c facilities and access to them
> d managers' authority
> e number and payment of staff
> f procedures and systems

1 The skunk works manager must be given practically complete control of the program in all aspects. He/She should report to a division president or higher.
2 Strong but small project offices must be provided.
3 There must be a minimum number of reports required, but important work must be recorded thoroughly.
4 There must be a monthly cost review covering not only what has been spent and committed but also projected costs to the conclusion of the program.
5 Push more basic inspection responsibility back to subcontractors. Don't duplicate so much inspection.
6 The specifications applying to the equipment must be agreed to well in advance of contracting.
7 There must be mutual trust between the military project organization and the contractor, with very close cooperation on a day-to-day basis.
8 Because only a few people will be used in engineering and most other areas, ways must be provided to reward good performance by pay not based on the number of personnel supervised.

20.2 Complete the sentences with the correct forms of expressions from B opposite.

1 The iPhone was seen to be a .... in design and ease of use, and other phones have had to catch up.
2 An .... in email and online advertising, Yahoo has been shouldered aside in recent years by Google.
3 When one company .... a successful business, competition inevitably intensifies. Consumers benefit from the resulting cuts in prices and improvements in quality.
4 So far Taiwan has always been a ...., making things invented elsewhere more cheaply.

20.3 Look at the following facts about the development of the market for online book sales. (They are not in chronological order.) Complete each fact with an appropriate form of an expression from C opposite.

1 Some smaller companies stopped selling altogether – they ....
2 There is a trend towards fewer and bigger companies in the market, a trend towards

....
3 Selling books online in the 1990s was new – it was an ....
4 Amazon and a few others lead the industry – they .... it.
5 The market is no longer young – it is now ....
6 The 'rules of the game' are now fixed – the structure of the industry is

....

Over to you

- Is it always difficult for large organizations to come up with innovative ideas and products?
- How does your organization produce new ideas?

21 Preparing for the future

A Scenario planning

Manuel Ricardo works on long-term strategy in a large oil company:

'My job is to contribute to long-term plans for our future activities. We have to **anticipate** – judge and estimate – what competitors' behaviour and activities will be. We also have to look at trends in the general **social and economic environment,** and be ready to **respond to changes** in society and changes in the economy as a whole. This is called **scenario planning.** In our organization, we imagine ways in which the energy industry might change and **evolve** – how the industry might develop – and what the place of oil will be in relation to alternative fuels in 20, 50 or 100 years from now.'

B Futurology

'I'm a kind of **futurologist** or **futurist.** Of course, **futurology** is not an exact science, but there are ways of **forecasting** or **predicting** the future in a structured manner. There is the **Delphi method,** where a **panel of experts make forecasts** about a subject independently, and the forecasts are circulated to the other members of the group. Each member then comments on the others' observations. The process is **iterative** – repeated several times. Opinions **converge** – become more similar – and experts **reach a consensus** – an agreement about what is likely to happen. The method can be used to make **predictions** in a number of different **applications** – uses.

'The technique is based on the idea that a **structured group** will produce more accurate results than an unstructured one or from individuals working on their own. It can be adapted for use in face-to-face meetings, and is then called **mini-Delphi** or **Estimate–Talk–Estimate (ETE).**'

C Risk management

'A related area is **risk management.** Operating in politically unstable countries is one of the most extreme examples of where we have to manage risk. The dangers there may include **nationalization of assets** by the government.

'Elsewhere, we may be accused of working with governments that people do not approve of. We have to think about the impact of this in terms of our reputation for **social responsibility** (see Unit 48).

'There is the danger of oil spills from ships transporting our oil, with the resulting pollution and associated costs of fines, cleaning up, etc. In addition, there is the much greater long-term cost of the negative effect this has on our **image** – the way the company is perceived. A badly handled oil spill is a **public relations disaster.**

'These are some of the potential **crises** we face. We try to have **contingency plans** or **crisis management plans** for all the risks we can think of.

'If our computer systems are damaged, for example in a fire, we have **business continuity plans,** involving back-up machines on another site so that we can carry on working normally.'

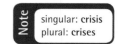

Note
singular: **crisis**
plural: **crises**

21.1 Manuel Ricardo is talking about the oil industry. Match the underlined words relating to the expressions in A and B opposite that he is referring to.

1 'In studying the trends in the <u>wider picture</u>, we may find that there is increasing consumer demand for alternative fuels such as wind energy, and we have to take account of this change in consumer expectations.'

2 'Of course, <u>people in my profession</u> take into account all the factors we can in making our forecasts, but what we do is an inexact science.'

3 'One of the problems with <u>this approach</u> is that the <u>members</u> will come up with the same ideas as the other participants. There is always a danger when you have <u>a view that everyone shares</u> that you exclude other possibilities.'

4 'When you make <u>these</u>, you can't avoid looking to the past.'

5 'Of course, <u>it</u> is an inexact science – the only thing you can say for sure is that the future will be like the past, but different.'

6 'In <u>this area</u>, some of our competitors are talking about scenarios over periods up to 300 years!'

7 <u>This process</u> of finding ideas and submitting them to others who then challenge them and send them back with comments can be very useful. (3 expressions)

8 It's very difficult to predict how industries will <u>change and develop</u>, and even more difficult to predict new industries that might emerge.

21.2 Look at C opposite. The questions are from shareholders at a tobacco company's annual general meeting. The answers are from the company's chief executive. Match the questions with the answers.

1 'Would you be prepared if the company's executives were kidnapped when working abroad?'

2 'Do you approve of the government's initiative on preventing children under 16 from smoking?'

3 'What are you doing to protect the company's image in health issues generally?'

4 'Is there a risk of nationalization of the company's assets by foreign governments?'

5 'Are you sure that you have done everything to prevent damage to the company's reputation in extreme or unusual situations?'

a 'Yes, we are fully aware of our social responsibility in this area.'

b 'Protecting the image of any tobacco company is difficult, but we support, for example, the European Union's plans for stricter health warnings on cigarette packets. We know our image will suffer if we don't.'

c 'Yes, we have the best public relations firm in the business who know exactly what to do to prevent public relations disasters.'

d 'No, the trend now is for governments to sell state-owned assets in the tobacco industry, rather than buy them!'

e 'Yes, we have contingency plans to deal with that. A special crisis management team will meet to deal with the situation.'

Over to you

- What is the biggest risk for your organization or one you would like to work for?
- How has your organization handled risks in the past? What lessons has it learnt?

22 The four Ps and beyond

A The four Ps

Susanna Chang is marketing manager at a mobile phone company:

'Of course, marketing is often defined in terms of the following:

- **Product** – deciding what products or services to sell. The word 'product' for us can refer to a product or a service, or a combination of these. We have to decide what our **offers** or **offerings** – products, services and combinations of these – will be.

- **Pricing** – setting prices that are attractive to customers and that are profitable for the company.

- **Place** – finding suitable **distribution channels** and **outlets** to reach these customer groups.

- **Promotion** – all the activities, not just **advertising** and other forms of **communication**, used to support the product. This includes everything from pre-sales information to after-sales service.

'These are the traditional **four Ps** of the **marketing mix** – the factors that we use in different combinations for different products and different potential buyers (see Unit 24).'

B Three more Ps

'But in services such as mobile phone communications, we also have to think about the following:

- **People** – The people **in contact with** our customers must have the right **attitude** – way of behaving, etc. – whether in our shops or in our call centres. They have to be **helpful, well-trained** and **highly informed** about our products and **highly motivated** to sell them. They are the public face of the company, not only during the **sales process** but afterwards. Customers can come back with their phones to get more "training" from our sales assistants on how to use them. This **after-sales service** is all part of the overall **sales support**.

- **Process** – This is the whole series of events from initial interest in our company's services, purchase of a phone, connection, invoicing, etc. This should be as **efficient** – well-run, problem-free, etc. – as possible and contribute to a positive **customer experience**.

- **Physical evidence** – Customers can see our phones in our shops or on our website, but they have to be convinced of the benefits of our service as a whole. Until they do, the service remains **intangible** – not visible. We provide physical evidence of services by giving in-store demonstrations of people using our phones, accessing the Internet, etc.

'So my job is much more than organizing advertising campaigns. I work with engineers, finance people and other senior managers to find offerings that will appeal to customers.'

22.1 Susanna Chang is talking about her organization. To which 'P' of the marketing mix in A opposite is she referring to in each of her statements?

1 We want to offer calls at a lower cost than our competitors.

2 We don't put our own brand on mobile phones – we sell phones from different manufacturers for use on different call plans: both pre-paid and monthly-billed customers.

3 We advertise more and more on the Internet.

4 We have our own high-street outlets, but we don't sell through other chains.

5 We phone existing customers to try to persuade them to buy more sophisticated phones where they can download other services.

6 We sponsor sports events.

22.2 Look at B opposite. Complete the section headings (a–c) with the three Ps from B opposite. Then complete the gaps (1–7) with expressions from B. Use some expressions more than once.

a ....

A service can't be experienced before it is delivered. This means that choosing to use a service can be perceived as a risky business because you are buying something (1) ....
This uncertainty can be reduced by helping customers to 'see' what they are buying. Facilities such as a clean, tidy reception area can help to reassure them.

b ....

Anyone who comes into (2) .... with your customers will make an impression, and that can have a profound effect, positive or negative, on customer satisfaction. It is essential that all employees who work with customers are the right kind of people for the job. They must be highly informed and (3) .... , be appropriately trained, and have the right (4) .... in dealing with customers. The level of after-sales (5) .... and advice provided by a business is one way of adding value to what you offer, and can give you an important edge over your competitors.

c ....

The (6) .... of giving a service, and the behaviour of those who deliver it, are crucial to customer satisfaction. Issues such as waiting times, the information given to customers and (7) .... staff are all vital to keep customers happy. Customers are not interested in the details of how your business runs. What matters to them is that the business works for them.

Over to you

- Think of a product that you bought recently. Describe your purchase in terms of the four Ps in A opposite.
- Now describe a service you have bought recently in terms of the additional Ps in B opposite.

23 Customer satisfaction

The four Cs

Susanna Chang, mobile phone marketing manager (see Unit 22), continues:

'The whole marketing effort can be looked at from the point of view of customers, rather than the company, with the **four Cs**:

- **Customer solution** – we aim to find a solution to a customer "problem" by offering the right combination of product(s) and service(s) to satisfy particular customer needs. For example, pay-as-you-go was a dream solution for parents worried about children running up big phone bills.

- **Customer cost** – the price paid by the customer for the product. It includes the "price" related to not buying another product of the same or another type. For example, someone who buys a sophisticated mobile may not then have the money to buy a laptop computer that they wanted.

- **Convenience** – distributing our products in the way that is most convenient for each type of customer. We have to decide, for instance, how many new shops to open and where they should be. We also have to think about the people who prefer to buy online.

- **Communication** with the customer – customers are informed about products through advertising, and so on, but the communication is two-way. Customers also communicate with us, for example through telephone helplines. This is a good way for us to find out more about what our customers want. We can then change or improve our offering, and get ideas for new offerings.

'Thinking of the marketing mix in these terms helps us maintain a true **customer orientation** or **customer focus**.'

B Customer expectations

When customers get what they hoped for, their **expectations** are **met** and there is **customer satisfaction**. Products, sadly, often **fall below expectations**.

When expectations are **exceeded** – you get more than you expected – there may even be **customer delight** (see Unit 12), but this partly depends on how **involved** you are in the purchase. There is a difference in your degree of **involvement** when you buy different products. For example, there is low involvement when you buy something ordinary like petrol, and high involvement when you purchase something emotionally important such as a family holiday.

C Customer dissatisfaction

Research shows that 95 per cent of dissatisfied customers don't complain; they just change suppliers. Satisfied customers create new business by telling up to 12 other people. Dissatisfied ones will tell up to 20 people*. **Word-of-mouth** is a powerful form of advertising.

Some say that encouraging **customer loyalty** or **allegiance** is important for profitability. They say that **customer retention** – keeping existing customers – is key. Getting **repeat business** is five times cheaper than finding new customers. (For another view, see the article opposite.)

Customer defection must be reduced as much as possible of course, but a company can learn from **lost customer analysis** – analysing its mistakes by asking those who do leave why they **defected**.

Services like mobile phone and cable TV companies have to reduce **churn** – the percentage of customers who change suppliers or who stop using the service altogether each year. This is very costly; the companies would prefer, of course, to keep existing customers and add more in order to build their **customer base**.

*Philip Kotler and Kevin Keller: *Marketing Management*, Pearson, 2008.

23.1 A new customer for Sky satellite television services is talking. Look at A opposite and find which 'C' he is referring to in each of the sentences.

1 I wanted the satellite dish to be installed at a time that suited me.

2 I had some questions about how to use the service, so I looked at the Sky website. It answered all my queries.

3 The cost is very reasonable considering all the channels you get.

4 I wanted a TV service with good reception. The ordinary TV signal in my area is very bad.

23.2 Match the two parts of these sentences containing expressions from B opposite.

1 The systematic analysis of customer claims constitutes an important source of information on customer
2 Dreze has researched customer
3 The company's acquisition of its rival led to customer
4 Maintaining customer
5 You can sometimes obtain customer

a loyalty programs for years and says the best programs allow customers to earn points outside the business but redeem them inside.
b satisfaction, or more likely, on customer dissatisfaction.
c delight by delivering more than you promise.
d defections, due to declines in service quality.
e allegiance results from continuing to provide excellent service, which dissuades your customers from wanting to go elsewhere.

23.3 Look at C opposite. Then read the article and find the following:

1 five industries
2 three types of customers, and the behaviour of each type
3 one finding of the McKinsey research into loyalty
4 four findings of the research by Werner Reinatz and V. Kumar

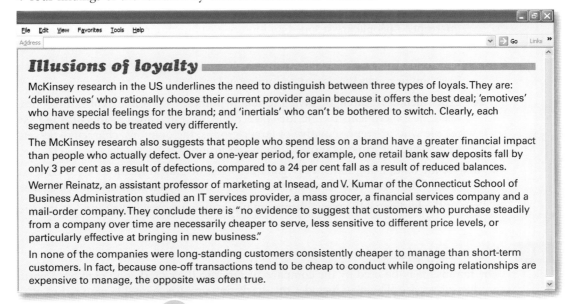

Illusions of loyalty

McKinsey research in the US underlines the need to distinguish between three types of loyals. They are: 'deliberatives' who rationally choose their current provider again because it offers the best deal; 'emotives' who have special feelings for the brand; and 'inertials' who can't be bothered to switch. Clearly, each segment needs to be treated very differently.

The McKinsey research also suggests that people who spend less on a brand have a greater financial impact than people who actually defect. Over a one-year period, for example, one retail bank saw deposits fall by only 3 per cent as a result of defections, compared to a 24 per cent fall as a result of reduced balances.

Werner Reinatz, an assistant professor of marketing at Insead, and V. Kumar of the Connecticut School of Business Administration studied an IT services provider, a mass grocer, a financial services company and a mail-order company. They conclude there is "no evidence to suggest that customers who purchase steadily from a company over time are necessarily cheaper to serve, less sensitive to different price levels, or particularly effective at bringing in new business."

In none of the companies were long-standing customers consistently cheaper to manage than short-term customers. In fact, because one-off transactions tend to be cheap to conduct while ongoing relationships are expensive to manage, the opposite was often true.

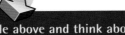

Over to you

Look again at the article above and think about your own loyalty to a particular brand as a consumer. Are you a 'deliberative', an 'emotive' or an 'inertial'? Describe your behaviour.

24 Knowing your customers 1

A Market intelligence and market research

Market intelligence is knowing about the **latest trends** in a **market** – the people or organizations who buy or might buy something. These trends include changes in buyers' needs, new products that competitors are developing, and so on. Some intelligence can be gathered by salespeople reporting what they see going on when they visit customers, etc. Or it might be gathered by companies sending **mystery shoppers** – researchers who pretend to be real consumers – who go into shops to see how the company's products are displayed, how salespeople behave, etc.

However, finding out fully about a market requires systematic **market research** or **marketing research**. A specialized company that carries this out is a **market research firm**.

Research can be carried out using **secondary data** – information that already exists and is publicly available – and **primary data** – information collected for a specific purpose.

B Research stages

Research takes place in these stages:

a **Define the problem** and **the research objectives** – identify the exact purpose of the research.

b **Develop the research plan** – decide how the research is to be carried out.

c **Collect the data** – gather the information. Primary data can be collected through:

  - **observational approach** – for example, watching how shoppers behave in shops when choosing between different products.

  - **focus group** – a small group of people is invited to discuss a product, service, organization, etc. with a **moderator** – a specialist in running group discussions like this.

  - **online focus group** – a group of people discuss the product, etc. online in a **chat room** discussion between several people on the Internet.

  - **survey research** – a **questionnaire** is given to people face to face, for example in **mall intercepts** – people are stopped and interviewed in shopping centres or, again, on the Internet. Website users are increasingly receiving questionnaires in this way.

  - **behavioural data** – information about what people actually buy, rather than what they say they buy or might buy (see **data mining** in Unit 26).

  - **experimental research**, involving **testing hypotheses** – possible explanations or causes – in scientific experiments to find the correct one. Research such as this may use **samples** of people who are representative of larger groups; the opinions, characteristics, etc. of the sample are the same as those of the wider group.

d **Analyse the data**, using **statistical techniques** – mathematical methods are used to analyze large amounts of data and **draw conclusions** from it – find key information of use to marketers.

e **Present the findings** – the **researchers** communicate what they have found in their research to the organization.

C Marketing plans

The findings may be used by the company as input to their **marketing plan** for a particular product or service. The plan includes the **marketing mix** (see Unit 22) required to achieve desired results. This type of plan is **tactical** or **operational** – relating to the selection, timing and spending on each element of the mix.

A grand plan affecting a company's whole future direction is its **strategic marketing plan**.

24.1 Complete the sentences with appropriate forms of expressions from A opposite.

1 What makes a good ....? The best notice both small details and the big picture. They focus on their own experience, but also what is happening at the next counter.

2 Salespersons may not like having to spend time on a task for which they do not receive any payment. In order to organize the .... function of the sales force, sales managers should explicitly include this responsibility in the salesperson's job description.

3 We conducted .... collection using interviews and .... collection using published material.

4 Even in a relatively youth-oriented industry, such as athletic footwear, seniors spent nearly 13 per cent more in the past year than they did two years ago, according to data from the NPD Group, a New York ....

5 The .... in pet food emphasize not only natural ingredients but also an increased obligation to identify the precise origins of those ingredients.

24.2 Match these stages (1–5) in a market research project with the stages (a–e) in B opposite.

1 Researchers stopped people in the street and asked them into the rooms to taste three different new instant coffees. They asked which one they preferred and got them to answer a questionnaire.

2 Information from the tastings was analyzed – not only the numbers of people who preferred each type of coffee, but also their professions, social class, etc.

3 Managers from the market research firm were invited by Nestlé to its offices in Zurich. The research firm recommended that the coffee to be marketed should be the least strong of the three that had been tested, along with many other conclusions that would affect the marketing plan.

4 Researchers decided that they would need a sample of at least 1,000 coffee drinkers in each major European country. They rented rooms in buildings on busy streets in Paris and other European capitals where they could get people to taste the possible new types of coffee.

5 A foods company wanted to find out if there would be a market for a new instant coffee in Europe. It contacted Nielsen, a market research firm.

24.3 Look at C opposite. Does each of these examples relate to a) an operational/tactical marketing plan, or b) a strategic marketing plan?

Following market research:

1 Northwest Airlines merged with Delta Airlines to guarantee their future.
2 Ford selected the TV programmes during which its new Fiesta model would be advertised.
3 IBM sold its PC business to Lenovo.
4 Nokia designed mobile phone models specifically for satellite navigation as well as making calls.
5 Apple cut the price of its iPod.

Over to you

Describe one type of market research that your organization, or one you would like to work for, carries out, and some of its findings.

25 Knowing your customers 2

A Segmentation

A **segment** is a group of customers or potential customers with similar characteristics, needs and requirements. **Segmentation** allows marketers to identify and **differentiate** between the needs of the customer groups that make up a particular market. Marketers may offer different products to different segments, or they may offer the same product, marketing it in different ways. For example, HD (high-definition) television screens are marketed differently for households and professional users such as cafés and bars. They are **positioned** in different ways for each segment.

Segmentation, identifying particular **target groups**, can be done in various ways.

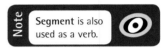
Note: **Segment** is also used as a verb.

B Customer groups

Customers can also be divided up by **behavioural segmentation** – why, when and how often they buy a particular product, their attitude towards it, etc. Identifying people who drink Coke at home rather than in cafés is an example of behavioural segmentation based on **situation of use**.

In **demographic segmentation**, customers are divided up on the basis of **age, occupation** and **social class** – middle class, working class, etc. A company may intend its products to **appeal to** a particular **demographic** – to be attractive to one of these groups.

People from a given social class may spend their money in particular ways, but it can be more useful to look at people's **lifestyles** – the overall pattern of how they live, what they buy, etc. Here, **values, opinions, activities** and **interests** are important.

Psychographics is the activity of attempting to categorize people in this way. For example, the VALS system* divides people into groups such as:

a **actualizers** – successful, active people with cultivated, expensive tastes
b **strugglers** – poorer, elderly people who are loyal to familiar brands
c **experiencers** – young, enthusiastic people who spend a lot on clothes, music, etc. without planning for a long time what they are going to buy
d **believers** – conservative people who prefer familiar products and established brands
e **makers** – practical family-oriented people who buy practical, functional products such as tools
f **strivers** – people without much money, but who buy stylish products to imitate those with more money

C New technologies, new concerns

In retailing, **radio-frequency identification** (**RFID**) can be used to **track** – follow – purchases made by individual customers even more closely than **loyalty cards** (see Unit 26). Each product is identified by a **tag**. **Electronic readers** can **scan** tags in one go to see what is in a shopping trolley, a kitchen cupboard, etc. This information can be used to build **profiles** – detailed descriptions – of individual shoppers.

On the Internet, the technology exists to analyze **traffic** to a particular **website** by tracking the way that **visitors** use it and **interact** with it. How many people just look around and leave without buying anything? How many **conversions** – visitors who go on to buy something – are there? How many **virtual shopping carts** are **abandoned** – how many start a purchase without completing it?

And the software exists to track the overall **internet usage** of individual users – all the sites that they visit, how long they stay on each site, etc. Marketers can use this information to build profiles of different user groups.

Of course, all these things raise concerns in the areas of **privacy** and **confidentiality**.

*You can take the VALS questionnaire and get your own VALS profile on the Internet.

25.1 Use expressions from A and B opposite to complete these statements by people working for different organizations. You can use some expressions more than once.

1 'I work for a food products company. We make a powder that can be added to hot milk to make a nutritious drink. It is used to make two different products and sold under two different names – to mothers who feed it to their babies and to old people who drink it to get important vitamins. This is the basis of our .... Of course, these are two entirely different ....?'

2 'We sell car insurance. We calculate the premiums using applicants' postcodes because this tells us about the areas our customers live in and their .... We are great believers in ....?'

3 'I work for a political party. When we knock on people's doors and ask them to vote for us, we never try to persuade people who are hostile to us. We concentrate on those who are favourable to us in some way, even if they haven't voted for us before. This .... allows us to target our resources better.'

4 'I work on health campaigns to discourage people from smoking. One of the most important .... is young people from 12 to 18. We want to discourage them from taking up smoking in the first place.'

25.2 Look at B opposite. Match the consumers (1–6) with the VALS types (a–f)in B opposite.

1 a father of three children who spends a large part of his weekends in do-it-yourself stores
2 a middle-aged person who goes out to buy a vacuum cleaner, chooses a Hoover and avoids the new 'hi-tech' brands like Dyson
3 a professional person in her 30s earning €80,000 a year who buys opera tickets at €100 each
4 a single woman of 22 who spends a large proportion of her income eating out and on clubbing without thinking much about her spending
5 a woman in her late 20s who spends 30 per cent of her income on expensive clothes brands so as to feel more at ease with colleagues who are earning more than her
6 someone with a basic pension struggling to reach the end of the month, who buys food brands that she knew in her childhood

25.3 Use expressions, and expressions grammatically related to them, from C opposite to complete the text.

More enterprise features

Google Analytics now makes the features that experts demand easy to use for everyone. Gain rich insights into your website (1) .... with Advanced Segmentation, Custom Reporting, Motion Charts and more.

IMPROVE YOUR ONLINE RESULTS

Learn more about where your (2) .... come from and how they (3) .... with your site. You'll get the information that you need to write better ads, strengthen your marketing initiatives and create higher-converting websites. Learn more about the benefits. Google Analytics is free for everyone, whether you are an advertiser, publisher or site owner.

TEST YOUR WEBSITE AND INCREASE (4) .... RATES

You can now use your Google Analytics login to access Website Optimiser. Find out which page designs, headlines and graphics (5) .... the most visitors.

Over to you

Think of a product you have bought recently and analyze your purchase in terms of some of the different types of segmentation.

26 Knowing your customers 3

A Data and databases

'Hi, I'm John. I'm head of **data management** at a big supermarket chain. Customers can get money back by using our **loyalty card** when they go shopping. Loyalty cards allow customers to collect **points** that can be **redeemed against** future purchases, either with us or with other retailers in the same scheme.

'This gives us masses of data about our customers' **buying habits** which we then **hold** on our **database**. We can follow what each of our customers buys and **enrich the database** with this information.'

Here are some frequent combinations with 'data':

data	**analysis**	finding useful information in data (see Unit 24)
	management	the way data is collected, organized, used, etc.
	mining	finding useful information in large amounts of data, using advanced techniques
	protection	preventing access to data by unauthorized people and organizations
	warehousing	keeping data safely

B Customer relationship management

'Of course, with all the information we have on our computers in our **data warehouses**, powerful computers are needed to analyze it. This analysis is called **data mining**. We look for particular patterns in **consumer behaviour**. The data can be used to **target** particular types of customer. We build **consumer profiles**. For example, if someone has bought organic food in the past, special offers are sent to them so that they get reduced prices on future purchases of organic food.

'All this is part of the wider picture of **customer relationship management** (**CRM**) – getting to know your customers. The computer programs that we buy to do our data mining are referred to by their sellers, often companies who specialize in this, as **CRM software packages** or **CRM solutions**.

'Dealing with customers as individuals is our ultimate goal, but we are still a long way from this ideal of **one-to-one marketing**. This has also been described as **segment-of-one marketing**. The computer maker Dell may be on its way to this ideal; it puts together its products according to the **specifications** – requirements – of individual customers in a process of **mass customization**.

'There are issues of **privacy** and **confidentiality** that we have to be careful about – customers have the right to check the information that we hold about them. We must be careful to obey the law on **data protection**.'

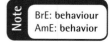

Note: BrE: behaviour AmE: behavior

26.1 Read this article relating to the ideas in A and B opposite. Decide if these statements are true or false.

The first paragraph:

1 could be referring to banks, supermarkets and mobile phone operators.
2 is about companies who understand CRM and use it successfully.
3 says that some companies have quite basic methods of understanding their customers.

The second paragraph:

4 says that really understanding data about customers means being able to act on it.
5 refers to a supermarket that introduced loyalty cards just to increase customer loyalty.
6 has an example about sales of a product that were rising, and this caused the supermarket to stock more in order to attract more customers of the same type.

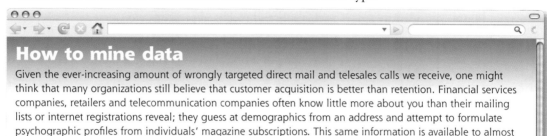

How to mine data

Given the ever-increasing amount of wrongly targeted direct mail and telesales calls we receive, one might think that many organizations still believe that customer acquisition is better than retention. Financial services companies, retailers and telecommunication companies often know little more about you than their mailing lists or internet registrations reveal; they guess at demographics from an address and attempt to formulate psychographic profiles from individuals' magazine subscriptions. This same information is available to almost any company. There is nothing unique about this data, and little that can help one company differentiate their unique offer from another.

The major problem for businesses is to understand what the data they have really means and then turn that into actionable information. The supermarkets introduced loyalty cards for a better reason than just providing a small discount to the consumer. They hoped to get some loyalty and some useful data to analyze purchase profiles and customer characteristics. For example, a British supermarket was about to stop selling a line of expensive French cheeses that were not selling well. But data mining showed that the few people who were buying the cheeses were among the supermarket's most profitable customers, so it was worth keeping the cheeses so as to retain these customers.

26.2 Match the two parts of these sentences containing expressions from C opposite.

1 We store data in a way that ensures the strongest
2 Linkages between customer satisfaction, customer loyalty and customer relationship management (CRM) have been created.
3 In future, computers will be able to follow us down the High Street, checking which shops we go into and what we buy.
4 If customers can't opt out, then that breaks European data
5 Bell Canada has adopted a faster, more flexible CRM

a Over time, emphasis has shifted away from raw satisfaction measures towards loyalty and CRM.
b Critics find the prospect of 'one-to-one marketing' somewhat disturbing.
c protection law, which demands that companies can't store your info without asking your permission.
d safeguards are in place to protect privacy and confidentiality.
e solution in less than two months. The objectives were to ensure customer service and support through quick implementation.

Over to you

Think about your organization or one you would like to work for. What kind of information does it hold about its customers?

27 Brands and branding

A Brand equity

A **brand** is a name given to a product or group of products so that they can be easily recognized. 'The most distinctive power of professional marketers is their ability to **create, maintain, protect** and **enhance** – strengthen the power of – **brands**,' says Philip Kotler*.

Here are some frequent combinations with 'brand'. These are some of the issues in **branding** – the art and science of using brands:

brand	image	what people think of when they think of a brand
	loyalty	the degree to which people continue to buy a brand
	awareness	the degree to which people know about a brand
	identity	what a brand means, represents, etc.
	recognition	the degree to which people recognize a brand
	equity	the value of a brand to its owners, as sometimes shown on a firm's balance sheet

> **Note** The combinations with **brand** are given in descending order of frequency.

B Brand positioning and differentiation

A firm can **position a brand** by emphasizing its characteristics and benefits in relation to other brands – this is **brand positioning**. A company can **position its products** in a particular way in relation to each other and/or to competing products – **product positioning** – or it can **position itself** in relation to other companies. This can be represented on a **positioning map**.

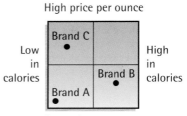

Here is an example of a positioning map for different brands of breakfast food.

Differentiation is when a company designs a product in a way that distinguishes it from competitors' brands and communicates the comparative benefits to customers in its sales documentation, advertising, etc. For example, Air New Zealand ran a series of advertisements with scenes 'filmed recently in our cabins'. By showing these authentic scenes, the airline wanted to **differentiate** itself as genuinely more caring towards customers, more human, etc.

C Brand stretching

A **flagship brand** is the most important brand owned by an organization – for example, 'Coke' is the most famous of the many soft drink brands owned by Coca-Cola. A **generic brand** is one used on a variety of different products. For example, the brand name 'Nestlé' is used on all the food products the company owns, even if another brand name is also used on some of the products.

Brand stretching or **brand extension** is when a company uses an existing brand name for new types of product. Consumers are expected to **associate** some of the same characteristics with the new product – think of the product in the same ways – but there are limits to this. Brand stretching can lead to **brand dilution**, making the brand less powerful, and thus can **damage the core** – main – **brand**.

*Philip Kotler and Kevin Keller: *Marketing Management*, Pearson, 2008.

27.1 Match the two parts of these sentences containing expressions from A and B opposite.

1 We saw Formula 1 motor racing as a cost-effective opportunity of increasing our brand
2 Taco Bell's strong brand
3 Simon and Sullivan (2007) define brand
4 Pharmaceutical companies sold prescription drugs at college health centers at large discounts so as to grab customers at a young age to build brand
5 Cingular has done a tremendous job of building brand
6 It's true that BMW's brand

a image evokes food dripping with sour cream and cheddar cheese.
b recognition over the past few years, but the name change makes sense now because AT&T needs to have a single, unified brand.
c awareness worldwide.
d identity is to do with more aggressive, more fashionable, more exciting, sportier cars than competing luxury brands.
e equity as the profits from branded products over and above the profits that would result from the sale of unbranded products.
f loyalty that might last a lifetime.

27.2 Look at B opposite. Complete each sentence with the correct form of the word in brackets.

1 Las Vegas has successfully .... (position) itself as an attractive destination for conventions.
2 SGI is .... (position) the Altix as a workhorse that will run with a minimum fuss rather than as a breakthrough machine designed to set supercomputer records.
3 The brand .... (position) has shifted with a new marketing strategy, significantly enhancing the fashionability of the Burberry brand.
4 Superior products and processes provide a means to .... (differentiate) the corporation from its competitors.
5 The term '...............................' (differentiate) is preferable because it throws the emphasis on the need to be 'better' than rival products not just in some general way but in precisely specified ways.
6 The marketers of all these different brands of vodka will say, 'Well, ours tastes better' or 'Ours is special this way or that way' – they're all trying to .... (differentiate) their brand.

27.3 Look at C opposite. Was each of these brand extensions successful, do you think? Give reasons for your thinking.

1 Ivory soap extended to dishwashing liquid and gentle care clothes washing detergent.
2 Bic pens extended to perfume using the 'small disposable pocket items' association.
3 Coke extended to New Coke.
4 Dole pineapple juice extended to fruit juice, fruit salad and frozen fruit bars.
5 Woolite fabric wash extended to carpet cleaner spray.
6 Campbell soups extended to spaghetti sauce.

Over to you

Think about your organization or one you would like to work for. What are its brands? What are its flagship brands? Are there any examples of brand extension?

28 Global brands

A Steps abroad 1

Katrin Braun is marketing manager for a German company that makes fork lifts:

'We started to get inquiries from Asia so we **appointed** – found and used – **agents** there who could help us with **indirect export**. They **represented** us and sold our machinery. These **exclusive agents** each had their own **sales area** – the agent in each area was the only person allowed to sell our products there.

'Sales grew, and we moved on to **direct export** – we no longer used agents but handled exports ourselves. We had an **export manager** based here in Germany, but she spent ten months a year travelling in our different markets.'

Fork lifts

B Steps abroad 2

'Then we started **licensing** our production techniques to companies abroad – we sold them the **rights** to **manufacture** our fork lifts **under licence** for their markets. In China, for example, we had a **licensing agreement** with a company to produce and market our fork lifts there. But in India, we signed a **joint venture** agreement with an established materials handling company who knew the market well. We worked with them as equal partners. We set up a special company and we each invested the same amount of money in the project. In addition, personnel from both companies were involved.

'The agreement worked very well for five years, but then we decided to make a **direct investment** in India; we decided to build a fork lift production plant near Hyderabad and market our products ourselves.'

> **Note**
> BrE: **licence** – noun, **license** – verb
> AmE: **license** – noun and verb

> **Note**
> Alternatives to **licensing agreement** in this context are **licensing arrangement**, **licensing deal** and **licensing pact**. The four expressions are used in this order of frequency.

C Think global, act local?

'We have **global offerings** – we offer exactly the same products all over the world – as requirements in fork lifts are the same everywhere. We treat the world as a **homogenous** market – we don't need to **adapt** our fork lifts to individual markets. Companies that do this talk, informally, about **glocalization**.

'AFL is now a **global brand** – our products are enjoyed in 120 countries all over the world.'

28.1 Complete the emails from a Hong Kong manufacturer of air conditioners called Sophaircon with correct forms of expressions from A and B opposite. (Use some expressions more than once.) Then put the emails into their probable chronological order.

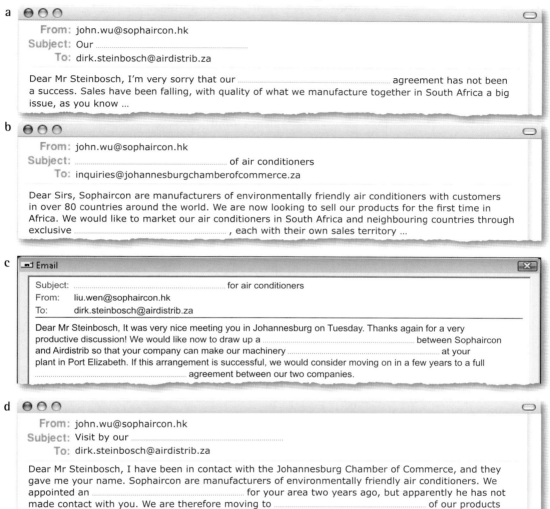

a

From: john.wu@sophaircon.hk
Subject: Our ....
To: dirk.steinbosch@airdistrib.za

Dear Mr Steinbosch, I'm very sorry that our .... agreement has not been a success. Sales have been falling, with quality of what we manufacture together in South Africa a big issue, as you know ...

b

From: john.wu@sophaircon.hk
Subject: .... of air conditioners
To: inquiries@johannesburgchamberofcommerce.za

Dear Sirs, Sophaircon are manufacturers of environmentally friendly air conditioners with customers in over 80 countries around the world. We are now looking to sell our products for the first time in Africa. We would like to market our air conditioners in South Africa and neighbouring countries through exclusive ...., each with their own sales territory ...

c

Email

Subject: .... for air conditioners
From: liu.wen@sophaircon.hk
To: dirk.steinbosch@airdistrib.za

Dear Mr Steinbosch, It was very nice meeting you in Johannesburg on Tuesday. Thanks again for a very productive discussion! We would like now to draw up a .... between Sophaircon and Airdistrib so that your company can make our machinery .... at your plant in Port Elizabeth. If this arrangement is successful, we would consider moving on in a few years to a full .... agreement between our two companies.

d

From: john.wu@sophaircon.hk
Subject: Visit by our ....
To: dirk.steinbosch@airdistrib.za

Dear Mr Steinbosch, I have been in contact with the Johannesburg Chamber of Commerce, and they gave me your name. Sophaircon are manufacturers of environmentally friendly air conditioners. We appointed an .... for your area two years ago, but apparently he has not made contact with you. We are therefore moving to .... of our products into Africa and our ...., Liu Wen, is planning to visit South Africa next month. Would you be interested in meeting him to discuss possible requirements for our machinery?

28.2 Look at C opposite. Does each of the companies (1–3) below a) have a standard global offering, or b) adapt its products to specific markets?

1 a car company that offers different interiors for northern Europe, where customers prefer a more 'cosy' feel
2 a soft drinks company that makes its products sweeter for some markets
3 a do-it-yourself store chain that sells the same product range in stores on five continents

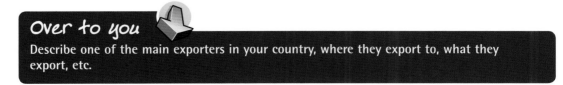

Over to you

Describe one of the main exporters in your country, where they export to, what they export, etc.

29 Supply chain management

Manufacturing

Here are some frequent combinations with 'manufacturing':

manufacturing	sector	the sector that makes things, rather than other sectors of the economy
	plant	a factory
	jobs	work making things, rather than in other sectors
	productivity	the amount produced by each worker, or group of workers – their **output**
	capacity	the amount that can be made at a particular plant, or at plants as a whole
	operations	activities related to making things
	process	all the stages involved in making something

Manufacturing plant sounds more modern than **factory** or **works**. **Fab plant** is used to talk about one where hi-tech manufacturing of **silicon chips** – the main components of computers – takes place. An **assembly plant** is one where products such as cars are put together on **assembly lines**.

A new plant is built and production is **ramped up** – progressively increased. Perhaps the plant will **operate at full capacity** – produce as much as it is able to – or **below capacity**. A plant that is not operating at all is **idle**.

Manufacturing plant

Manufacturing operations depend on networks of **suppliers** of **raw materials**, **components**, etc. that have to be ordered and delivered at the right time. These suppliers make up the **supply chain**, and organizing and managing it efficiently is **supply chain management** (see Unit 30).

Vertical integration

When Ford started making cars, it raised its own sheep to provide wool for the seat covers! This is an example of **vertical integration** – when a company produces everything internally that it needs, owning all the stages of the supply chain itself.

Many organizations **outsource** some of their requirements and **buy** them **in** from outside (see Unit 31). The buying-in process is known formally as **procurement**.

In advanced manufacturing, suppliers are **integrated into** a manufacturer's information systems. They often deliver required parts **just-in-time**, eliminating the need for **warehousing – handling** and **storage** in expensive **warehouses**. Managers from the manufacturer often supervise the supplier's own **production lines**. This leads to **clusters** – groups – of suppliers located very near the manufacturer, their main or only customer. Plants such as these that provide components to only one nearby manufacturer are **captive plants**.

Retailing

Services such as **retail** that involve the movement of physical goods also depend, of course, on managing the supply chain efficiently. The efficient **transport** or **distribution** of goods, and their storage, especially in **automated warehouses** managed by sophisticated computer programs, is known as **logistics** (see Unit 30).

29.1 Match the two parts of these sentences containing expressions from A opposite.

1 The $40 million perfume bottle manufacturing
2 Our improved financial results are due to better manufacturing productivity,
3 North Kentucky has lost about 1,700 manufacturing
4 Many Hong Kong manufacturers have adopted advanced technology and machinery in the manufacturing
5 In the manufacturing
6 Hoover has twice as much manufacturing
7 Gruma, with 2006 revenue of $2.8 billion, has manufacturing

a led by Eric Steenburgh, our Chief Operating Officer.
b jobs during the year, continuing a decade-long decline.
c plant in Covington, Georgia is the only one that French glass manufacturing giant Saint-Gobain operates in North America.
d sector, electronics has become a major export activity.
e capacity as is needed; the North Canton plant has 900,000 square feet of unused space.
f operations on five continents, and its products are sold in more than 50 countries.
g process to improve efficiency and product quality.

29.2 Complete the article with these expressions from A and B opposite. Use one expression twice.

| captive plants | integrated | just-in-time | process | suppliers | warehouse |

When Western businesspeople went to Japan, they discovered the interlocking relationships between companies and their **(1)** .... , often funded or owned by a common umbrella organization, the Keiretsu.

These company partnerships were quite natural, and as the geniuses at Toyota carried out decades of warfare on waste in every part and **(2)** .... of their business, what could be more wasteful than supplies on **(3)** .... shelves for eventual use? Out of Japan came **(4)** .... supplies, nerve-wracking for traditional Western factory managers. It is still exciting to see less than an hour's supply of car seats stored in a Japanese auto plant, already stacked to match the colour of the cars that are on the production line.

Behind the handshake between need and supply was something more than **(5)** .... computer systems. When Japanese auto companies started manufacturing in Britain, they trained some local UK suppliers to their rigorous needs. But the vital components were made in new **(6)** .... built by their usual Japanese **(7)** .... close to the British plant.

29.3 Complete the table containing expressions from B and C opposite.

Verb	Noun(s)
retail	................., retailing
warehouse	................., warehousing
transport	................., transportation
distribute	
	outsourcing

Over to you

Think of a manufacturer in your country and describe its probable supply chain.

30 Logistics

Logistics

The Council of Supply Chain Management Professionals (CSCMP) in the US has defined **logistics** as '… that part of **supply chain management** (see Unit 29) that plans, implements, and controls the efficient, cost-effective **forward** and **reverse flow** and **storage** of goods, services and related information between the point of origin and the point of consumption in order to meet customers' requirements'.

Another definition by CSCMP is 'the management of **inventory – stocks** – at rest or in motion'. The inventory referred to here can be of **raw materials** or **components**:

- **work-in-progress** – for example, some cars are transported between quite distant plants for different parts of the manufacturing process

- **finished goods**

A manager who works in logistics, or an academic who studies the subject, is, formally, a **logistician**.

> **Note**
> BrE: **stocks** (countable) **stock** (uncountable),
> AmE: **inventory**
> BrE: **work-in-progress**,
> AmE: **work-in-process** or **inventory-in-process**

B Word combinations with 'logistical'

The related adjective is **logistical**, or much more rarely, **logistic**. Here are some frequent combinations with 'logistical'. It's interesting to note the negative nature of some of the most frequent words following 'logistical'.

logistical	nightmare
	problem
	difficulty
	challenge
	hurdle
	obstacle

C Reverse logistics

Reverse logistics 'involves the flow of materials back to the distribution, production or supply stages where **valuable outcomes** result from their return'*.

Sustainable development requires manufacturers to be responsible for their products **from cradle to grave** – from their production to their **disposal** or **recycling**.

Waste disc drives for recycling

One initiative in this area is the European Union **directive** – set of rules – on **waste electrical and electronic equipment (WEEE).** The directive gives guidance on:

- **Reuse** involves using the product again without going through one of the steps below.

- **Repair** involves fixing or replacing broken or non-functioning parts or components for use by the original or another buyer.

- **Refurbishment** involves restoring the product back to the original specifications. **Refurbished** products often have reduced capabilities and limited additional service life.

- **Remanufacturing** aims to **upgrade** the product – improve its quality and performance, for example with additional **functions** and **features.**

- **Recycling** aims to **salvage** – save for future use – as much value as possible from **retired** – no longer used – products. This involves reusing parts and components from products that have been **dismantled** – taken apart – and by recovering materials.

*David L. Rainey: *Sustainable Business Development*, CUP, 2006.

30.1 Match these people and things (1–7) with expressions in A opposite. You can use more than one expression with four of the items.

1 finding the best way of getting goods to the supermarkets in a supermarket group
2 a university professor who lectures on supply chain management
3 the subject taught by the professor in 2 above
4 aircraft wings to be used in the construction of a plane
5 washing machines on a truck going out of the factory gate, rather than components being delivered to make them
6 the cotton to be used in making thread for clothes
7 books in a bookshop waiting to be sold

30.2 Match the two parts of these sentences containing expressions from B opposite.

1 At present internet sales of meat are restricted to Britain because of the logistical	a nightmare for railroads this year, slowing grain shipments.
2 There are a variety of logistical	b challenge for working parents, as well as a financial burden.
3 Poor weather conditions, company mergers and booming grain export demand have combined to create a logistical	c difficulties and additional costs owing to its need for access to water.
4 The plant's lack of a waterside location created logistical	d obstacles to opening up a show that has not been performed for two weeks, from restarting complicated machinery to doing the dry cleaning.
5 Providing child care is a logistical	e problem of exporting small orders of fresh meat.

30.3 Look at C opposite. Then use the words below to complete the article.

> dismantle   disposal   recycle   refurbishment   remanufacturing   waste

Xerox equipment recovery and parts reuse/recycling

Xerox is a pioneer in the (1) .... of retired copying equipment into new products for sale to customers. As part of the company's (2) '............................. - free initiative', Xerox established a customer-product take-back process. The initiative included designing new products with (3) .... in mind and creating a remanufacture and parts reuse production capability and marketing effort. Xerox understood that retired copying equipment presented opportunities for creating value and improving the total solution for customers and stakeholders. Taking back end-of-life equipment relieved the customer of the cost and effort of (4) .... Xerox received equipment that had been in use and could study the implications and impacts of earlier design and production decisions. It had 'evidence' that could help current designers create improved products and better solutions. Xerox designers also received the insights they needed to make their products easier to (5) .... , refurbish and (6) .... Solutions to the end-of-life consideration have to be built in during front-end design and production. Xerox has become a master at thinking about the total solution.

Over to you

What are the main logistical nightmares of your organization or one you would like to work for?

31 Outsourcing and offshoring

A Outsourcing

Outsourcing is when organizations pay **subcontractors** – outside suppliers – to do work that was previously carried out **in-house** (see, for example, the first three combinations below). These activities may be described as **non-core** – not a part of the organization's **core competences** or **competencies** – the skills that allow it to maintain its **competitive edge** (see Unit 17). For example, Kodak considers that its core competence is electronic imaging and has kept this in-house; it **subcontracts** or **farms out** many other activities.

A key problem is identifying what is core and non-core. A company must undertake **transaction cost analysis** of each activity to see whether it would be cheaper to outsource and benefit from a supplier's **expertise** – skills and knowledge – because it does not have this expertise and is unwilling or unable to develop it strategically. The company has to decide which **capabilities** – skills – are central to its particular **corporate culture** – the way it does things, how its employees think, etc.

Here are some frequent combinations with 'outsourcing':

business process		administrative tasks
information technology (IT)		computer-based tasks
logistics	outsourcing	transport and warehousing
strategic		outsourcing that is important for the company's long-term goals
offshore		offshoring (see below)

B Business process outsourcing

Business process outsourcing (BPO) includes:

- **back office outsourcing** which involves **business functions** such as:
  a **purchasing** – buying in materials, etc.
  b **payroll** – payment of employees' salaries
  c **billing** or **invoicing** – preparing invoices and sending them to customers

- **front office outsourcing** which involves **customer-facing services**, such as:
  d **technical support** – maintaining products bought by customers, training customers, etc.
  e **marketing**

C Offshoring

Outsourcing to companies abroad is **offshoring**. Financial institutions were among the first to **offshore** their back office operations, with call centres and IT services moving to countries such as India and the Philippines.

Knowledge process outsourcing (KPO) relates to tasks such as research and development in pharmaceuticals, design and development in the car and aircraft industries, medical services, and legal support services. This work requires highly qualified employees, sometimes referred to as **knowledge workers**. There are, of course, **cost savings** when using workers in these areas in developing countries.

This is all part of the trend of companies to **globalize** (see Unit 54).

31.1 Replace the underlined expressions with appropriate forms of expressions from A opposite.

1 'These are something that really benefit our customers and our competitors can't easily imitate them.'
2 'They are very reliable. They provide the services more cheaply than if we did them here – their level of knowledge and skills is greater than ours. Anyway, these are not strategically important activities for us.'
3 'It has shown that it would be cheaper to manage our IT networks ourselves, rather than getting another organization to take care of them.'
4 'Only we know how to make this paint, and this gives us a great advantage. But if our rivals steal our industrial secrets, we will lose it.'
5 'The way we do things round here is based on advanced pharmaceutical research by the best minds in Europe.'

31.2 Which area of BPO (a–e) in B opposite is referred to in each of these situations (1–5)?

A company started outsourcing to different specialized firms and found that:
1 employees started to complain that overtime payments had been miscalculated.
2 its product brochures were much better and led to more sales.
3 the machines that it sold were better maintained.
4 customers complained that they were being bullied for payment.
5 the cost of its company cars had gone down.

31.3 Look at A and C opposite. Then read the article and say if these statements are true or false.

Even if the business advantage of offshoring is too compelling to ignore, the CEO will also have to deal with the human implications of offshoring decisions – namely the fear and anxiety created in those directly affected and in those who remain. For those directly affected, the first question will be: 'What will happen to me?' The CEO has a responsibility to create some options for these people, in terms of training, in terms of helping them find other jobs and in terms of financial compensation. The survivors will be watching closely how fairly their colleagues are treated: 'Today it was them, but tomorrow it could be us.' The survivors will be more interested in the question: 'Now what?'

Here, the CEO must explain the decision against the wider perspective and explain how the offshoring of non-core activities can help to boost the core activities and secure remaining jobs. For example, the offshoring of manufacturing frees capital for investment in new infrastructure or to increase spending on R&D. This helps the company stay ahead of the competition.

1 The CEO has to deal only with the technical implications of offshoring decisions.
2 Employees affected by offshoring decisions think mainly about their own situation.
3 The article mentions four areas where companies can help employees whose jobs are outsourced.
4 Those left in an organization after some of its activities have been outsourced will be more confident about the future.
5 The CEO should explain how outsourcing can help to make remaining jobs more secure.
6 The article mentions three areas where spending can be increased following offshoring of some activities.

Over to you

Is outsourcing an issue in your country? Why? / Why not? Give examples.

32 The evolving Web 1

A Broadband Internet

High-speed **broadband access** to the Internet, making it easier to **download** text, pictures and video, etc. has now become well-established.

Higher **bandwidth** – connection speed – allows better use of some **applications** such as **webcams**, for two-way video communication, and **video-conferencing**, where people in two or more locations can see and talk to each other.

Internet TV is also emerging, with users able to watch television as it is **streamed** over the Internet, and with **video-on-demand** (**VOD**) services such as the BBC's iPlayer to watch programmes later.

Internet access is increasingly available on **wireless LAN** (**local area network**) systems, also known as **Wi-Fi**. To access the Internet in this way, you have to be in a particular **hotspot** – a place such as a café, airport terminal, etc. equipped with the network.

B Mobile Internet

This relates to accessing the Internet via **mobile devices** such as mobile phones and **personal digital assistants** (**PDAs**), also referred to as **handhelds**. In this area, a new category of computer has emerged: the **netbook**, a small, portable laptop computer with no moving parts, specifically designed to **browse** or **surf the Internet**. The standard mobile communications technology for doing this is **3G**.

Mobile devices increasingly come **loaded** – equipped – with different applications or **apps** – programs for different uses, for example **email**, a **music player** such as Apple's iPod, etc. Another of these applications is **SatNav** – **satellite navigation** using **GPS** (**Global Positioning System**) – with **mapping** to see where you are and to **navigate** – plan and follow routes.

C Moore's law

As ever, **Moore's law** is playing its part in bringing down the price of different devices. This is the principle that the **computing power** of a particular size of **computer chip** – the basic component of computers – will roughly double every 18 months. This means that the cost of a particular unit of computing power will continue to halve every 18 months for the foreseeable future. The law is named after Gordon Moore, co-founder of the chip company Intel, who made the prediction in 1965.

32.1 Use expressions from A and B opposite to complete these sentences.

1 Akimbo offers individual TV shows as well as .... TV 'channels' like the Anime Network.

2 American Airlines replaced its network, including all its computers, and put in higher .... to carry data, pictures and graphics.

3 Eleutian Technology is a company with 120 employees that uses Wyoming teachers to teach South Koreans how to speak English via ....

4 Many day-care centers offer .... Most of the cameras don't offer streaming video, but the quality is generally good enough to pick out individual children.

5 Microsoft has enabled the Xbox to .... movies and television shows.

6 Streaming video differs from .... in that it's not downloaded to a computer. Rather, it streams, playing only once on a computer, while downloads are generally accessible more than once.

7 The New York Giants set up a .... broadband network for fans who want to access the Web on their laptops or mobile devices during the game.

32.2 Read this advertisement and answer the questions using expressions from A and B opposite.

> We are proud to introduce the Optimum 3000. It's not just a mobile phone – it's in a class of its own: it's a communications device, a music player and an Internet browser. The Optimum 3000 has the latest 3G mobile technology and the best wireless technology. Its many other features include GPS and games that you can buy and download from the Optimum site.

1 Which technology does it use to make calls and access the Internet?
2 Which technology does it use in hotspots?
3 Where can you buy new applications for it?
4 What do you use to avoid getting lost?
5 What do you use to find and access different websites?

32.3 Use Moore's Law in C opposite to do the following calculation. In 1979, the cost for a particular size of computer memory chip was US$12,500. What was the cost for the same unit in 2009? Choose from these options (a–c).

> **a** $1000   **b** $10   **c** 10 cents

Over to you

- Do you think mobile devices are suitable for accessing the Internet?
- What sort of services would you like to access – for example, football-action video replays, internet shopping, weather forecasts?

33 The evolving Web 2

A Web 2.0

The Internet is evolving. Many internet companies went out of business when the **dotcom bubble burst** in 2000–1.

What has emerged is **Web 2.0**. 'Web 2.0 is the business revolution in the computer industry caused by the move to the Internet as a **platform**, and an attempt to understand the rules for success on that new platform.' [*] It emphasizes:

- **communication**
- **information sharing**
- **interoperability** – the ability of different computers and computer systems to work together
- **collaboration** – users working together, for example on **wikis** – websites that anyone can **edit** – contribute to and change; the most famous wiki is the online encyclopedia Wikipedia

B Keeping in touch

Instant messaging allows internet users to send short messages to each other that are received immediately.

Social networking sites allow users to **post** – make available – details and pictures about themselves in their **profiles**, say who their friends are, etc.

Some are **external social networking sites** open to everyone. There are also **internal social networking sites** open only to particular groups, for example medical workers in a particular speciality, who exchange information and advice with each other in a **specialized forum**. Here, users may be **vetted** – checked – to see if they are properly qualified.

Video-sharing sites such as Youtube have created another **online community** – internet users seen as a group. Users **upload** videos they have made to the site for all to view. (When users upload material copied from elsewhere, there are problems – see Unit 37.)

Other online communities make up the **blogosphere** and include:

- **blogs** – online diaries written by **bloggers**, with readers able to react and comment
- **chat rooms** – users conversing with each other in written form to **socialize**
- **forums** – where people discuss a particular subject

C Website attractiveness

Websites are judged by their **attractiveness** – how nice they are to look at – and their **user-friendliness** – how easy they are to use. By their nature, some applications are more **interactive** than others, requiring more activity on the part of the user.

Many websites are free to use and they **generate revenue** – make money – with advertising. Advertisers, like site owners, want to know how many **hits** they are getting – how often the site is **visited** – or in other words, the amount of **traffic** they have, as well as the number of **unique users** – different **visitors** to the site. There is also the number of **page views** – the total number of times that people look at the site's pages. Another factor is whether a site is **sticky** – whether users stay on the site for some time. The related noun is **stickiness**.

There are specialized **internet ratings agencies** that measure user numbers, stickiness, etc. One task of **website management companies** is to ensure that when people enter particular words in a **search engine** like Google, a site is near the top of the **rankings** – the list of sites that appear first.

Website developers are always looking for the next **killer app** – the next very popular and profitable application.

[*] Tim O'Reilly's definition of a term first used by Dale Dougherty and Craig Cline.

33.1 Complete the sentences, using appropriate forms of expressions from A and B opposite.

1 I'm an IT manager and when we buy a new internet application, I want to be sure that it will work with the applications that we already have. What I want is ....

2 As a recruiter for IBM, I check different .... to see if anyone applying for a job with us has .... his or her .... there. You can see them doing stupid things sometimes!

3 I follow politics closely, and it's good to see politicians in embarrassing situations, so I use .... quite a lot. Some of the videos that are .... are very funny.

4 I'm a doctor, and I'm treating someone with a rare tropical disease, so I joined an .... to find out more about it from colleagues. It's good to feel part of an .... but at the same time to know that the other users are properly ....

5 I run a website that anyone can access and change – it's a .... and it's great for .... with other people.

6 'I'm a big fan of Web 2.0. Instant .... and social .... are great for .... – people can keep in touch with each other so easily.

33.2 Complete the table with words from C opposite.

Adjective	Noun
attractive	
	interactivity
user-friendly	
sticky	

33.3 Replace the underlined expressions in this dialogue between two company managers with appropriate forms of expressions from C opposite and the table in 33.2 above, using any necessary verbs.

Amar: People say that our website isn't very attractive.

Britt: I know. We must do something about it. The number of **(1)** <u>different visitors</u> is relatively high, but **(2)** <u>overall number of visits</u> to the site is very low, and so is the number of **(3)** <u>pages visited</u>.

Amar: Another problem is that the site is not **(4)** <u>one where visitors stay a long time</u>.

Britt: Yes, and people say it's not very **(5)** <u>easy to use</u>.

Amar: Yes, and we must find ways of **(6)** <u>making</u> more <u>profit</u> from it.

Britt: Yes, we must find ways of making sure that we come near the top of the **(7)** <u>list</u> when people search on the Internet for the names of the types of products that we sell.

Amar: Yes, time to change the **(8)** <u>firm that takes care of our website</u>, I think.

Britt: Right!

Over to you

Should recruiters look at social networking sites to check the information that candidates have posted about themselves? Why? / Why not?

34 Knowledge and the Internet

A Knowledge creation

Ikujiro Nonaka and Hirotaka Takeuchi suggest a model of **knowledge creation** – the way that knowledge in a company is built up. They see this as a process that is continually growing and developing. To understand and manage it effectively, they suggest **the SECI model**. They see this as a repeated process that will build up an organization's knowledge over time.

These steps are to be found in a **learning organization,** one that is able to produce **innovation** – new ideas and products (see Unit 20). Knowledge is a company's **intellectual capital**.

a **Socialization**: spreading **tacit** – unspoken – knowledge by sharing experience in working on something.

b **Externalization**: developing concepts, often with **analogies** – when one idea is used to increase understanding of another – that allow them to be communicated.

d **Internalization**: through **learning by doing** and **hands-on experience**, the knowledge becomes part of the individual's **knowledge base** – what they know – and thus becomes an **asset** – something valuable – for the organization.

c **Combination**: sorting, adding and combining ideas to 'make' new knowledge.

B Intranets

One way of making knowledge available to everyone in a company is through a **company** or **corporate intranet** – a website specifically for a company's employees. For example, in project development, they can look at how past projects were organized, how much they cost, etc. They can see new ideas that were proposed but that were never taken up. Employees can **tap into** a vast amount of information. There can be **chat rooms** and **forums** (see Unit 33) for discussion of ideas and the spreading of knowledge.

A possible problem is managing this knowledge and making it available in usable ways. The information has to be well-organized, otherwise there is a danger that people will be overwhelmed by **information overload**. There has to be **metadata** – information about where the **content** is to be found.

C Global communities

Rob McEwen is the CEO of Goldcorp Inc, a gold mining company:

'We completely changed our approach to knowledge. We were having trouble finding gold in a particular place, so we made all the information we had accessible on a **collaborative site** on the Internet. Until then, a lot of this information had been **proprietary** – we owned it and didn't share it.

'This is **mass collaboration, collective intelligence, crowd intelligence** or **crowdsourcing**, call it what you will; anyone who wants to can **collaborate on** an online project. We gave prize money for successful suggestions about where to find gold, but there are cases, such as the online encyclopaedia Wikipedia, where **networks** of people do this for enjoyment, recognition by others, or opportunities to socialize with others. They may be referred to as **prosumers** – contributors to the "products" that result.'

34.1 Match the expressions (1–4) with the stages (a–d) in A opposite.

1 A manager compared the flow of components through the production process in terms of a river.
2 A production worker showed a new employee how to do a particular part of the production process.
3 An employee found some useful data on the Internet and combined it with data from within the company in order to solve a problem.
4 Employees worked together to apply new knowledge on production techniques to their own production line.

34.2 Match the two parts of the sentences containing expressions from A and B opposite.

1 I feel that this experience really helped build my knowledge
2 Alavi and Tiwana* define knowledge
3 People and intellectual
4 A-Space will operate like a corporate
5 People who feel overwhelmed by information
6 The County Intelligence Initiative taps

a capital are the most important assets of the modern corporation.
b intranet, where companies post important documents, or special skills of certain employees.
c into the expertise of local people and allows local and county governments to share data.
d creation as the 'development of "new" organizational know-how and capability.'
e base for the engineering task ahead of me.
f overload will believe the research showing that worldwide information production is increasing at an average rate of 30 per cent each year.

*In Ronald J. Burke and Cary L. Cooper (eds.): *Building More Effective Organizations*, CUP, 2007.

34.3 Complete the article with these expressions from C opposite.

collaborate	collaborative sites	proprietary
collaborating	networks	prosumers

Wikinomics

With collective intelligence, employees drive performance by working together and
(1) .... across organizational boundaries. Information is no longer
(2) .... Customers become **(3)** .... by co-creating
goods and services rather than simply consuming the end product. So-called supply chains work more effectively
when the risk, reward and capability to complete major projects – including massively complex products like cars,
motorcycles, and airplanes – are distributed across planetary **(4)** .... of partners.
Smart companies are encouraging, rather than fighting, the growth of massive **(5)** ....
– many of which emerged from the fringes of the Web to attract tens of millions of participants overnight. Even
competitors are agreeing to **(6)** .... on path-breaking science initiatives that accelerate
discovery in their industries.

Over to you
How is knowledge shared in your organization, company or school?

35 Internet security

A Attack and defence

Melissa Vorster is a consultant on **internet security**:

'I work with companies to try to prevent **hackers** from **infiltrating** – illegally penetrating – the companies' computer systems in order to steal or destroy the information on them. Hackers may write programs designed to **overload** an organization's system with requests for information so that users cannot access it. This is a **denial of service attack**, and it causes huge inconvenience for customers and lost business for companies.

'Another problem is **viruses**. A virus is a small program designed to make computers malfunction, despite the **firewalls** and **anti-virus programs** that we **install** as the technical defences to prevent computers being **infected**. Computers may also be **hijacked** – used to send viruses on to other computers. Virus programs designed to do this are **Trojan horses**. These are just some examples of **malicious software** or **malware**.'

B Cybercrime

'**Cybercrime** is criminal activity on the Internet. Companies that sell goods and services over the Internet need to reassure customers that their credit card details will not be stolen by **cybercriminals**. Confidential information is **encrypted** or **coded** so that it cannot be read by others. Companies that sell on the Internet will display the level of **encryption** that users of their site benefit from.

'Internet bank accounts are protected by **passwords**. **Phishing** is when criminals try to obtain this information by sending emails that pretend to be from someone's bank, telling them to reconfirm their **security details** – passwords, etc. – and allowing criminals access to the account. Or they may manage to put **spyware** on your computer that records passwords, etc. as you type them. This is **identity theft**.

'You might get an email telling you that you have won a lottery or that someone's uncle has died and left money that you can claim. These, of course, are **scams**.'

C Privacy and confidentiality

'When someone uses the Internet, they leave an **electronic trail** – a record of the sites they visit – and if they buy something, their personal details. This raises issues of **privacy** and **confidentiality**. Who should have the right to access and analyze this information?

'This is all part of the debate about the powers of **surveillance** – the powers to watch and examine the activities of private individuals – that **law enforcement agencies,** such as the police, should have. Critics say that the authorities should not **snoop into** people's private lives; they say that there are big issues of **civil liberties** at stake. These are freedoms that ordinary people should have without being watched by **Big Brother** – a term from George Orwell's novel *1984* describing a society that was under constant surveillance.'

35.1 Look at A and B opposite. Complete the article with these expressions.

> identity theft   infected   infiltrated   malware   scams   security

Cybercrime booming

Computer security firm McAfee says that cybercriminals were "cashing in on consumer anxiety to profit from 'get rich quick' **(1)**................................". And another computer **(2)**................................ group, Sophos, said it now found a new infected website every 4.5 seconds. Each of these websites could lead to the user having his or her computer **(3)**................................, with the risk of **(4)**................................, said Sophos in its latest Security Threat Report.

Sophos said that there were now five times more infected emails being sent than at the beginning of the year. Sophos added that the US remained the biggest source of **(5)**................................ websites (37 per cent) followed by China (27.9 per cent) and Russia (9.1 per cent). It further said that **(6)**................................ – malicious software – was a growing problem for Apple Macintosh users.

35.2 Which expressions in B opposite are people talking about here? Use the clue in brackets to help you.

1 'They took my details and applied for a credit card in my name.' (specific crime)
2 'I change mine to each of the sites I use every couple of months.' (letters and/or numbers)
3 'I get these emails, supposedly from my bank, asking me to confirm my security details, but you can see they're not really from the bank.' (specific crime)
4 'Some experts say that in this area we're losing the battle against these guys.' (2 expressions: the activity, and the people involved in it)
5 'I trust the website because I know they use the most advanced technique to keep my details safe.' (method for doing this)
6 'The site asks me for my password and the name of my favourite film.' (information)
7 'It's scary – it lets others know exactly what you're typing.' (software)

35.3 Complete the sentences with expressions from C opposite.

1 Cisco, a maker of telecommunications equipment, sells technology used by .... around the world in Internet surveillance.
2 Much of what people do online – their search engine queries and the ads they click on – is logged by internet companies, generating intense criticism from groups that compare such activity to George Orwell's ....
3 The human resources department should ensure .... and .... of employees' personal information under the Data Protection Act.
4 The Center for Democracy and Technology is a Washington policy center that tries to protect .... in the digital age.
5 People think they have anonymity on the Internet, but they don't realize they leave an ....
6 The US 6th Circuit Court of Appeals in Cincinnati ruled that federal prosecutors should get permission in the form of a search warrant before they .... into someone's email.

Over to you

Do you / Would you feel safe using internet banking? What can you do to minimize the risk?

36 Internet selling

E-commerce

E-commerce sites are used to sell over the Internet. Sites specialize in either **business-to-consumer (B2C)** transactions or **business-to-business (B2B)** ones. **E-procurement** is when businesses, government organizations, etc. obtain supplies and services using the Internet.

Here are some frequent combinations with 'e-commerce':

e-commerce	**portal**	a 'gateway'	for selling on the Internet
	platform	a computer system used	
	site	a website	
	application	a particular type of site	
	solution	a technical means used	
	software	programs used	

B B2C

Business-to-consumer e-commerce has come to be dominated by a few big companies like Amazon, which used its initial strength in selling books to extend to all sorts of other products. Amazon is a **pure-play** – exclusively – **online seller**; it has no **bricks-and-mortar outlets** – no traditional shops. This is **pure e-tailing**.

Other retail organizations are **clicks-and-mortar outlets,** combining e-commerce with sales through traditional outlets. The Tesco supermarket chain uses e-commerce in conjunction with its existing operations; it did not have to invest in a whole new expensive **infrastructure** of new computer systems, warehouses, etc. to take care of **e-fulfilment** – the processing and delivery of orders.

Price comparison sites allow you to **shop around** and compare prices of different sellers without having to go to each site individually. **Screenscrapers** go to different sites and compare prices for the same products or services, for example flights or insurance, and allow you to buy through the screenscraper site.

> **Note**
> BrE: e-fulfilment
> AmE: e-fulfillment

C B2B

In business-to-business e-commerce, groups of companies can set up **e-marketplaces, trading hubs** or **trading platforms.** These are sometimes used to organize **reverse auctions** on the Internet – the supplier offering the lowest price gets the contract. But this can go against a wide range of close, long-term **supplier relationships** (see Unit 29).

There are **private e-marketplaces** where a single company deals with suppliers in this way. Some companies prefer to use this form of e-commerce because they do not want to indicate their requirements to their competitors, thus revealing their current activities. There are also **consortium e-marketplaces** where **key buyers** in an industry get together to organize buying and selling on a collective basis.

36.1 Match the two parts of the sentences containing expressions from A opposite.

1 Customers expect e-commerce
2 Insurance firms have configured their e-commerce
3 Often e-commerce
4 iMerchants.com was Asia's first e-commerce
5 IBM probably leads e-commerce software and support activities by

a portal, or internet gateway.
b platforms to support online searching, online claim processing, and online commenting, as well as online sales for some products.
c providing solutions that can be used immediately, and also by providing data center management services.
d sites to entertain, inform and make transactions easy.
e applications are developed first by large firms whose size enables them to achieve greater cost savings and efficiency gains.

36.2 Look at B opposite. Then read the article. Match each paragraph (1–4) with its summary (a–d).

a a Ryanair spokesman's explanation of its actions
b Ryanair's cancellation of bookings made on price comparison sites, some of its reasons for doing this, people's objections to these cancellations
c how customers buy tickets directly on price comparison sites, and the number who do this
d further reasons given by Ryanair, and an example of action it has taken against one screenscraper

Ryanair blocks 'illegal' bookings

[1] Ryanair is to cancel thousands of its own customers' bookings after they were made through internet travel agents whose activities it says are illegal. The airline is targeting price comparison websites on which you can buy Ryanair flights without having to go directly to the Irish firm's site. Ryanair says this is against its terms and conditions, and the technology used slows down its site for other users. But travel agents said the move was 'foolish' and 'unreasonable'. Consumer groups said they were 'stunned' by the move.

[2] So-called screenscraping websites account for about 0.5 per cent of Ryanair's bookings, equivalent to about a thousand a day. These websites use a technology that allows their booking tools to marry up to those of Ryanair and other low cost airlines,
and execute a sale. The customer, however, never leaves the original price comparison site.

[3] But Ryanair insists these sites' activities are illegal and passengers using them are being forced to pay more for fares and other services. Ryanair has taken legal action against Italian company BravoFly to force it to stop screenscraping the airline's website.

[4] Ryanair defended its decision to cancel bookings made this way, saying it was 'a quick and effective way of discouraging this unlawful activity'. A spokesman said: 'We hope that by getting rid of screenscrapers we will speed up passenger processing times on Ryanair.com as well as ensuring that Ryanair passengers are not paying unnecessary handling charges or higher fares.'

36.3 Replace the underlined expressions with expressions from C opposite.

1 <u>They</u>'re important if you want to develop a good understanding with the company that you're buying from – it's not just a question of price.
2 <u>These guys</u> all know each other and understand each other's needs in relation to suppliers.
3 We're thinking of setting up <u>one of these</u> not only to buy products, but to share information with the companies that we buy from.
4 We don't really like <u>them</u> – price shouldn't be the only thing that determines whom to buy from.

Over to you

Have you bought something recently over the Internet? What was your experience of the site, the payment process, delivery of goods (if you ordered a product rather than a service), etc?

37 Intellectual property

A Downloading

Joe Reggiano is a music industry executive:

'We don't sell as many compact discs these days. Internet users can **download** music from **online music stores** such as iTunes for very reasonable amounts. We **license** the stores to do this. We even organize downloads of concerts just after they have happened. So the whole **business model** in our industry is changing. This is the new way to **generate revenue** – make money – with our **content**, in other words our music, pay **royalties** to its **creators** – the performers – and make a profit and stay in business.

'Of course, **illegal downloading** and **file sharing**, when people make copies for their friends on **peer-to-peer (P2P) sites,** is still going on. But we think that legal downloading is a better alternative for consumers.'

B Copyright infringement

Julia Kaprisky is a film industry executive:

'We have problems with films appearing on the Internet even before their **release** – before they come out in cinemas. And when they do come out, there are people who **pirate** our films by using cameras in cinemas. This **piracy** is **infringing our copyright. Content providers** like film companies face a big challenge through **copyright theft** such as this. Our **assets** – our films – are our **intellectual property**. The companies can only be profitable if these assets are **copyrighted** and **protected**.

'Everything on the Internet is in **digitized** form – the language of computers and the Internet. People can make perfect copies of music or films without any loss of quality. We have technical means of **encryption** so that records and films cannot be copied. We also use a system of **electronic** or **digital watermarks** – technical means to identify the source of all material. But of course, there will always be people who find ways of breaking this encryption; our defences will have to become more and more technically advanced.'

| Note | Another form of **digitized** is digitalized. | |

C Digital rights management

Julia Kaprisky continues:

'There is a lot of discussion about **digital rights management (DRM)**. Some people say that films and music should not be **copy-protected**, but we argue that films need to make money and be profitable if we are going to be able to pay film makers, actors, etc. and to invest in new films.

'We want a system of digital rights management to make sure that people pay for the films that they watch. We want total **copyright protection** for all our products whereby we receive payment for all use of our property. We want to fight any idea that a record or film can be "free".'

37.1 Complete the table with words from A, B and C opposite.

Verb	Noun
copyright	
	download
encrypt	
	infringement
pirate	
protect	

37.2 Now match the nouns in 37.1 above with these definitions.

This is when:

1 legal means are used to prevent a film or recording from being copied (2 words)
2 technical means are used to prevent a film or recording from being copied
3 a rule or law is broken
4 a film or a recording is obtained from a website
5 a film or recording is copied illegally

37.3 Complete the extracts with these expressions from A and B opposite

copyrighted	downloading	file sharing	peer-to-peer	revenue
digital watermarks	encrypting	intellectual property	pirates	

1

Radiohead invited fans to digitally download their seventh album for whatever price they chose from its website, radiohead.com. This initiative contrasted sharply with what happened last week in a US District courtroom in Duluth, Minn. There, the record industry won a $220,000 judgement against a local woman it sued for .... 24 .... songs and making them available for .... with others.

2

So far this school year, 1,287 Ohio University students have been caught breaking copyright and .... laws on the university's computer network. The Recording Industry of America has targeted songs swapped over .... sites where students make their music collections available while they pick from collections of others.

3

The Motion Picture Association of America said that American film and record industries lost an estimated $2.3 billion in .... to copyright .... in China last year, with only one out of every ten DVDs sold in China a legal copy.

4

The record industry has spent a lot of time and money coming up with ways to plug 'leaks', such as .... advance CDs with ...., so sources of leaks before the official release date can be traced.

Over to you

Do you think it's acceptable to download music from file-sharing sites on the Internet?
Why? / Why not?

38 Financial performance

Please study the input and exercises in the units in this *Company Finance* section (Units 38–45) in the order given, as each unit relies on knowledge of previous units.

A Finance

Finance is the way money is made, lent, used, etc. To describe the **financial** situation of a government, organization or person, you talk about their **finances**. The way that something is paid for is the way that it will be **financed** – its **financing**. A **financier** is someone who works in finance at a high level, providing money for particular companies, projects, etc.

Financial reporting is the information that a company gives about its finances. **Financial performance** is how well, or badly, a company is doing from a financial point of view.

B Financial reporting

Maria Malone is the **chief finance officer (CFO)** of a large international media company, based in the UK, with activities in television and publishing. She's talking to new trainees in the **finance department**:

'As with all companies, investors and analysts want to know how the company is being run and how their money is being used. Each year we produce an **annual report** with three key sets of figures:

- profit and loss (P&L) account
- balance sheet
- cashflow statement

'These are the three key **financial statements** in financial reporting. They give the basic information about our **financial results** (see Units 39–41).'

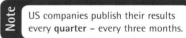

> **Note** US companies publish their results every **quarter** – every three months.

C The financial year

'Our **financial year** ends on 31 March, although other companies choose other dates. Soon after this, we publish **preliminary results** or **prelims**. The **full report and accounts** are published a few months later. As a UK company, we also publish **interim results** or **interims** after the first six months of our financial year.'

D Shareholders, bondholders and lenders

'We use **shareholders'** money from the **shares** that we **issue** to operate and invest in the business. Some of the **profit** we make is normally paid out to them, usually in the form of **dividends** in relation to the number of shares that they each hold. Our shares are **traded** – bought and sold – on the London **stock market**.

'We borrow money in the form of **bonds**. We pay percentage **interest** on those bonds and then later repay the **principal** – the amount of money originally lent to us. Our bonds are traded on **bond markets**.

'We also **borrow** money from banks in the form of **loans,** and we pay interest on this **lending**.

'Of course, our shareholders, **bondholders** and **lenders** all take a keen interest in our accounts!

'The results we publish can affect **share prices**; good results cause prices to rise if the market believes the company is **undervalued**. However, poor results often cause a drop in share price, as investors feel the company is **overvalued**.'

38.1 Complete these sentences with appropriate forms of expressions from A opposite.

1 The separation between shareholders and managers allowed for firms to be .... without further involving the .... in the running of the corporation.
2 The firm helped companies that could not obtain .... from conventional banking sources.
3 The company is in a terrible state – its .... are in crisis and production is falling.

38.2 Complete the crossword with the correct form of words from A, B, C and D opposite.

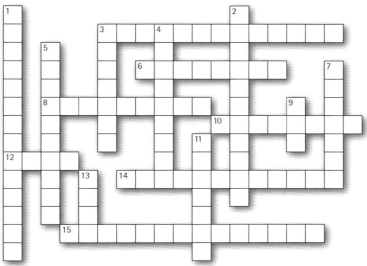

Across
   3 and 7 down One of the three key financial statements (6,3,4,7)
   6 What you get for lending money (8)
   8 What you normally get if you own shares (9)
   10 Another of the three key financial statements: .... statement (8)
   12 Final information about a company's performance is found in the .... report and accounts (4)
   14 The third of the key financial statements (7,5)
   15 Information about the first part of the year (7,7)

Down
   1 The executive in charge of money: chief .... (9,7)
   2 If you think a company's shares are cheaper than they should be, they are .... (11)
   3 Results that are not final (7)
   4 The adjective from *finance* (9)
   5 The owner of bonds (10)
   7 See 3 across
   9 Abbreviation for 1 down
   11 People and institutions that lend money (7)
   13 Money borrowed from a bank is a .... (4)

Over to you

• Why do companies spend money on making their annual reports look attractive? Who are they intended for?
• Why might a company see its annual report as a marketing tool?

39 Profit and loss account

A Accruals accounting

Maria Malone (see Unit 38) continues:

'The **accruals principle** or **accruals method** means that events in a particular **reporting period**, for example sales of goods or purchases of supplies, are recorded in that period, rather than when money is actually received or paid out, which may happen in a later period.'

B Profit and loss

'The **profit and loss (P&L) account** records the **profit** – the money we make – or the **loss** – the money we lose – during a particular reporting period, using the accruals principle.

'In our case, our accounts show **sales** from books, magazines, television advertising, etc. during the period. Then we show the **cost of goods sold (COGS)**, for example **labour costs** – cost of employees' salaries – and the cost of materials.

Designing a book

'Then we take away **general expenses** – the costs related to making these sales such as salespeople's salaries, rent for buildings, etc. There is also the cost of **depreciation** – this is not an actual sum of money paid out, but is shown in the accounts to allow for the way that equipment wears out and declines in value over time and will have to be replaced (see Unit 40). This leaves us with our **operating profit**.

'Then we subtract the **interest payable** on money we have borrowed in the form of bonds and bank loans. This gives the **profit on ordinary activities before tax** or **pre-tax profit**.

Making a television programme

'Sometimes there are **exceptional items** to report, for example the cost of closing a particular operation, but fortunately this does not happen very often.

'Of course, we pay tax on our profits and in the UK this is called **corporation tax**.'

> **Note**
> Sales are also referred to as **turnover** in BrE. The profit and loss account is called the **income statement** in the US.

C Earnings

'From the **profit after tax**, we usually pay **dividends** to shareholders, and you can see the figure for **dividends per share**. However, when business is bad, we may not do this – we may **pass, omit** or **skip the dividend**. Profit after tax is also referred to as **earnings**.

'Naturally, we don't pay out all our profit in dividends. We keep **retained earnings** – some of the profit to invest in our future activities (see Unit 41).

'You can look at profitability in terms of **earnings per share (EPS)**, even if some of these earnings are **retained** – kept by the company and not paid out in dividends.'

> **Note**
> **Pass, omit** or **skip a dividend** occur in this order of frequency. There is no difference in meaning.

39.1 Match words from the box to make expressions in A, B and C opposite. The first one has been done for you as an example.

> accruals   exceptional   interest   payable   profit   retained
> account   expenses   items   period   profit and loss
> earnings   general   operating   principle   reporting

39.2 Now complete each sentence with the correct expression from 39.1 above.

1 Our .... runs from 1 April to 31 March.
2 The company's .... before exceptional items has increased by 10 per cent this year.
3 We have decided to keep £250,000 from our profits as .... and not distribute this to the shareholders.
4 One of the .... in the profit and loss account this year related to the restructuring costs of our operations in Korea.
5 With the ...., of course, postponing or bringing forward cash payments has no effect.
6 During the early months of the loan, the amount of .... each month on this type of loan is relatively high.
7 The .... eventually arrives at a figure for profit to shareholders, after the deduction of all expenses including debt interest and taxes.
8 The cost of new operations in Argentina caused .... to increase to £60.5 million from £51.9 million.

39.3 Are the statements containing expressions from B and C opposite true or false in the context of a company's profit and loss account?

1 The cost of goods sold is the total cost related to selling something.
2 Selling and general expenses include the salaries of the salesforce.
3 Depreciation represents an actual amount of money paid out to suppliers of equipment.
4 Operating profit is the same as pre-tax profit.
5 If a company has a bank loan and/or has borrowed money in the form of bonds, it has to show interest payable in its accounts.
6 Exceptional items are paid out every year and relate to the normal operations of the business.
7 A figure for profit after tax relates to what is left after corporation tax has been paid.
8 If a company shows a figure for retained earnings from a particular period, it has paid out all the profit from the period to shareholders.
9 EPS and dividends per share are the same thing.

Over to you

Describe the profit (or loss) of a company in the news recently.

40 Balance sheet 1

A Assets

A company's **balance sheet** gives a 'snapshot photo' of its assets and liabilities at the end of a particular period, usually the 12-month period of its financial year. But the snapshot could be taken on any day of the year.

An **asset** is something that has value or the power to earn money for a business. These include:

1 **current assets:**

- **cash** at the bank
- **securities** – investments in other companies
- **stocks** of **raw materials, unfinished goods, finished goods** that are going to be sold, etc.
- **debtors** – money owed to the company by customers, not including **bad debts** that will probably never be paid

Stocks

2 **fixed, tangible** or **physical assets:** equipment, **machinery, buildings** and **land** (see Unit 43)

3 **intangible assets:** for example **goodwill** – the value that the company thinks it has as a functioning organization with its existing customers – and in some cases **brands** (see Unit 27) because established brands have the power to earn money, and would have a value for any potential buyer of the company

Items are **carried** – shown – on the balance sheet at particular amounts. However, there are some things of value that are never shown on a balance sheet, for example the knowledge and skills of the company's employees.

> **Note**
> BrE: **stocks**; AmE: **inventories**
> BrE: **debtors**; AmE: **accounts receivable** or **receivables**

B Depreciation

Of course, some assets such as machinery and equipment lose their value over time because they **wear out** and become **obsolete**. Amounts relating to this are shown as **depreciation** or **amortization** in the accounts. For example, some computer equipment is **depreciated** or **amortized** over a very short period, perhaps as short as three years, and a **charge** for this is shown in the accounts. The value of the equipment is **written down** or reduced each year over that period and **written off** completely at the end.

The amount that is shown as the value of an asset at a particular time is its **book value**. This may or may not be its **market value** – the amount that it could be sold for at that time. For example, land or buildings may be worth more than shown in the accounts because they have increased in value. Equipment may be worth less than shown in the accounts because its value has not been depreciated by a realistic amount.

> **Note**
> **Depreciate** and **depreciation** are usually used in BrE, **amortize** and **amortization** in AmE.

40.1 Complete the assets table for a UK company with expressions from A opposite, and the relevant figures, using the information below. (The other half of this balance sheet is in Unit 41.)

- Paradigm has goodwill – in the form of hundreds of satisfied customers – worth an estimated £30 million. This is its only intangible asset.
- It has investments of £12 million in other companies.
- It has raw materials, unfinished goods and finished goods together worth £7 million.
- It owns equipment and machinery with a book value of £18 million.
- It owns land with a book value of £62 million.
- The company has £22 million in its accounts at the bank.
- The company owns offices and factories with a book value of £188 million.
- Various people and organizations, including customers, owe £15 million.

 Paradigm Manufacturing

Balance sheet at 31 March

ASSETS (millions of pounds)

(a)	22		
(b)	**(c)**		
Stocks	7		
(d)	**(e)**		
Total current assets		56	
(f)	**(g)**		
(h)	**(i)**		
Equipment and machinery	18		
Total fixed assets (book value)		268	
(j)	**(k)**		
Total intangible assets		30	
TOTAL ASSETS			354

40.2 Using the information in B opposite and in the table in 40.1 above, decide if these statements about Paradigm's assets are true or false.

The figure for:

1 cash relates only to banknotes in the safe on the company's premises
2 equipment and machinery is the price it was bought for, minus amounts for depreciations
3 stocks relates only to finished goods waiting to be sold
4 land and buildings is the exact amount they could definitely be sold for
5 goodwill is an estimated value that a buyer of the company might or might not agree to pay
6 debtors is a reasonable estimate of how much it will receive from them

Over to you

Think of a company that you're interested in. What are some of its main assets? Which of them might be shown on its balance sheet?

41 Balance sheet 2

A Liabilities

A company's **liabilities** – everything it owes – are its debts to suppliers, lenders, bondholders, the tax authorities, etc.

1 **Current liabilities** are debts that have to be paid within a year, for example:

- **creditors** – money owed to suppliers, etc.
- **overdrafts** – when the company spends more money than it has in its bank accounts
- **interest payments** that have to be paid in the short term
- **tax payable** – money owed to the tax authorities

> **Note**
> BrE: **creditors**
> AmE: **accounts payable** or **payables**

2 **Long-term liabilities** are debts that have to be paid further into the future, for example **long-term bank loans** and **bonds**.

B Shareholders' equity

When you deduct a company's liabilities from its **assets** – everything it owns – you are left with **shareholders' equity**, **owners' equity** or **shareholders' funds**. (The last of these is used particularly in UK company accounts.)

In theory, this is what would be left for shareholders if the business stopped operating, paid all its debts, obtained everything that was owed to it, sold all the buildings and equipment that it owns, etc.

Shareholders' equity as shown in a company's accounts includes:

- the capital that shareholders have invested
- the profits that have not been paid out in **dividends** to shareholders over the years, but that have been kept by the company as **reserves** or **retained earnings** (see Unit 39).

41.1 This is the other half of the balance sheet in Unit 40. Complete the assets table with expressions from A opposite and the relevant figures, using the information below.

- Paradigm has a bank loan of £40 million to be repaid in five years.
- It has issued £200 million worth of shares.
- It has issued bonds for £60 million that it will have to repay in seven years.
- It has retained earnings of £21 million.
- It has to pay £7 million in interest on its bank borrowing and bonds.
- It owes £10 million in tax.
- It owes £12 million to suppliers and others.
- On one of its bank accounts, Paradigm has spent £4 million more than it had in the account.

Paradigm Manufacturing

Balance sheet at 31 March

LIABILITIES (millions of pounds)

Creditors	12		
(a)	(b)		
(c)	7		
(d)	(e)		
Total current liabilities		33	
Bank loan repayable in five years	(f)		
(g)	60		
Total long-term liabilities		100	
(h)	(i)		
(j)	(k)		
Shareholders' funds		221	
TOTAL LIABILITIES PLUS SHAREHOLDERS' FUNDS			354

41.2 Using the information in B opposite and in the table in 41.1 above, decide if these statements about Paradigm's liabilities are true or false.

1 The item for creditors includes debts that will have to be paid relatively soon.
2 Overdrafts are a form of short-term loan.
3 In the coming year, Paradigm will have to pay more tax than it pays out in interest on its loans.
4 The figure of £12 million for creditors relates to money that it paid out to them in the previous period.
5 Shareholders' equity of £200 million is the current value of Paradigm's shares held by shareholders.
6 Retained earnings is the total of all the dividends that have been paid out to shareholders over the years.

Over to you
When a company goes bankrupt, i.e. goes out of business, what are its usual liabilities?

42 Cashflow statement

A Cash inflows and outflows

Remember that under the **accruals method** (see Unit 39), events in a particular **reporting period** are recorded in that period, rather than when the money is actually received or paid out, which may happen in a later period. And **depreciation** (see Units 39 and 40) represents reductions in the values of the firm's equipment, etc. although no actual cash leaves the company, of course.

However, the **cashflow statement** shows **cash inflows** and **outflows** – money actually coming into and going out of a company in a particular period.

A company can have **cashflow problems** even if it is profitable, for example if it is paying suppliers more quickly than it is being paid by customers. This is related to the **credit terms** that businesses have. In the UK, there is usually an agreed **credit period** of 30 days or more in which invoices must be paid. In some countries, this period is much longer.

> **Note**
> The forms **cashflow, cash-flow** and **cash flow** are about equally frequent.

B Types of cashflow

Net cashflow from operations is the money **generated** by the sales of the company's goods or services, minus the money spent on supplies, staff salaries, etc. in the period.

Net cashflow from investment activities is the overall result of the following:

- inflows – loans repaid and loan interest paid by borrowers; money received from sales of securities in other companies; sales of land, buildings and equipment
- outflows – loans made to borrowers; purchases of securities in other companies; purchases of land, buildings and equipment

Net cashflow from financing activities is the result of the following:

- inflows – money received through issuing new shares and bonds in the company; money received through short-term borrowing
- outflows – money repaid in short-term borrowing; dividends paid to shareholders

Adding and subtracting the figures above, the company calculates its **net cash position** at the end of the year. Investors check the cashflow statement to see how the company has obtained and used cash – how much it has made from its operations, raised through new share issues, etc.

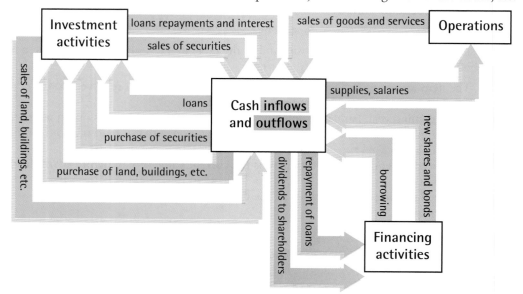

42.1 Use the information in A and B opposite plus the facts from the presentation below to complete the table about a fictional UK company called SBC.

> Last year, SBC had a net cashflow from its operations of £10.1 million. It bought a new office building for £8 million and new equipment for £1 million. The company lent £1 million to one of its directors so that she could buy a new house. SBC paid £10 million to buy shares in Company A and obtained £6 million for shares that it sold in Company B. It received interest of £500,000 on a loan it had made to another director and sold its old office building for £5 million.
>
> SBC obtained a bank loan for £500,000 that it will have to repay next year. It paid out £1 million in dividends to shareholders. It raised £1.25 million by issuing new bonds and £1.75 million by issuing new share capital. It also repaid a loan of £1.5 million that it obtained last year.

Cashflow statement for the year ended 31 December

(Millions of pounds. Negative figures are shown in brackets.)

Operating activities	**Net cashflow from operations**		**10.1**
Investment activities	purchases of securities	(10)	
	money received from sales of shares in other companies	**(a)**	
	loans made to borrowers	**(b)**	
	loans repaid and loan interest paid by borrowers	0.5	
	purchases of land, buildings and equipment	**(c)**	
	sales of land, buildings and equipment	**(d)**	
	Net cashflow from investment activities		**(e)** ....
Financing activities	money received through short-term borrowing	**(f)**	
	money repaid in short-term borrowing	**(g)**	
	money received through issuing new shares in the company	1.75	
	money received through issuing new bonds in the company	**(h)**	
	dividends paid to shareholders	**(i)**	
	Net cashflow from financing activities		**3.0**
NET CASH POSITION AT YEAR END			**(j)** ....

Over to you

What are typical credit terms in your country and some others that you know?

43 Comparing performance

A Profit and profitability

The **profit** made by a company in a particular period is also referred to as its **earnings** – profits after tax – or **net income** – money produced minus everything spent to produce it. There are different indicators of **profitability** – level of profit in relation to what is required to produce it. One measure is **EBITDA** – **earnings before interest, tax, depreciation and amortization** (see Unit 40 for these last two items). Comparing the EBITDA of different companies is a good way of comparing their fundamental **operating performance** before other financial and tax considerations are taken into account. It may be used to see if a company is good at **generating cash** or **cashflow** (see Unit 42).

> **Note**
> A company's **profit** (uncountable) from a particular period may also be referred to as its **profits** (plural). **Profits** is also used to refer to several periods or several companies.

B Investment ratios

Another way of comparing companies is by looking at **investment ratios** – the relationship of one key figure to another.

One important ratio is **return on assets (ROA)**, where you look at a company's profits for the year in relation to the value of its **assets** (see Unit 40) to see how well managers are using those resources. This is an indicator of how well the company is using its **capacity** – the maximum number of products it can produce in a particular period. Particular levels of ROA may indicate that a company is **operating at full capacity** or it may have **spare capacity**.

If a company uses relatively few resources compared to similar companies to generate a higher level of profits, you can say, slightly informally, that it is **sweating its assets**. But it may reach a point where it is not investing enough in new buildings, equipment, etc. There are limits to how far assets can be made to sweat!

And in companies that depend on **knowledge workers** (see Unit 31) for their success, **physical assets** are less important, so ROA is a less useful measure of performance here.

C Return on equity

Return on equity (ROE) measures how well a company's managers are using **shareholders' equity** (see Unit 41) to invest in activities and resources that generate profit for shareholders. For example, if in a particular year profit before tax is £50,000 and the company has shareholders' equity at that time of £500,000, it has ROE in that year of 10 per cent.

Like all ratios, this can be compared with figures from other companies in the same industry, or for the same company from year to year. One figure by itself doesn't mean very much.

D Leverage

To get a better return on equity, companies may borrow in the form of loans and/or bonds. The amount of a company's borrowing and the interest it pays on this in relation to its share capital is its **income leverage**. This ratio can be expressed as a percentage; for example, a company that makes £80,000 in operating profit in a particular period and pays £20,000 in interest has leverage of 25 per cent. This can also be expressed in terms of **interest cover** – the number of times it could pay the interest out of its operating profit; in this case four times.

A company with a lot of borrowing in relation to its share capital is **highly** or **heavily leveraged**. You can also say that it is **heavily indebted**. A company that has difficulty in making payments on its debt is **over-leveraged**. A company that reduces the amount of debt that it has **deleverages**.

> **Note**
> **Leverage** is also called **gearing**, especially in BrE. Companies may be said to be **highly geared**.

43.1 Complete the extract with these expressions from A opposite. Use one of the expressions twice.

amortization and depreciation   cashflow   EBITDA   net income

Sequoia has received investor inquiries as to why our cashflow has been so much better than reported net income. This is partly accounted for by non-cash factors such as **(1)** .... If we look at Sequoia's **(2)** ...., our excellent **(3)** .... is more understandable. Our **(4)** .... in the quarter was $93,000, but our **(5)** .... were $253,000 for the same period, or $160,000 higher.

43.2 Match the underlined words with the expressions in B and C opposite to which they refer.

1 <u>They</u>'re the most profitable assets at the market research firm AC Nielsen, rather than <u>machinery, buildings, and so on</u>, so <u>this</u> is not a very useful measure in judging its success.
2 British Rail was famous for <u>using its trains and other equipment in the most intensive way possible</u> – but the equipment broke down more often and wore out faster than it would otherwise. (2 expressions)
3 In manufacturing, <u>a return on money invested by shareholders</u> of 15 per cent would be quite a good figure.
4 Until recently in banking, a figure for <u>profits in relation to the money available to a bank</u> of 1 per cent was considered reasonable.
5 This money is <u>what shareholders have invested over the years, plus any profits not distributed in the form of dividends</u> and ROE is calculated to see how well it's being used.

43.3 Match the two parts of these sentences containing expressions from D opposite.

1 These bonds are often issued by highly
2 For building firms that were heavily
3 We needed to reduce debt and de-
4 High-risk bonds perform better when the economy is booming, helping heavily
5 The company is massively over-
6 Many firms are too highly

a leveraged, the slowdown was catastrophic – it's a bad time to be a builder but a good time to buy a house.
b leverage in order to survive.
c geared, having borrowed to expand their businesses in the boom and now, with incomes falling, interest payments that are difficult to make.
d leveraged and owes much more to lenders than its operations will ever bring in.
e leveraged small companies to make scheduled payments of interest and principal.
f indebted companies that then have trouble meeting interest payments.

Over to you

Is your organization (school, company, etc.) sweating its assets? Or does it have spare capacity? Give an overview of the situation.

44 Shareholder value

A Yield

Investors look at the **yield** of a company's shares – the **dividend per share** that it pays out in relation to the share price. For example, a company whose shares are worth €20 and that pays a dividend of €1 has a yield of 5 per cent.

Those investors interested in high **dividend payouts** look for **income shares** – shares that have high dividends in relation to their prices. Others look for **growth shares**, typically with lower yields, if they think the company's profits will grow over the coming years and that the shares will increase in value.

B Price–earnings ratio

But companies do not pay out all their **earnings** in dividends each period. Not all earnings are **distributed** to shareholders; companies keep some as **retained earnings** (see Units 39 and 41).

Investors want to know how well their money is working for them and one way of doing this is to look at the **earnings per share** (**EPS**). This is calculated by dividing the after-tax profit by the number of **shares outstanding** – the number issued and in existence. For example, if a company has an after-tax profit of €1 million and has four million shares outstanding, it has EPS of 25 cents.

Investors can also use the earnings per share to work out the **price–earnings ratio** (**PE ratio**) – this is the share price divided by the earnings per share. A company with EPS of 25 cents and a current share price of €5 has a PE ratio of 20.

This ratio gives an idea of how expensive a share is in relation to the profit the company is making. If investors are willing to pay for shares with a higher-than-average PE ratio, it may be because they expect the company to have higher-than-average profits growth in the future and they are thus willing to pay more for these higher predicted earnings.

C Maximizing shareholder value

Shareholders in a company obviously want to maximize their **return on investment** (**ROI**) or **return**. They increasingly look at how the company is managed in terms of **shareholder value** – the total amount the shares they hold are paying out in dividends – and the increase in the value of their shares during the time that they hold them.

If a company's shareholders could get the same or better ROI by putting their money on deposit in a bank, they will not be too pleased with the company's managers. So shareholders are watching senior managers' decisions increasingly closely. A company may say that it wants to **maximize shareholder value**, and use its assets and potential assets in the most profitable way. This implies key **strategic decisions** such as making the right **acquisitions**, and **divestment** (see Unit 19) of business units that do not make enough profit even if they are not actually loss-making.

> **Note**
> singular: **return on investment**; plural: **returns on investment**

44.1 Complete the crossword with the correct form of words from A, B and C opposite.

Across
 2 See 12 across
 6 The number of a company's shares in existence is the number .... (11)
 7 The share price divided by the profit 'belonging' to that share (2,5)
 8 A company may keep these for a rainy day (8,8)
10 Some profits are .... to shareholders, some not (11)
12 and 2 What many investors want companies to do (8,11,5)
13 Occasions when one company buys another, or the companies bought (12)
14 Abbreviation relating to profit per share (3)
15 and 9 down Choice that a company makes hoping to become more profitable (9,8)

Down
 1 and 3 Companies' profitability in relation to what investors have put in (7,2,10)
 4 If a company doesn't keep all the profit from a particular period, there's a .... (8,6)
 5 Describing shares that increase in value (6)
 8 An abbreviation relating to what you get back (3)
11 Describing shares that produce good dividends (6)

44.2 Complete the sentences with appropriate forms of expressions from C opposite.

 1 The role of the Chief Financial Officer is to enable the best use of capital so as to
....
 2 Consider the outsourcing of a large part of the manufacturing load and the consequent
.... of many plants.
 3 Nokia made a .... to concentrate on telecommunications and become
a leading supplier of mobile telephone technology and networks.
 4 Programs that provide childhood nutrition, education and agricultural know-how can pay
big dividends – the .... often exceed 20 per cent a year.
 5 There is room for growth because there are many small companies available as
.... targets.

Over to you

It often makes sense to maximize shareholder value by divesting loss-making businesses
and investing in other areas, but is this always easy to do? Why? / Why not?

45 Accounting standards

A   Audits and their transparency

Every company appoints **auditors** – specialist external accountants – who **audit** its accounts. The auditors approve the accounts if they think they give a **true and fair view** of the company's situation. If not, they specify the **qualifications** they have about the accounts. If auditors do this, it certainly gets investors worried!

Companies that give **misleading** – false – **information** in their accounts are said to **cook the books**. They may **overstate** or **understate** particular amounts – indicating that they are more or less than they really are. Companies that do this are guilty of **fraud**.

But auditors complain that there may be an **expectation gap** between what they are required by law to do and what clients and investors sometimes expect them to do; auditors say that they should not be expected to pick up every problem.

Following the scandal of Enron and other **corporate collapses** in the US, investors became increasingly worried about **accounting irregularities** or **false accounting**, and they are demanding that auditors should be more strictly **regulated** – the authorities should **supervise** them more closely.

Regulators – government agencies checking that the law is applied – are demanding more **transparency**; they say audits should ensure that the company's accounts should give a clear picture of its true financial situation.

They are particularly concerned with:

- **auditor rotation** – the principle that companies should be obliged to change their auditors regularly
- **conflict of interests** – some say that a company's auditors should not be allowed to do its consultancy work, for example giving tax advice or doing management consultancy

B   International standards

In the UK, the way accounts are presented is governed by regulators such as the **Financial Reporting Council (FRC)**.

In the US, they have the **Generally Accepted Accounting Principles (GAAP)**, promoted by the **Financial Accounting Standards Board (FASB)**.

People and institutions invest in companies worldwide. Therefore it is important for financial reporting to be in a form that means the same thing to people all over the world. This is why accountants worldwide are moving towards **International Accounting Standards (IAS)** – **standards** or rules that companies all over the world will, ideally, end up using.

These standards will eventually be accepted by **bodies** – organizations – such as the **International Organization of Securities Commissions (IOSCO)** representing stock markets all over the world, including the all-important **Securities and Exchange Commission (SEC)** in the US. This acceptance will facilitate investment by allowing investors from every continent to understand and trust the accounts of companies, wherever they are based.

The SEC has come under attack for not using its **regulatory powers** – its right to control financial activities – to prevent the excesses that led to the banking crisis of the years 2007–9. Critics said that its **oversight** – control – of the financial services industry was not strict enough.

45.1 Complete the article with these expressions from A opposite. Use one expression twice.

> audits   fraud   overstated   understated
> cooked the books   irregularities   regulators

Inquiry launched in PWC's auditing of Satyam's accounts

Regulatory authorities in India have ordered an inquiry into PriceWaterhouseCoopers' auditing of Satyam, the company at the heart of the country's biggest ever alleged fraud, which commentators are calling India's Enron.

Shareholders have lost more than $2 billion since Satyam's chairman Ramalinga Raju resigned on Wednesday after issuing a statement admitting he had (1) .... the company's cash reserves and (2) .... its liabilities. Many of the losers are said to have been reassured their investments were safe by PWC's presence.

Mr Raju's detailed confession of how he says he (3) .... has now raised serious questions over how $1 billion in non-existent cash reserves could have been overlooked on PWC's watch as auditors. In a statement, Mr Raju said it was with "deep regret .... and a tremendous burden that I am carrying on my conscience, that I would like to bring the

following facts to your notice: The balance sheet carries inflated (non-existent) cash and bank balances of Rs50.4 billion" (nearly £1 billion).

He also detailed $78.3 million of "non-existent" interest, and an (4) .... liability of $256 million. He denied personally profiting from the alleged (5) ....

PWC's role will now be investigated by India's Institute of Chartered Accountants.

PriceWaterhouseCoopers said: "Over the last two days, there have been media reports with regard to alleged (6) .... in the accounts of Satyam Computer Services. The (7) .... were conducted by PriceWaterhouse in accordance with applicable auditing rules and were supported by appropriate audit evidence. PriceWaterhouse will fully meet its obligations to cooperate with the (8) .... and others."

45.2 Now answer these questions about the article in 45.1 above.

1 Has the fraud been proved in a court of law?
2 How much have shareholders lost?
3 Are cash reserves assets or liabilities?
4 Why had shareholders felt confident?
5 Does Mr Raju feel bad about what has happened?

45.3 Look at B opposite and answer the questions using abbreviations. Which body or set of rules would be most involved with, or relate mainly to the following?

1 a company whose shares are listed on the New York Stock Exchange and that is accused of accounting fraud
2 the way that something is presented in a UK company's accounts
3 discussions between stock exchanges around the world on standardizing procedures
4 the way multinationals around the world account for profits from overseas subsidiaries
5 the way that something is presented in a US company's accounts

Over to you

Describe a case of false accounting that you remember. What happened to the people involved?

46 The business cycle

A Key indicators

To assess the state of a country's economy, commentators look at **key indicators** such as:

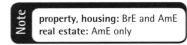

a the **jobs market** – how many people are **in employment** and how many are **out of work** or **unemployed**.
b **disposable incomes** – what people have available to spend after buying essentials such as food, electricity, etc.
c **retail sales / consumer spending** – how much people are spending in the shops. This is related to **consumer borrowing** – how much people have borrowed in loans, on their credit cards, etc.
d the **property** or **housing market** – **house prices**, and the price and availability of **mortgages** – loans to buy property. **Interest rates** decided by a country's **central bank** – how much it costs to borrow money – are very important in this context.
e **inflation** – how fast prices are rising.
f **financial markets**, including the **stock market** for company shares.
g the **trade balance** – how much the country is importing and exporting. If it exports more than it imports, it has a **trade surplus**; if it imports more than it exports, it has a **trade gap**.
h **exchange rate** – the value of a country's **currency**.
i **government spending** – the amount that the government is paying for everything that it provides. There is a **budget surplus** when a government takes in more in taxes than it spends; there is a **budget deficit** when a government takes in less in taxes than it spends.

> **Note** property, housing: BrE and AmE
> real estate: AmE only

B The business cycle

Economic growth is when a country's economic activity increases. Typically, when the economy **recovers** from a **trough** – its lowest point – there is a period of **recovery** when growth starts to **pick up** – speed up. This is followed by a phase of **prosperity** when people and companies have money to spend and feel confident about the future. These two phases make up a period of **expansion**.

The economy then **peaks** or reaches its **peak** – highest point – and starts to **decline** – grow more slowly. The economy may even **shrink** in a period of **contraction** or **contract** in a **slowdown** – get smaller – before it **reaches a trough** or **bottoms out** and starts to grow again. This is the **economic** or **business cycle**.

C Boom and bust

When the economy is **booming** – growing fast – commentators start to talk about the **risks** or **signs of overheating**, with key indicators getting out of control, and a loss of **economic stability**. They talk about the need for a **soft landing**, with the government aiming to bring economic activity back to more **sustainable levels** – ones that can be continued – without the economy going into **recession** – technically, a period of declining activity lasting two consecutive quarters (six months) or more.

A long period of **severe recession** is a **depression** or a **slump**. This whole process is referred to, slightly informally, as the **boom and bust cycle**.

46.1 Match these headlines (1–9) with the issues that they relate to (a–i) in A opposite.

1 Shares in biggest one-day rise for 10 years

2 Average house price now €203,000

3 Jobless at lowest for 12 years

4 CONSUMERS IN RUSH TO MALLS

5 Dollar falls to 15-year low against yen

6 Average pay rises 3 per cent – gas, electricity fall

7 TRADE GAP WIDENS BY RECORD £500 MILLION

8 Government borrowing rises to unprecedented levels

9 Consumers and firms hit by price jump shock

46.2 Use nouns from B opposite to complete the labels in this diagram.

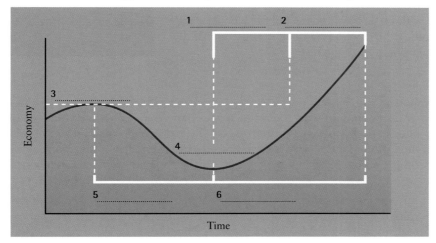

46.3 Use correct forms of expressions from C opposite to complete these sentences.

1 Britain's economy .... for most of the 'Blair decade', growing by 3 or 4 per cent per year.

2 The Chinese Central Bank raised interest rates, a move aimed at reducing the risk of .... in an economy that is growing at more than 11 per cent per year.

3 The president said he is concerned but believes the market will find a .... without substantial government intervention, and will not go into a recession.

4 Government spending went well beyond sustainable levels during the boom and this threatened ....

5 The Turkish economy had a sudden reversal and experienced a severe ...., following growth of 8 per cent the previous year.

6 In the gold industry, ... cycles last an average of ten years.

Over to you

At what point in the business cycle is your country right now? What is the state of some of the key indicators?

47 Bursting bubbles

A Bubbles

A **bubble** is a period when **demand** for something – the number of people who want to buy it – grows too fast, leading to prices also rising too fast.

Here are some frequent combinations with 'bubble':

economic financial	
speculative	**bubble**
real estate housing property	
mortgage	

Then the **bubble bursts,** with demand falling very fast. Prices **crash,** with buyers wanting to sell for whatever they can get, including those who had bought **at the top of the market** – when prices were highest.

B The credit crunch

The **credit crunch** of 2007–9 was part of a wider **banking crisis.** US banks had lent too much money to mortgage borrowers who could not repay. These were called **sub-prime** or, informally, **NINJA** – no income, no job or assets – **mortgages.** The banks had **repackaged** and **sold on** these mortgages in the form of new **securities** – lending – to other financial institutions, who then lent money to yet others on the basis that they would get their money back from repayments of the original mortgages.

However, the buyers of these securities did not know that the mortgages were **high-risk.** When house buyers started to **default on** – stop repaying – their **loans,** the lenders were in trouble. These **defaults** meant that what banks thought were valuable securities were in fact **toxic** – worthless – **assets.**

Some commentators blamed **light-touch regulation** of banks; they said that the government **regulators** had not been strict enough. And they criticized **ratings agencies** – commercial organizations that publish risk levels for different securities, who had underestimated the risks.

Banks said that they wanted to **deleverage** – rely less on borrowed money. Some financial institutions were in danger of going out of business, and governments in some countries had to **rescue** them. Banks refused to lend to each other and to companies and individuals, causing problems in the **real economy,** with businesses and individuals unable to borrow money in the ways that they had been used to. This in turn led to a **full-blown** – total – **economic crisis.**

C The real economy

Following the credit crunch, governments around the world were worried about **deflation** – a period of falling prices and falling demand, which would be very difficult to end. So they produced **stimulus packages** – actions designed to increase economy activity, for example by lowering taxes in order to give people more money to spend. They reduced **interest rates** to nearly zero, meaning that borrowing money was almost cost free. They started **printing money** – putting more money into the economy than really existed – in order to increase demand. But critics said that this last move could be dangerous because of the risk of **galloping inflation** – prices rising very fast – or even **stagflation** – inflation with no economic growth.

47.1 Match the two parts of these sentences containing expressions from A opposite.

1 During the real estate
2 One striking difference between the current crisis and recent financial
3 Students and factory workers were putting much of their savings into stocks, threatening to create a speculative
4 The bursting of the housing
5 No-proof loans fed the mortgage
6 When Hong Kong's property
7 Yubari continued building tourist sites even after the collapse of Japan's economic

a bubble because buyers listed incomes much higher than what they really earned.
b bubble also represents a period of lost wealth, even for people who keep their homes.
c bubble burst, revenue was slashed and the government incurred a budget deficit of HK$32 billion.
d bubble, as the nation tried to spend its way to recovery.
e bubble that could end in a damaging and politically explosive crash.
f bubble, lenders and mortgage brokers sometimes encouraged homeowners to borrow more based on inflated home values.
g bubbles is that this time it is the developing world that is best positioned to weather the current storm.

47.2 Look at the expressions in B opposite. What are these things examples of?

1 the Financial Services Authority, responsible for seeing that UK bank finances are healthy
2 Standard and Poor, an organization that judges how likely it is that loans will or will not be repaid
3 manufacturing, retail, etc. as opposed to financial services
4 when banks are left to decide for themselves which activities are too risky to get involved in, rather than being told what to do by the government
5 when banks and companies borrow less
6 when a housebuyer stops repaying their mortgage
7 debts that lenders discover are never going to be repaid, having previously believed that they would be
8 when many companies go out of business, unemployment rises to 10 or 20 per cent, and the government doesn't really know what to do

47.3 Complete the table with words from A, B and C opposite.

Noun	Verb
crash	
default	
	deflate
deleveraging	
	regulate
rescue	
	stimulate

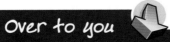

Over to you
How did the credit crunch affect your country?

48 Corporate social responsibility

A Ethics

Ethics (countable) are moral beliefs about what is right or wrong. **Ethics** (uncountable) is the study of this.

The related adjective is **ethical**. Here are some frequent combinations:

ethical	**behaviour**	doing things that are morally right
	lapse	temporary failure to act in the correct way
	dilemma	a choice between two actions that might both be morally wrong
	standard	a rule for moral behaviour in a particular area
	stance	a stated opinion about the right thing to do in a particular situation
	issue	an area where moral behaviour is important

B Accountability and transparency

Individuals and organizations should be **accountable** – completely open about what they do and able to explain their actions. **Dealings** – business transactions – should be **transparent** – not hidden or secret – and explainable in a way that can be understood by outsiders. Companies may say that their managers and employees should **act with integrity** and, more formally, **probity** – complete honesty – and that they do not tolerate any form of **professional misconduct**. People expect the behaviour of organizations to be **above board** – completely open and honest.

C Corporate social responsibility

Companies have long had **codes of ethics** and **codes of conduct** saying how their managers and employees should behave. Now they are looking at these issues in more systematic ways. They are designating executives to oversee the whole area of **corporate social responsibility (CSR)**, which relates to the following areas, among others:

a **employment and community**: they want to pay attention to things that affect the well-being of everyone, not just their employees, in the areas where the company has its plants, offices and other activities.

b **environmental protection**: they want to conduct business in ways that protect the **environment**, for example to ensure that the company does not cause **pollution** of the air, rivers, etc. and does not **endanger** plant and animal life or contribute to **climate change** (see Units 50 and 51).

c **winning new business**: they want, for example, to get business without engaging in **corruption**, for example offering **bribes** – money given to someone so that they behave **unethically**.

Companies want to be seen as good **corporate citizens**, with activities that are beneficial not only for their **stakeholders** (see Unit 14) but for the community and society as a whole.

48.1 Match the two parts of these sentences containing expressions from A opposite.

1 'We are committed to the highest ethical
2 Is ethical
3 There were questionable ethical
4 They tightened the city's ethics policy after a string of ethical
5 'As a bank with a strong ethical
6 He's dealing with the ethical

a stance, we are always looking to reduce the amount of paper we use.'
b lapses came to light, including city managers hiring their relatives.
c behaviour in business affairs different from everyday behaviour in the family or community?
d dilemma of whether to disclose to a buyer that the house might soon be demolished to make way for a new road.
e standards and to promoting our medications only for approved uses,' the company spokesperson said.
f issues, including whether he helped a company that hired his brother as a lobbyist.

48.2 Complete the sentences with expressions from B opposite.

1 His lawyers have argued that the transactions were completely above .... and approved by the other directors.
2 The code of professional conduct requires directors to act with .... and ...., and to accept that failure to comply carries the threat of fines.
3 It faces the most serious charges of .... yet brought against a big accountancy firm, with claims that it deliberately concealed evidence of fraud.
4 We are totally .... about the methods that we use, so it would be hard for us to hide the fact if we were not giving the correct numbers in our findings.
5 The city's officials ought to be held far more .... than they are today for what they spend and how.

48.3 Match the ideas (1–5) in the article with the points (a–c) in C opposite.

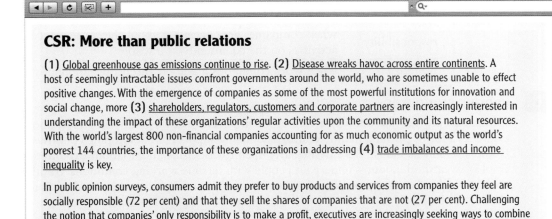

CSR: More than public relations

(1) Global greenhouse gas emissions continue to rise. (2) Disease wreaks havoc across entire continents. A host of seemingly intractable issues confront governments around the world, who are sometimes unable to effect positive changes. With the emergence of companies as some of the most powerful institutions for innovation and social change, more (3) shareholders, regulators, customers and corporate partners are increasingly interested in understanding the impact of these organizations' regular activities upon the community and its natural resources. With the world's largest 800 non-financial companies accounting for as much economic output as the world's poorest 144 countries, the importance of these organizations in addressing (4) trade imbalances and income inequality is key.

In public opinion surveys, consumers admit they prefer to buy products and services from companies they feel are socially responsible (72 per cent) and that they sell the shares of companies that are not (27 per cent). Challenging the notion that companies' only responsibility is to make a profit, executives are increasingly seeking ways to combine (5) economic gain with social well-being in ways that will produce more customer loyalty, better relationships with regulators, and many other advantages. CSR practices may, in fact, prove pivotal to the success of a company.

Over to you

Think of a particular ethical issue that concerns you. Write a letter to a company asking what its policy is on this issue.

49 Social reporting

A Social reporting

Since the 1970s, businesses have been increasingly aware of the importance of social and environmental issues for their reputation. There has been a trend towards commissioning **social audits** relating to their **social performance** – these audits evaluate the effect of their behaviour in relation to their employees and to society as a whole. A new dimension in this is companies' attitudes to the now urgent issue of **climate change**.

Social audits are part of **social reporting** – when a company regularly gives information about the social impact of its activities – and supporters say that it is as important as financial reporting. They say that it provides important information for all of a company's **stakeholders**. This is part of the wider picture of **stakeholder theory** – the idea that companies have responsibilities not only to employees, customers and shareholders, but to all members of society affected by their activities.

Critics say that a social audit may just be a **public relations exercise**, with no real benefits.

B Word combinations with 'social'

Here are some frequent word combinations with 'social:'

social		
	issues	areas of concern, such as unemployment, poverty, etc.
	justice	the idea that people should be treated fairly and equitably
	programs	actions by a government to reduce poverty, unemployment, etc.
	responsibility	when companies are concerned about the consequences of their activities on the community as a whole
	welfare	when work conditions are good and people are happy

C Labour standards

Companies are also increasingly aware of the importance of their suppliers' reputation. For example, a lot of clothing manufacturing is done by suppliers in developing countries. Companies in this industry are particularly open to criticisms about **labour exploitation**. Some employ **sweatshop labour** – underpaid people with terrible **working conditions**. Another aspect of this is lack of **worker representation**, for example in workplaces where **trade unions** (see Unit 5) are banned.

But many point to progress by leading companies in this area in improving **labour standards** – for example, ensuring that their suppliers are paying their workers fairly, that they have a good **health and safety record**, with low levels of illness and accidents, and so on. Companies and their suppliers also do not use **child labour** – they ensure that workers are above the legal minimum age. They know that, increasingly, they have to be seen to be **socially responsible**.

However, critics say that companies with lower profiles may not be observing these standards.

49.1 Complete these extracts with expressions from A opposite.

1 The management has to be aware of its wider responsibilities to the community, not just employees and shareholders, when presenting new proposals. This is sometimes called ....

2 There is a risk that companies in industries that are more renowned for polluting and exploiting than caring and sharing could adopt .... and use it to highlight their more ethical activities, purely as a ....

3 The investment fund Jupiter says it will operate a 'best in class' approach, allowing investment in any UK company that has a good record of .... within its peer group.

4 Auditors should also be required to report to a wider interest group than just the shareholders. These .... could include bankers, customers and suppliers, potential shareholders, employees and even government departments.

5 A group of experts looking at how company law operates is already considering whether companies should be forced to publish annual .... , giving details of their social and environmental policies.

49.2 Complete these sentences with expressions from B opposite.

1 The Social Venture Network applies capital to enterprises that reduce poverty and advance social .... (2 expressions)

2 Organizations have benefited by adopting strategic approaches to environmental and social ....

3 Different individual self-interests can have a negative effect on corporate profits and hence reduce overall social ....

4 The federal government is facing a harder time obtaining resources to fund social ....

5 Toyota is seen by many as the automaker most successful in creating an image of environmental sensitivity and social ....

49.3 Match these expressions from C opposite with the newspaper headlines.

a worker representation	c health and safety record
b child labour	d sweatshop labour

1 **Underage children found working in clothing factory**

2 **PLANT'S UNION REPRESENTATIVES SACKED**

3 **Workers get 20 US cents an hour for 12-hour day in grim conditions**

4 **Factory accidents '30 per cent above national average'**

Over to you

Find out about social responsibility issues in a company that you are interested in.

50 Green issues

A Environmental damage

For 40 years, governments in many developed countries have imposed **stringent** – strict – **environmental regulation** to combat **environmental pollution** – damage to the land, sea, etc. caused by industry. For example, companies should not **pollute** the air with **toxic emissions** from chimneys or with **effluent** – toxic liquids that they **discharge** into rivers or the sea. They should **dispose of waste** in acceptable ways.

Critics who say that manufacturing is often moved to countries with less strict regulations complain that pollution is being **exported**.

Nuclear power plants are required to monitor levels of **radioactivity** – a form of energy that can harm humans, animals, etc. – but critics say that even minimum levels of radioactivity are unacceptable. And some **pollutants** are **carcinogenic** – they cause cancer. The nuclear energy debate has now been reactivated in the context of **climate change**. Supporters of nuclear power say that it can help to combat **global warming**.

B Eco-friendly products

Deep-sea fishing has to be done in a way that maintains fish stocks and avoids **overfishing**. Agricultural products should be produced in ways that can be continued and that avoid **overfarming**.

Ideally, those engaged in **logging** that causes **deforestation** should have an incentive to maintain future timber stocks through **reafforestation**.

Another aspect of **sustainability** is **renewable resources**, including **alternative energy sources** such as **wind power, solar power** from the sun and **tidal power** from the natural rises and falls in sea level. These are together known as **renewables**.

These are some of the **environmental** or **green issues** that governments and companies are facing. Companies may say that their products and activities are **eco-friendly**. (**Eco-** is used in many other combinations to refer to the environment.)

All this is part of the idea that businesses should be run in ways that are **sustainable** – in ways that maintain the resources that they rely on. Companies may say, for example, that their products come from sustainable forests or their seafood from sustainable fishing methods.

Some companies produce reports on these issues that give a more favourable impression than is justified by the facts. This is called **greenwash** by critics.

For more on sustainability, see Unit 59.

> **Note**
> BrE: reafforestation
> AmE: reforestation

C Recycling

Products should be made of materials that are **recyclable** – reusable in new products. The European Union, for example, has regulations about the **proportion** or percentage **content** of products and packaging that must be reused and **recycled**. **Household** and **industrial waste** should also be recycled. Some companies, for example, are recycling their products by reusing parts in new products (see Unit 30). All this is part of the wider picture of **corporate social responsibility** (see Unit 48).

50.1 Complete the table with words from A, B and C opposite.

Noun	Verb	Adjective
carcinogen	–	
discharge		–
disposal	.... (of)	–
environment	–	
.... , ...		polluting
recycling		.... , ...

50.2 Use correct forms from the table in 50.1 above to complete the sentences.

1 Environmental requirements will force the county to remove .... from waste water that is discharged into the Santa Cruz River.
2 Of the 186 million empty water bottles that are thrown away each year, 61 million bottles are ....
3 The EU's Electronic Equipment Directive makes manufacturers responsible for the collection and .... of electronic products.
4 The introduction of stringent rules and heavy fines has led to less waste being .... into the sea.
5 The Food and Drug Administration continues to find traces of .... chemicals in imported fish.

50.3 Complete these extracts with appropriate forms of expressions from B and C opposite.

1 Illegal .... around the world robs US companies of $460 million a year in lost sales, according to a study by the American Forest & Paper Association.

2 Haiti has begun importing wood directly from Delaware because extreme .... has eliminated 95 per cent of its trees.

3 .... in deep waters is putting at risk the least sustainable of all fish stocks – their numbers are declining rapidly.

4 The Chinese government has set itself the target of producing 16 per cent of energy needs from .... resources by 2020.

5 Critics call the ads .... , a thin attempt to make companies' activities more eco-conscious than they are.

Over to you

What steps have been taken in your area to help the environment? What else should be done?

51 Climate change

A Global warming

Since the beginning of the **industrial revolution** about 250 years ago, **emissions** from the burning of **fossil fuels** such as oil and coal have led to increasing amounts of **carbon dioxide** and other **greenhouse gases** in the atmosphere. This **greenhouse effect** has led to **global warming** – an increase in temperatures around the world. Experts predict serious consequences if this continues, with, among other things, **storms** and **rising sea levels** causing **floods**, and **droughts** – periods of low or no rainfall. This in turn will lead to severe effects on **infrastructure** – transport, communication, etc. – with large numbers of people forced to move away from affected areas.

B Carbon management

Individuals and companies are increasingly aware of their **carbon footprint** – the amount of carbon dioxide that their activities produce – and take measures to reduce it. Governments talk about the need to reduce **carbon levels** and have signed **climate treaties** – international agreements – that oblige countries to take measures to reduce the amount of carbon that they **emit**. The first of these was the **Kyoto protocol** of 1997, designed to put the **United Nations climate change convention** into effect. Change has been slow, however, and in 2007 the UN Intergovernmental Panel on Climate Change forecast that by 2100 **global temperatures** would increase by between about 3 and 7 degrees Celsius.

C Carbon trading

The maximum amount of carbon that a company is allowed to produce is **capped** – limited to a particular level. With **carbon trading**, a company can emit more than this by buying **carbon credits** from another company that emits less than the permitted amount. These credits can be **traded** – bought and sold.

With **carbon offsets**, the carbon dioxide produced by a company's activities or products can be **offset** – compensated for elsewhere. For example, a car company can arrange for trees to be planted to **absorb** the equivalent amount of carbon that its cars produce. If by doing this the amount of carbon produced does not increase, the company can claim that its activities are **carbon-neutral**.

D Carbon capture

Some scientists say that the above measures will not be enough to reverse climate change. They say that the greenhouse gases already in the atmosphere need to be removed from it, for example by **capturing** it and storing it underground. This is **carbon capture** or **carbon sequestration**.

51.1 Complete the article, using expressions from A opposite. Use some expressions more than once.

NATIONS MUST 'ACT NOW' ON CLIMATE CHANGE

Countries must begin adapting to the effects of climate change as a matter of urgency or face serious effects from **(1)**.., a leading industry group warned on Thursday. Water and sewage infrastructure, the electricity network and transport were all at risk from the effects of **(2)**.. gases, including droughts, floods and severe **(3)**.., said the Institution of Mechanical Engineers, an international body for the engineering industry. It urged governments around the world to face up to the challenge of adapting to the effects of climate change, rather than putting all their efforts into cutting **(4)**.. .

Environmental groups have been reluctant in the past to support the cause of adaptation in developed countries, out of concern that it would be seen as a fallback option that would remove the need for them to cut greenhouse gas **(5)**.. . But they have supported allocating funds from rich countries to the developing world in order to help poor countries to adapt to climate change, which they otherwise would not have the funds to do.

(6).. that is in use today is likely still to be in use many decades from now, the IMechE pointed out, and so it is important for companies developing such **(7)**.. today to build the probable effects of climate change into their plans.

51.2 Relate the underlined words to nouns in B, C and D opposite.

1 I'm trying to reduce <u>mine</u> by taking the train more and flying less.
2 <u>They</u> are already much higher than predicted ten years ago.
3 Critics say that these <u>agreements</u> are useless while coal is still being used as a fuel.
4 <u>This</u> is very expensive, but removing carbon from the atmosphere can be done. (2 expressions)
5 <u>It</u> needed to be replaced by a stricter agreement, limiting emissions even further.
6 Land Rover has a scheme for <u>these</u>, whereby the emissions during a car's first 40,000 miles are compensated for by projects reducing the use of burning wood as fuel in East Africa.
7 Companies can trade <u>these</u> so that some companies emit more carbon dioxide and some less, but the overall level is the same.

51.3 Use appropriate forms of verbs from B, C and D opposite to complete these sentences.

1 Engineers are now able to .... carbon dioxide and store it underground.
2 Companies can .... their emissions by commissioning activities that reduce carbon emissions elsewhere.
3 Carbon dioxide can be .... from the atmosphere by plants.
4 Governments can legally limit the amount of carbon a company can .... by .... it.
5 Carbon credits can be .... between companies.

Over to you

What steps have you taken, or might you take, to reduce your carbon footprint?

52 Corporate governance

A Board organization

Corporate governance is the way a company is organized and managed at the highest level. This can have a critical influence on the company's performance.

A company's **board of directors** or **corporate board** includes the following **board members**:

- **executive directors**, the **chief executive officer** (**CEO**) and other senior managers such as the finance director.

- **non-executive directors**, **non-execs** or **independent board members** – outsiders with relevant management experience who are invited to sit on the board, bringing their expertise and an external view. Large investors in a company like pension funds may also have **seats on the board** so that they can influence how the company is run.

In some countries such as Germany, there are two boards. Above the **management board** is a more senior **supervisory board**, some of whose members are not shareholders. These boards are a company's **governance bodies**.

Commentators talk about the quality of a company's **stewardship** – the way that it is guided, managed and protected.

In the banking crisis of 2007–9, there were complaints that banks' board members had not been active enough in questioning the actions of banks' CEOs, actions that led to the collapse of their institutions.

B Separation of roles

Another key issue in corporate governance is whether the most senior job in a company should be split into two or not. Should the roles of **chairman** or **chairwoman** and chief executive officer be held by one person, or should there be a **separation of roles**?

Some people say that these two functions should be separated in order to avoid concentrating too much power in one person's hands. Supporters of combining the two roles, however, say that this gives the company stronger **leadership**.

C Rewards for success (and failure)

Executive pay – or, more formally, **executive remuneration** or **compensation** – is becoming an increasingly sensitive issue. Top executives are **rewarded** for success in the form of high salaries and **share options** (BrE) or **stock options** (AmE) – the chance to buy shares in the company cheaply. Executives say in their defence that share options are one of the **incentives** that can make them perform better. Company boards may appoint a **remuneration committee** to make decisions in this area. **Remuneration consultants** are brought in to advise on **remuneration packages** for senior managers.

Executives may also be seen as being 'rewarded' for failure, with high **payouts** or **payoffs** when they leave the company following poor performance.

And there is increasing anger about the senior managers of banks receiving **bonuses** – extra payments – when their institutions have had to be **bailed out** – rescued – by governments.

Following the banking crisis of 2007–9, senior bankers especially have been described, informally, as **fat cats**, implying that they do not deserve their continued high salaries and bonuses following the damage they have done to the institutions that they lead.

52.1 Complete the sentences with appropriate forms of expressions from A and B opposite.

1 Under Terry Semel's .... , Yahoo increased its revenue ninefold and more than tripled the number of employees to 12,000.

2 It's obligatory for corporations in Germany to separate .... into a, more senior, ... board (Aufsichtsrat) and a .... board (Vorstand), with the requirement that a third of the members of the .... are not shareholders.

3 The reform of the corporate .... has three aims: the emphasis on .... (non-executive directors); the focus on evaluating the activity of all board members; and the drive to separate the functions of chairman and CEO.

52.2 Complete the table with words from C opposite.

Verb	Noun
remunerate	
compensate	
	reward
incentivize	
pay out	
pay off	
	bailout

52.3 Now replace the underlined expressions in the sentences with appropriate forms of expressions from the table in 52.2 above.

1 In <u>these</u>, such as the ones in 2008, governments have to lend vast amounts of money to the banks to prevent them from collapsing.

2 The average CEO in the US is now paid 500 times more than the average employee, so <u>this</u> is very controversial. (2 expressions)

3 Everyone agrees that executives should have <u>these</u> as motivation to produce good results, but when they are given bonuses just for average performance, there is anger.

4 There is also anger when executives leave their organizations following poor performance, but they receive huge <u>ones</u> even so. (2 expressions)

Over to you

What are the governance bodies of your company or one that you would like to work for?

53 Ethical investment

A Activist shareholders

The biggest shareholders in many companies are **institutional investors** such as **investment funds** – funds that group together the money of many different investors. There has been criticism that institutional investors are not active enough in the companies that they invest in – for example, when they do not vote at shareholders' meetings.

And in the banking crisis of 2007–9, there was criticism that shareholders had not challenged the decisions being made by the banks' executives. Critics say that **good corporate governance** (see Unit 52) requires **activist shareholders** who take a more active role in the way that the companies that they invest in are run.

B Controversial products

George Unwin is a fund manager for an **ethical investment fund**:

'People and organizations who put their money into our fund want us to invest it in ethical ways. We want to avoid companies that have a bad record on social and environmental issues. We particularly want to avoid certain sectors: tobacco, arms manufacturers, nuclear power or uranium producers. So we put our clients' money into funds that do not invest in these activities.

'In selecting companies to invest in, we look closely at how they are managed. We are particularly interested in issues of corporate governance. We believe that well-managed companies are more profitable to invest in. As ever, **transparency** and **accountability** (see Unit 48) are key.'

C Socially responsible investment

There is more and more relevant information about ethically run companies that people can put their money into. In the UK, **FTSE4Good** is an **index** of **ethically managed companies**. In the US, there are the **Dow Jones Sustainability indexes**:

- **DJSI World** – containing the shares of 300 companies from 23 countries that lead their industries in terms of sustainability
- **DJSI Stoxx** – 180 companies from 14 European countries

Sustainability is the idea that businesses should be run not for short-term profit, but in a way that takes account of the long-term interests of society and the environment. (For more on this, see Units 50 and 59.) DJSI defines **corporate sustainability** in these terms:

a '**Strategy**: integrating long-term economic, environmental and social aspects in their business strategies while maintaining global competitiveness and brand reputation.
b **Financial**: meeting shareholders' demands for sound financial returns, long-term economic growth, open communication and transparent financial accounting.
c **Customer and Product**: fostering loyalty by investing in customer-relationship management, and product and service innovation that focuses on technologies and systems, which use financial, natural and social resources in an efficient, effective and economic manner over the long term.
d **Governance and Stakeholder**: setting the highest standards of corporate governance and stakeholder engagement, including corporate codes of conduct and public reporting.
e **Human**: managing human resources to maintain workforce capabilities and employee satisfaction through best-in-class organizational learning and knowledge-management practices and remuneration and benefit programs.'

The FTSE4Good and DJSI indexes give the overall value of the share prices of the ethical firms, and we can compare the performance of individual firms against them.

This is part of the movement towards **socially responsible investment (SRI)**.

53.1   Look at A and B opposite. What are these things examples of?

1 A company that gives full details of its directors' pay, benefits and pension arrangements, giving information in its annual report beyond what is required by law.
2 A fund that promises not to invest in companies that make weapons.
3 An oil company that says it will take full responsibility for the environmental consequences of its production activities.
4 Pension funds and insurance companies that invest on the stock market and elsewhere.
5 A company that has a board structure that follows best practice in this area.
6 People who own shares in a company and want to prevent the company operating in a country whose government they disapprove of.

53.2   Complete the table with words from B and C opposite.

Noun	Adjective	Adverb
ethics		ethically
	transparent	transparently
	accountable	–
	sustainable	sustainably

53.3   Now complete the sentences with appropriate expressions from 53.2 above.

1 Does the chief financial officer provide .... real-time information for internal · decision-making and for governance purposes?
2 The present-day idea that the corporation is .... to outside shareholders was unknown in the nineteenth century.
3 Asda has committed itself to supplying only .... caught fish.
4 Sales managers may influence salespersons to behave more or less .... toward their clients.
5 Shell views openness and .... as an essential part of the long-term energy solution for the global business environment.
6 Toyota mapped out the company's strategy for .... growth in the 21st century. It included balancing the needs of people, society, the economy and the global environment.

53.4   Match what these executives say (1–5) with the points (a–e) in C opposite.

1 We have taken steps to evaluate the effectiveness of our employee training programme.

4 We follow all the latest recommendations on structuring our board of directors in the most responsible and effective way.

2 With the latest software, we can anticipate what our customers are going to require from us six months from now.

5 Our profits and growth exceed our competitors' performance.

3 We really have to take account of the long-term environmental impact of our activities.

Over to you

'The only responsibility of companies is to make a profit.' What do you think?

54 Globalization

A Paths to prosperity

In terms of economic development, the world is divided into:

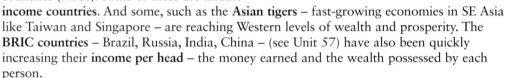

- the rich **industrialized countries** or **advanced economies** of the **West**. (The West is taken to include countries such as Japan and Australia.)

- the **developing countries** or **less-developed countries (LDCs)** at various stages of **industrialization** – they are **newly industrialized countries (NICs)**. Some of these are **middle-income countries**. And some, such as the **Asian tigers** – fast-growing economies in SE Asia like Taiwan and Singapore – are reaching Western levels of wealth and prosperity. The **BRIC countries** – Brazil, Russia, India, China – (see Unit 57) have also been quickly increasing their **income per head** – the money earned and the wealth possessed by each person.

- countries with **rural economies** – based on agriculture – and very little industry, where most people are very poor. These are sometimes referred to as the **Third World**.

People who want to emphasize the difference between the industrialized and the less-developed countries of the world often refer to the **North** and the **South**.

B GDP and GNI

The **prosperity** of a country is measured in terms of **GDP (Gross Domestic Product)**, which is the value of its **economic output** – all the goods and services produced there in a year. **GDP per capita** is the total output of a particular country divided by the number of people living there.

High national income can mean high **living standards** – high levels of wealth for people. This depends on the **income distribution** of particular countries – the way that money is divided among the people of a country.

Prosperity can also be measured in terms of **GNI (Gross National Income)**. This includes money coming into a country from investments abroad, minus money leaving the country to go to investors from abroad. This is the new name for what used to be called **GNP (Gross National Product)**.

C Globalizing trends

Globalization is the tendency for the **global economy** to function as one unit, with increasing **interdependence** between different parts of the world – what happens in one place affects what happens in another.

These are some of the factors that are driving globalization. Its supporters say that growth and prosperity will continue to spread thanks to:

- **free movement of capital** – money for investment can be easily moved around the world

- **trade liberalization** or **free trade** – obstacles to international trade are gradually being removed

- **shipping costs** that are ever-declining thanks to the efficiency of **containerization**

- **telecommunications** and **computing costs** that have fallen dramatically

But the **credit crunch** (see Unit 47) of 2007–9 strengthened criticism of globalization, with some politicians wanting to protect particular companies from foreign competition, for example with **tariffs** – taxes on imported goods. This is **protectionism**.

54.1 Complete the crossword with the correct form of words from A and B opposite.

Across

2 Very poor countries considered together (5,5)

4 Levels of material comfort: living .... (9)

7 Where most activity happens outside towns: .... economies (5)

9 Advanced economies are .... (14)

10 Poorer countries considered together: the .... (5)

14 All goods and services produced in a particular period (8,6)

16 Rich countries considered together, even if they are not all located there: the .... (4)

18 and **15** down .... countries are between the rich and the poor ones (6,6)

Down

1 and **5** Old name for GNI (5,8,7)

3 How money is divided between people: income .... (12)

6 Wealth (10)

8 Abbreviation for gross national product (3)

11 Singapore, Taiwan and others: Asian .... (6)

12 The 'L' of LDC (4)

13 Rich countries considered as a group: the .... (5)

17 Abbreviation for gross national income (3)

54.2 Match these sentences with expressions in C opposite.

1 The charge for transporting a whole container of goods across the Pacific can be as little as $50.

2 The cost of a three-minute phone call from London to New York in 1930 was £200 in today's money. The same call costs much less than £1 today.

3 There are no taxes on goods traded within the European Union.

4 We can invest in many Asian countries and bring back our profits without penalty.

5 We should impose special taxes on foreign-made steel.

6 The US imports more than it exports, much of it from China, and China buys American debt.

Over to you

Can the level of development of a country be measured by GDP alone? If not, what other factors should be taken into account?

55 Investment and debt

A Direct investment

Foreign direct investment (FDI) is when companies put money into investment projects in other countries. With free **cross-border capital flows**, they can **repatriate** their profits to their own country, or **withdraw** their **investment** altogether.

There is debate about whether governments should try to limit **capital flows** – **inflows** and **outflows** – with **capital controls** or whether they should follow the global trend towards **liberalization**.

Some economists say that too much liberalization of capital flows leads to **instability** in a country's economy, with **foreign exchange crises** which lead to **devaluation** – its currency becomes worth less in terms of others. For example, some say that China's growth has benefited from the fact that its currency is not freely **convertible**. This lack of **convertibility** prevents the capital outflows that some other Asian economies have suffered from at various times.

B Borrowing

The **International Monetary Fund (IMF)** and the **World Bank** play an important role in the development of less-developed countries. A main function of the World Bank is to lend money to countries so that they can obtain the conditions for economic growth. For example, the World Bank sponsors **infrastructure projects** – road building, water supply systems, etc. and projects in health, education and agriculture.

An infrastructure project – ditch-digging

But developing countries may build up **unsustainable** levels of debt and be unable to repay these debts. The IMF has **debt reduction programmes** for **Heavily Indebted Poor Countries (HIPCs)** that will reduce the amount of money that they owe. The IMF also contributes to work on the **Millennium Development Goals** – specific targets relating to **poverty reduction** and the **stimulation of growth** in poorer countries.

C Word combinations with 'debt'

Here are some frequent combinations with 'debt':

debt	**load / burden**	an amount of debt owed by a company, country, etc. seen as a problem
	service	making repayments on a debt
	rescheduling	when lenders agree for a debt to be repaid at a different time
	restructuring	when lenders agree for a debt to be repaid in a different way
	relief	when lenders agree that debts do not have to be repaid in full, or can be repaid later than originally agreed
	forgiveness	when lenders agree that debts do not need to be repaid

Note Debt load is more frequent than debt burden, and debt rescheduling is more frequent than debt restructuring.

55.1 Complete the sentences with expressions from A opposite.

1 China remains the largest recipient of .... among developing economies. But after a decade when heavy .... from abroad were credited with bringing the country out of poverty, that investment is levelling off.

2 .... were imposed as an obstacle to foreign investment in the country.

3 There has been a .... of the Liberian dollar since last year. One US dollar used to be worth 35 Liberian dollars but is now worth 60 Liberian dollars.

4 Almost everywhere we see a lowering of barriers to the international transfer of capital, goods, services, culture and information. The prevailing trend almost everywhere is towards

....

5 Investors should keep in mind the political and economic .... in many emerging markets.

55.2 Replace the underlined expressions below with expressions from B opposite.

1 <u>It</u> demands both economic growth and specific anti-poverty policies.

2 Critics say that the country's social welfare policies will be <u>impossible to continue</u> if oil prices fall.

3 Among the Brazilian government's <u>plans</u> are a $2 billion plan to expand subway services in the cities of São Paulo, Rio de Janeiro and Brasilia.

4 The government has shifted the emphasis of policy from the control of inflation to <u>making the economy bigger</u>.

5 Despite all the promises made by rich nations, <u>these countries</u> are still suffering under the burden of unpayable debts.

6 When we worked on <u>these objectives</u> in the year 2000, clean water was one of the goals.

7 <u>These institutions</u> spread particular economic policies around the world, usually in exchange for a badly needed loan, or a condition attached to a loan.

55.3 Match the two parts of these sentences containing expressions from C opposite.

1 Those with the heaviest debt	a rescheduling agreement with its 225 creditor banks.
2 Maryland aims to keep debt	b burden got the worst interest rates, sometimes more than twice as high as other borrowers.
3 The airline has said a successful debt	c service to no more than 8 per cent of the state's tax.
4 The company is negotiating a debt-	d restructuring would prevent it from going bankrupt.
5 Celebrities have taken up the cause: Bono campaigns for debt	e cards alone, peaked at around $40,000.
6 The couple's debt load, on credit	f relief and Angelina Jolie puts African hunger on MTV.

Over to you

Should the debt of developing countries be completely forgiven? Why? / Why not?

56 Trade

A Dismantling the barriers

Free trade areas or **blocs** such as

- the **EEA** (**European Economic Area**) – containing the European Union plus some other countries
- **NAFTA** (**North American Free Trade Area**) – Canada, US and Mexico
- **GAFTA** (**Greater Arab Free Trade Area**)
- **Mercosur** – a grouping of South American countries

have **dismantled** – abolished – **trade barriers** between their member countries, or moved towards dismantling them. These barriers include:

- **tariffs** – taxes on imported goods
- **quotas** – limits on the number of goods that can be imported

Supporters of **free trade** believe that there is increased prosperity for all if goods and services can be freely bought and sold all around the world. The **World Trade Organization (WTO)** is working to remove or dismantle trade barriers and to resolve **trade disputes** – disagreements about trade.

However, countries of the North have yet to **open up their markets** fully to agricultural goods from the South. WTO negotiations are permanently ongoing. The latest stage of negotiations is referred to as the **Doha round**, after the Gulf city in Qatar where they began in 2001.

B Protected industries

American steel executives complain that they have higher costs than many other steel-producing countries and that they can't compete with their prices. They say that some countries are **dumping** their steel – selling it for less than it costs to produce. So they asked the government to impose tariffs on imported steel.

But steel producers in other countries feel that the US is engaging in **unfair trade practices**; from their point of view it's **protectionism**. They say that they believe in free trade, and that they should be allowed to compete in an open world market for steel.

And even within free trade areas, during the economic crisis of 2007–9 there have been calls by some politicians for companies to **repatriate** production to their home countries in order to qualify for financial assistance from the government.

C Fair trade

Claire Longdon is a consumer in Britain:

'I believe in **fair trade**. When I buy products, especially **commodities** like coffee or bananas, I look for the **fairtrade mark**. The **Fairtrade** organization makes sure that **producers** and **growers**, often **smallholders** – small farmers – are paid a fair price, not just the market price, which can be catastrophically low. Producers are encouraged to form **co-operatives** – organizations jointly owned by them – in order to sell their product without going through the usual **middlemen** – wholesalers.

'Prices can fall dramatically when there is **overproduction** around the world, causing a **glut** in a particular commodity, but Fairtrade guarantees prices paid to producers.'

56.1 Complete the sentences with appropriate forms of expressions from A and B opposite.

1 US and EU business leaders now need to focus on removing .... between the two blocs rather than aim to create a single .... area.

2 He said raising prices by increasing .... on Japanese luxury cars would give Detroit's Big Three automakers an excuse to increase their own luxury car prices.

3 The BRIC economies have been growing and .... their markets. They offer many new opportunities.

4 The European Union warned that South Korea should open up its car market, accusing the country of ....

5 If the Commerce Department rules that Mexico is .... tomatoes, consumers can expect higher tomato prices because the US will impose .... on them, limiting the numbers that can be imported.

56.2 Look at C opposite. Then read the article and decide if the statements below are true or false.

Smallholders farm a route out of poverty

Smallholders are too often overlooked by companies and policymakers alike, but they could hold the key to helping solve the food crisis and tackling poverty. Just 15 years ago, Rwanda was utterly devastated. They are now rebuilding their economy, with organized smallholders at its heart. Just 15 years ago, Maraba village was one of the country's poorest; their low-quality coffee was sold straight off the bushes to passing middlemen.

Today, the Maraba farmers have organized themselves into a Fairtrade-certified cooperative, have four washing stations (the first stage in processing coffee), have trained the first generation of cuppers, or tasters, who are constantly improving quality, and are commanding record premiums for their prize-winning beans. They are roasting and selling their coffee all over Rwanda as well as exporting it through Union Handroasted to UK shop shelves.

These are the most innovative farmers I have ever met – constantly researching new ways to improve productivity, such as making organic compost, or to add value, such as roasting at a village level, using traditional techniques. And they have sparked an economic revival that sees Maraba now among the more prosperous villages in Rwanda, as evidenced by the bustling bank and choice of hairdressing salons, while the farmers are now building and running a nursery school.

It is an economic revival that, with the right support, smallholders could lead worldwide. Some 450 million smallholder farming households cultivate two hectares or less, and with their families they make up a third of all humanity. Increasing their incomes will therefore be vital to improving the incomes of the poor. Indeed, because smallholders tend to spend more income on local goods and services, they could be the impetus that stimulates virtuous economic circles in local economies.

1 Rwandan smallholders have only recently started growing coffee.
2 They have started selling their produce abroad as well as across Rwanda.
3 They have improved the quality of what they grow.
4 They have not always been prosperous in relation to others in Rwanda, but now they are.
5 Smallholders around the world, and their families, represent one-third of everyone alive today.

Over to you

Do you / Would you buy Fairtrade products? Why? / Why not?

57 The BRIC economies

A Emerging economies

The **BRIC economies** – Brazil, Russia, India and China – are the world's largest **emerging economies**. Between 2002 and 2007, annual **GDP growth** averaged 10.4 per cent in China, 7.9 per cent in India, 6.9 per cent in Russia and 3.7 per cent in Brazil. They have fast growth, strong **economic foundations**, with large **trade surpluses** – they export more than they import – and as a result, healthy **foreign currency reserves**: $1,528 billion in China, $464 billion in Russia, $266 billion in India and $179 billion in Brazil. All this has made the BRIC countries into those with the most economic potential. By 2041, the combined BRIC economies are expected to be bigger than those of Germany, France, Italy, Japan, the UK and the US put together.

B Similarities

The term BRIC was used for the first time in a Goldman Sachs report in 2001. The report said that in BRIC nations, the number of people with an annual income of over $3,000 would reach 800 million people by 2013. It predicted a big rise in the size of the **middle class** in these countries, and it calculated that the number of people in BRIC nations earning over $15,000 may reach over 200 million, thus showing a big increase in **demand** not only for **basic goods** but for **higher-priced goods** as well.

According to the report, first China and then a decade later India will begin to dominate the world economy. Yet despite this growth, the average **wealth level** of individuals in the more advanced economies will continue to exceed the BRIC economy average by a big margin; Goldman Sachs estimated that by 2025 the **GDP per capita** or **income per head** in the six biggest EU countries will exceed $35,000, but only about 500 million people in the BRIC economies will have similar income levels, with many people there still very poor.

C Differences

Some say that the term BRIC is misleading, because each of the four economies is different; for example, see the table opposite for their widely varying GDP figures.

China and to a lesser extent India are **manufacturing-based economies** and big importers of **raw materials**, but Brazil and Russia are big exporters of **natural resources**.

India's new wealth is also based on **offshoring** of services, everything from call centres to medical services (see Unit 31).

Russia's wealth is mainly based on exports of **hydrocarbons** – oil and gas – with prices that change very quickly; when prices go down, the Russian economy suffers. Brazil's is largely based on **agricultural products** even if it is also a manufacturer of hi-tech products such as aircraft.

In **demographics** – population – India and Brazil are growing, but China and Russia are getting smaller because of **declining birth rates** and **ageing populations**, which will have long-term consequences for economic growth. A smaller percentage of the population will be working, supporting those who no longer work.

And the potential of the **Next Eleven (N-11)** countries identified by Goldman should not be ignored. These are at differing stages of **economic development: least developed country** (Bangladesh), **developing countries** (Egypt, Indonesia, Iran, Nigeria, Pakistan, Vietnam), **newly industrialized countries** or **NICs** (Mexico, Philippines, Turkey) and **developed country** (South Korea).

The criteria for selection were: their **economic stability** – lack of sudden changes; **political maturity** – efficient government; **openness of trade and investment policies** – i.e. lack of **protectionism**; and the quality of **education**.

57.1 Use information from A, B and C opposite to complete the table.

	Brazil	Russia	India	China
GDP	$1,845bn	$2,089bn	$3,094bn	$7,245bn
GDP growth 2005–7				
Foreign currency reserves				
Main sources of wealth				
Average age of population: getting older or younger?				

57.2 Complete the definitions with these expressions from A and B opposite.

basic goods   GDP   trade surplus
foreign currency reserves   middle class   wealth level

1 .... are the necessary commodities and food that people need.
2 A country has a .... when it sells more products abroad than it imports.
3 A country's .... is the value of all the goods and services produced there.
4 The .... is the part of society whose members are well-educated, and who usually have office jobs and a reasonable level of disposable income.
5 .... are the amounts of other countries' money that a particular country possesses, for example as a result of international trade.
6 The .... of a particular economy is how much money people have on average in comparison to those in other countries.

57.3 Look at C opposite and answer the questions.

1 Why is Russia's economy so exposed?
2 Why are China and India on the one hand, and Russia and Brazil on the other, different in their sources of wealth?
3 Why is an ageing population important to consider when making economic forecasts?
4 Which groups are the N-11 countries divided into? How many are there in each group?
5 Which of these criteria for economic success are not mentioned: functioning government; plentiful raw materials; resistance to protectionism; quality of schooling?

Over to you

Make an economic forecast for a country that you know, based on the criteria in this unit.

58 International aid

Humanitarian aid

When there are extreme situations, **aid agencies** such as Oxfam or Médecins sans Frontières play an important role. These situations include: war; **natural disasters** such as **earthquakes, floods, epidemics** – widespread disease; and **famine** – when people do not have enough to eat, for example following **crop failure,** when crops are not produced as usual. **Emergency relief** is provided in the form of supplies, medical assistance, and so on. This is part of **humanitarian aid.**

Aid agencies are **NGOs (non-government organizations)** even if in some cases they are totally or partially funded by governments.

Development aid

Aid agencies also contribute to economic development through specific **development projects.** These projects may use **intermediate technology** – equipment and machinery suited to local conditions that local people can operate and maintain.

Some of these projects are designed to improve **infrastructure** – a country's water supplies, roads, etc.

Some provide **seed money** for small businesses – the money they need to start up – until they become **viable** and able to develop by themselves.

This is **development aid,** referred to technically as **official development assistance (ODA).**

The aims of aid

Development aid often also comes from **donor countries.** Some countries are more **generous** than others, giving a higher proportion of their national **wealth.** The places to which aid is sent and the uses to which it is put are influenced by **pressure groups** such as the NGOs mentioned above.

Governments receiving aid are **recipients.** Some donors give **tied aid** – they require the recipients to use the money to purchase equipment, etc. from them.

Many would say that the purpose of aid is **poverty reduction.** But there is a lot of discussion about how this can be achieved. Some experts say that the best use of aid is to invest in projects that contribute to **economic development.**

58.1 Complete the sentences with expressions from A and B opposite.

1 International .... have promised about $600 million to help Afghans survive the winter.

2 Any opportunity to prepare for the effects of extreme changes in climate can help nations prevent heavy rains from becoming floods, a drought from becoming a .... , and an outbreak of disease from becoming an ....

3 Insurance companies have traditionally offered policies to farmers covering catastrophic weather and resulting major ....

4 Emergency .... all too often arrives in the wrong quantity at the wrong time, flooding in when no adequate channels exist to allocate it.

5 The squadron has a mission to provide .... aid in developing nations, as well as help with disaster relief.

6 Trickle Up is an organization that provides .... to people in developing nations who want to start small businesses.

7 Natural .... , such as the cyclone and flooding that hit Bangladesh recently, wiped out many people's stocks of food.

58.2 Match the newspaper headlines (1–7) with a word or expression from B or C opposite.

1 **New online tracking system in Ethiopia links coffee makers to markets**

2 **Sri Lankan women's group to start textile factory thanks to long-term loan**

3 **Hundreds of protestors call for the cancelling of Third World debt**

4 **Angola to receive cash from Italy to develop telecommunications, using Italian contractors**

5 **Use of clockwork radios revolutionizes life in remote villages**

6 **Madagascar's economy expanding at 6 per cent per year**

7 **Mobile phone use in Latin America doubles in three years**

Over to you

Can a country exist on humanitarian aid alone? Why? / Why not?

59 Sustainable development

Sustainability

Sustainability is the idea that the economy should be organized in ways that can be continued without causing **irreversible environmental damage, depletion of natural resources,** etc. Businesses should be run not for **short-term profit,** but in a way that takes account of the **long-term interests** of society and the environment, for example by not contributing to factors that cause **climate change.**

Developing countries are trying to attain the **living standards** of the industrialized world. Some experts warn that, in addition to the dangers of global warming, the world's natural resources are not sufficient for such large-scale economic development there.

Others argue that **renewable, non-polluting energy sources** such as **wind power, solar power** and **tidal power** will allow further economic growth without causing damage to the environment (see Unit 50). Some argue that **nuclear energy** will have a major role to play.

These are some of the issues surrounding **sustainable development** in the global economy.

B New technologies

Firms are reducing their **carbon footprint** (see Unit 51), but they are also looking at **new technologies** – methods – to reduce their **environmental impact** – the effect they have on the environment – in other ways. They are looking at ways of reducing and even eliminating entirely the **waste** that they produce. Today, there is debate about the relative merits of **recycling** and **incineration** – burning – of waste to produce energy in **incinerators**.

C The triple bottom line

SustainAbility*, a consultancy, says that the **triple bottom line** (TBL) makes corporations concentrate not just on the **economic value** they add, but also on the **environmental** and **social value** they both add and destroy. The TBL is used to sum up the values, issues and processes that companies must pay attention to in order to minimize any harm resulting from their activities and to create economic, social and environmental value. The three lines represent society, the economy and the environment. Society depends on the economy and the economy depends on the **global ecosystem,** whose health represents the **ultimate bottom line.**

*www.sustainability.com

59.1 Match these issues from A and C opposite with the newspaper headlines. Match some headlines with more than one issue.

| depletion of natural resources | nuclear energy | sustainability |
| environmental damage | renewable energy | triple bottom line |

1 **N-plant in radioactive leak scare**

2 **SAHARA SOLAR PANEL PLAN HOPES**

3 **Firm in all-round assessment of its activities**

4 **Books and newspapers 'do not deplete forests'**

5 **New coal-fired power station opens every week**

6 **Chemicals from plant found in river**

59.2 Look at B opposite. Then read the article and complete the table below.

JAPAN'S NO-WASTE APPROACH

At Toyota's Tsutsumi assembly plant in Nagoya, Japan's answer to Detroit, evidence of a more environmentally sensitive car industry is on display before you even walk through a door. What was once a vast, gray expanse of industrial might has come to life – literally. Large trees – 50,000 were planted in May – dot the visitor parking lot to offer a soothing greeting, Insulating vines wend their way up the outside of an employee locker building. Some 22,000 square meters of exterior walls are coated with photocatalytic paint that, Toyota says, mirrors the ability of 2,000 poplar trees to absorb nitrous oxide and process oxygen.

The roof of the visitor center is a mat of grass, designed to reduce waves of heat by 3 degrees C. Solar lights dot the streets and 800-kilowatt solar panels blanket the tops of buildings. Even the red roadside flowers were genetically engineered to absorb noxious emissions.

Behind Tsutsumi's facelift lies one of the globe's most visible bids to lighten the automobile's carbon footprint: the Prius. Hundreds roll off gleaming Line No. 2 here every day.

With the hybrid vehicle an Earth-friendly icon from Tokyo to Hollywood, Toyota decided it was important to have its back story match up. "Cars are a burden to the environment, but the hybrid helps," says Osamu Terada, leader of the sustainable plant initiative. "The plant is also important – we don't want manufacturing to cause a further burden."

Like the Prius, the Tsutsumi factory now relies on hybrid power, drawing 50 per cent of its electricity from solar panels and 50 per cent from capturing waste heat generated within the plant. The facility has reduced its carbon-dioxide emissions to half what they were in 1990, despite an increase in production. It eliminated production of landfill waste in 1999 and dispensed with incinerated waste in March 2008.

Initiative	Details including number (where stated) and benefit
trees in car park	50,000 – nice greeting for visitors
vines	
paint	
roof grass	
solar lights and panels	
roadside flowers	
waste heat	
landfill and incinerated waste	

Over to you

Are you optimistic or pessimistic about the capacity of the planet for future growth? Will the types of sustainable environmental practices described in the article in 59.2 above become widespread? Give your reasons.

60 Intercultural teams

Cultural issues

Culture is the 'way we do things round here'. 'Here' might mean a country, an area, a social class or an organization such as a company or school. It includes **values** – things that people think are important – and **beliefs** – things that people believe in. **Cultural differences** can arise when people from different cultures work together or do business together, for example in these areas:

a **Hierarchy** What is the **distance** between managers and the people who work for them, and how is this shown?

b **Roles of men and women** Are women often found at the highest levels of business and society? Are there jobs that are traditionally done by each gender? Is there a **glass ceiling** – a level of seniority in organizations beyond which women rarely go?

c **Conversation and discussion** What is the system of **deference** – showing respect – in communicating with more senior colleagues? How do people behave in different **settings** – formal, informal, social situations, etc.? What is their attitude to **turn-taking** – interrupting other people or letting them finish? How tolerant are they of **silence**? What is their attitude to **proximity** – how close people stand together? What kind of **gestures** and **body language** do they use? How much **contact** – handshakes, kissing – is there?

d **Attitudes to tasks** Are people **task-oriented** – focusing on the task at hand? Or are they **relationship-oriented** – focusing on the people that they are working with?.

e **Attitudes to time** – **planning, punctuality**, the working day/week/year, meals and breaks, **leisure time** – weekends, holidays, etc.

f **Relation of work and private life** What forms of **hospitality** are shown to customers/clients? Do businesspeople invite colleagues and contacts to their homes, or is everything done in the office, restaurants, etc?

International teams

A global car company has brought together some of its best engineers for a year at its research centre in Germany to work on a project developing a new electric car. Some are native English speakers, others not. Different cultures can have different interpretations of the same behaviour.

	Positive interpretations	Negative interpretations
Adnan always refers to head office before making a decision.	follows procedures	not independent, bureaucratic, rigid
Nadine calls the team leader 'sir'.	deferential, respectful of seniority	kowtows to authority – is too respectful of it
Carlos speaks English in a very formal way.	understandable by non-native speakers	unnatural, pompous – too formal
Susannah is always doing two things at once.	multitasker	doesn't concentrate, easily distracted
Sergei always leaves by 6 pm.	good work–life balance	lazy
Mia spends a lot of time at the coffee machine chatting.	sociable, congenial	time-waster, over-familiar – too friendly
Lee always says exactly what he thinks.	direct, sincere, efficient	tactless, rude, acerbic – very critical in a cruel way
Gina doesn't always follow procedures.	flexible, proactive	improviser, undisciplined, disorganized
Pekka doesn't say much about what he's working on.	modest, doesn't boast	uncommunicative

60.1 Match the points and subpoints in A opposite (a–f) with the organization described below.
The first one has been done as an example.

1 When a senior manager is talking, junior colleagues do not interrupt. *c – deference, turn-taking*
2 Managers and employees all have lunch in the same restaurant.
3 Clients are invited to karaoke bars until one or two in the morning.
4 Meetings always start and finish on time.
5 People are judged on their ability to get the task done.
6 Women rarely join the board of directors.
7 Changes in the company's activities are usually planned two years ahead.
8 When someone wants to underline a point in a meeting, they might bang on the table.
9 The office closes in August and everyone goes on holiday.

60.2 Look at A and B opposite. Then read the two articles and answer the questions.

> A major international oil company decided to merge its Belgian and Dutch operations
> into a single entity, based in Antwerp, Belgium. However, the Belgian and Dutch
> employees of the new company found it difficult to cooperate and, more seriously still,
> there were signs of poor communication, lack of trust and even discord among the two
> nationalities at the management level. The Belgians felt they had been taken over by
> the Dutch; they regarded their Dutch colleagues as often pompous and rude, and not
> taking enough account of the need to do things in Belgium the Belgian way. The Dutch
> on the other hand found the Belgians bureaucratic; they always seemed to want to
> check with the hierarchy before making decisions; at the same time, they seemed to be
> always improvising.

1 What did the oil company decide to do?
2 Why would you imagine that this would not be a problem? (This is not specifically
  mentioned.)
3 Which issues from A and characteristics from B are mentioned in the article?

> In one multinational team, some of the greatest difficulties between team members had
> everything to do with individual personality differences and very little to do with culture. It came
> as a great relief to the team to recognize that "unpleasant" characters exist in all cultures. Much
> of the tension generated by some individuals on the team was a result of their acerbic personal
> style. However, the team were almost unconsciously trying to tolerate unacceptable behaviour
> because they assumed it was culturally driven. Once the team realized that cultural difference is
> not an excuse for misbehaving or being inflexible it was as if a great weight had been removed
> from their collective shoulders.

4 What type of individual is the article about?
5 Are problems in international teams always related to cultural differences?
6 What was the outcome of knowing the answer to this question?

Over to you

Select three particular types of behaviour in the left column in B opposite. How would they
be perceived in your organization?

61 Intercultural meetings

A Meeting preparation

Just after they arrived in Germany, the team (see Unit 60) were to have their first formal meeting chaired by the team leader, Louise, an American engineer. Before the meeting, she made these personal notes on the agenda.

> ### Team meeting – Outline agenda
>
> 1 **Establish ground rules**[1] **for meetings**
> - Make clear that everyone is expected to make a **full contribution** to discussion **on an equal basis – no passengers**[2]
> - **Avoid digressions** in discussion – no **getting off the point**
> - …
>
> 2 **Team working**
> - **Allocate roles and tasks**[3] clearly.
> - Between meetings, team members expected to work with **maximum autonomy**[4] and **minimum day-to-day supervision**[5]
> - However, promise **support** where necessary. Encourage team to know when they need to ask for support.
> - Explain my **open-door** policy – team members can come in and talk when door is open. If closed, not.
> - …
>
> 3 **First stage of project**

[1]agree the basic rules
[2]everyone works

[3]decide who will do what
[4]independence
[5]being told what to do all the time

B Cultural preparation

To understand more about how his American boss Louise might run the meeting, Carlos read this article about business meetings in the US.

> When asked to describe meetings in the US, a word which Americans often use is **aggressive**. This **confrontational** approach (where openly and directly debating all the relevant issues even at the expense of personal relationships is valued), is very different to those cultures who always put **diplomacy** and **harmony** at the heart of their approach to meetings.
>
> Of course, many cultures mistakenly see this **direct approach** between colleagues as a sign of bitter, personal dislike. In the US, it is seen as a positive step towards addressing whatever the vital issues might be. Time-pressured, ambitious American business executives do not have time for the **vagueness**, diplomacy and **lack of focus** which they perceive as typifying meeting situations in such diverse cultures as the UK and Japan.

C Running the meeting

Louise **called** – told everyone to come to – **the meeting** and said these things to various participants.

a You're being rude. Could you **tone down your comments**, please?
b **You're getting off the point.** We don't need to hear about your living arrangements.
c **OK, now we have your detailed proposals, but we can't see the wood for the trees** – the proposals are too detailed.
d Please give me a yes or no answer.
e OK Carlos, **can we keep the humour for some other time?**
f **Let's keep the ball rolling here.** We need to keep going. Please say what you have to say.
g I know I'm the one in charge, but **come out and say what you think!**
h I know it's not on the agenda, but we need to discuss this now.

Note: BrE: humour AmE: humor

61.1 Look at A opposite. Here are some more notes (a–f) that Louise makes relating to the meeting agenda. Decide if each one refers to 1) Ground rules for meetings, or 2) Team working

> a Team to be encouraged to socialize together once a week in the evening –
>   no going home straight after work that evening!
> b People should come to meetings prepared, and with any information that will
>   be required.
> c No 'talking over' each other – each participant should be allowed to finish.
> d When working on tasks, don't expect the team leader to provide all the answers.
> e No making or receiving phone calls or text messages.
> f Team members to undergo three days' cultural awareness training to avoid
>   future misunderstandings at work.

61.2 Complete the table with words from B opposite.

Noun	Adjective
aggression	
confrontation	
	diplomatic
	focused
	harmonious
	vague

61.3 Now match the adjectives in 61.2 above with their meanings.

1 wanting to protect other people's feelings
2 pleasant and friendly
3 not wasting time
4 not clear

5 describing situations where there is
   argument and disagreement
6 angry and hostile

61.4 Look at C opposite. Match the different types of behaviour observed by Carlos during the meeting (1–8) with what the chair of the meeting said in reaction to each one (a–h).

1 has great respect for team leader and doesn't say anything unless invited to

2 keeps silent while others are talking and waits several seconds before he responds

3 doesn't say 'no' directly – I get the impression he thinks it's impolite

4 communicates in a very direct way, perhaps over-direct

5 came to the meeting with detailed proposals – maybe too detailed!

6 seems to think that meetings should be more like a social event – doesn't keep to the point

7 can't stand not following the agenda

8 I made jokes, but not everyone laughed

Over to you

Imagine that a visitor from the English-speaking world is coming to your country. Give some tips on what to expect and how to behave in meetings.

62 Intercultural networking

The right attitude

After six months on the design team in Germany, Carlos started to look for work elsewhere. He did this by **networking** – meeting people from the same profession at conferences and other events, including special **networking events** designed for this purpose. He found some tips for events like this, designed with a UK audience in mind.

a Be visible, proactive and friendly
b Not sure what to talk about?
c Create a dialogue
d Manage the business cards
e Follow up with people
f Be a resource
g Be adaptable
h Have fun!

Note
dialogue: BrE and AmE
dialog: AmE only

Good etiquette

Now look at the some of the notes that Carlos made about the above tips in an international context.

- **Proximity** (see Unit 60), **eye contact, etc.** – stand a reasonable distance from people, but not too far, and look them in the eye for about half the time

- **Deference** (see Unit 60) / **Forms of address** – show the right degree of respect and don't be over-familiar. Use first names only when invited to.

- **Avoid difficult, controversial** and **sensitive subjects**, e.g. politics and religion

- **Treat business cards with respect**

- **Communicate appropriately, at the right time, etc.** – don't talk too much, and don't digress and get off the point.

- **Be careful with humour** – probably better not to try to tell jokes at all with people you don't know

Business cards

In many English-speaking countries, business cards are treated rather casually. But in Asia, they are important. When someone **hands over** their card, **take it with both hands, look at it carefully** and **treat it with care and respect**. Feel free to **ask questions** (within reason, of course) about the information on it – it's good to **show interest** in this way, and it will help you to **understand the organization** that the person works for. **Do not write or make notes** on it. **Store it** in a specific place. Hand over your card in return, also with both hands; ensure that you always **have a supply with you**.

62.1 Match these items of advice (1–8) with the points (a–h) in A opposite.

1 Think about questions such as: 'What makes you interested in … ?', 'What are you hoping to get out of the meeting?' or 'Do you know any of the other people here?'

2 Not everyone is a natural networker, but we can all learn how to make more meaningful connections. Set a goal before each event that will keep you focused and interested, like meeting three new people and learning one interesting thing. And above all, enjoy yourself!

3 Try different ways of staying in touch with the person (phone, email, postcard, lunch, etc). Make sure that you have something specific to say, based on what you know about them.

4 Make the first move, in a friendly way. Expect to like people and to enjoy the event. If not, people will sense it and will not connect with you!

5 Keep your business cards in one pocket and the cards you collect in another pocket. Develop a system for keeping track of the people you want to follow up with (you can carry a pen to make a quick note on the card, or just tear the corner).

6 Find out what other people value or need most. Put people in your network in touch with each other. This creates a much stronger positive impression than trying to 'sell' yourself. Offer to email an article or resource you have that may be helpful for them.

7 Don't lecture. Make the goal in your conversations to connect rather than impress. Ask questions and find out more about the other person. Remember, you need at least six encounters before they remember you. Ask permission to stay in touch in a concrete way; suggest a time to call or send an email.

8 Find out the other person's communication or thinking style and adapt your own message to it. If the person likes facts, don't talk too much about abstract ideas; give them facts and figures.

62.2 Carlos spoke to an older Chinese engineer, Wang Ya, at a networking event in Asia, and later on the phone. Match what Carlos said (1–6) with the issues in B opposite.

1 We're getting on to politics. Let's not go there!

2 Ah, Canton. I was there last year for a conference. And here's my card.

3 Is this is a good time to call?

4 Shall we move over there? The people next to us are getting too close.

5 There was a Spaniard, an Italian and a Frenchman …

6 Please call me Carlos.

62.3 Look at C opposite. Were each of these actions at the networking event in Asia appropriate or inappropriate?

1 When Wang Ya handed over his card and Carlos saw that he worked in Canton, he made a comment about it.

2 Carlos then handed over his card with one hand.

3 Two other people were talking nearby. One handed over his card, and the other (following the advice in 62.1, point 5 above) tore the corner as a reminder to make contact later.

4 The second person then handed over his card in return; the first person looked at it carefully and put it in a special pocket in his briefcase.

Over to you

Give six pieces of advice to someone going to a networking event or making contacts at a trade show in your country.

63 Business writing 1

A CVs

RIKU HENDERSON

Career goals
Looking for **challenging**, **intellectually stimulating** development work in renewable energy. Would like to move into **team management**.

Skills
Enthusiastic **self-starter** – can work on projects with **minimal supervision**

Effective **multitasker** – good at **prioritizing tasks** and working on several at once

Experience of working with research teams from a **wide range of cultures**, with **good awareness of cultural issues – potential to become a team leader of international teams**

Experience
1999–now **Environmental research scientist**, Exxon Inc, Torrance, California

Professional development
March 2008 Future managers **development course – in-house training** organized by Exxon

June 2006 One-week course in intercultural training at Lancaster Associates, UK

Qualifications
1998–1999 **Master's degree** in Hydrocarbons, University of Vancouver, Canada
            Dissertation: "Energy use in low-carbon economies"

1994–1997 **Bachelor's degree** in Chemical Engineering, University of Tokyo

Languages
Native Japanese **speaker**, **fluent** English

Interests
Martial arts, baseball, Japanese cooking

Personal
Dual Japanese-Canadian **nationality**, born Tokyo, 3 April 1976

> **Note**
> BrE: CV, curriculum vitae; AmE: résumé, resume
> In the English-speaking world, it is becoming increasingly unusual to show **marital status / children** on CVs. Older people are sometimes advised not to put their **date of birth**. Riku above has put his **interests**, but showing these is optional. (Do not use 'hobbies'.) Also, at the top of the document, do not put **CV** or **Curriculum Vitae**, just put your name.

B Job enquiry

From: riku76@hotmail.com
Subject: Environmental scientists
Date: 20 March 2010
To: hr@singaporerenewables.sg

Hello. **I am writing with reference to** the article about renewable energy in last Tuesday's *Los Angeles Times*, in which your company was mentioned. The article said that you were looking for environmental scientists in the field of renewable energy, and I am writing to ask if you have **openings** for someone with my **background**.

As the attached CV relates, I have a Master's degree in Hydrocarbons, and I have worked for over ten years for Exxon at their research campus in Torrance, California. **I would now like to relocate** to Asia.

I will be in Thailand next month on vacation and would be available for a discussion any time between 15 and 30 April. I would be happy to fly down to Singapore from Thailand **at my own expense**. I believe **I have a lot to offer** a company such as yours. I have visited your company's website and like the look of what you do!

Looking forward to hearing from you.

Best regards

Riku Henderson

> **Note**
> How to end emails:
> More formal ◼︎◼︎◼︎◼︎◼︎◼︎◼︎◼︎◼︎ Less formal
> Best regards   Regards   Best wishes   All the best   Best

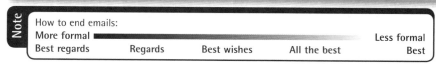

63.1 Look at the CV in A opposite. Then write one based on this information, using the same headings.

'Hi, I'm Ramesh Patel and I really like Bollywood cinema and rock music. I played in a rock band at university, and we played semi-professionally, but when I graduated after three years, in 2001, from New York University in Media Studies, I decided to do a Master's degree in Journalism just in case! I stayed another year at NYU to do this. The course was great, and we concentrated on broadcast media – something that I wanted to get into. I wrote a dissertation with the title "A comparative study of broadcast TV in three English-speaking countries: India, US, Australia". Anyway, the band broke up a year after we all graduated, so I was glad I had made the decision to pursue a "proper" career! I was born in Brooklyn on 19 May, 1980 and grew up there, but my parents were from India. I'm a US citizen and I'm bilingual, by the way. I started my first job in 2002, working as an assistant to news reporters on a Hindi-language channel for Star TV, based in Mumbai, but now I'd like to move on. I'm good at working in teams and would like to think that I'm a good communicator, thanks to all my media training. People tell me that I'm good at explaining complicated ideas clearly. I also like to think that I'm good at keeping calm and cool in front of the camera, even when things go wrong! My goal now is to work as a TV reporter for a TV company in an English-speaking country. Why not Australia?'

63.2 Look at B opposite. Then look at the email below. In some of the lines (1–11), there is one extra word that is unnecessary. Other lines, however, are correct. Tick the correct lines and cross out the extra words in the other lines.

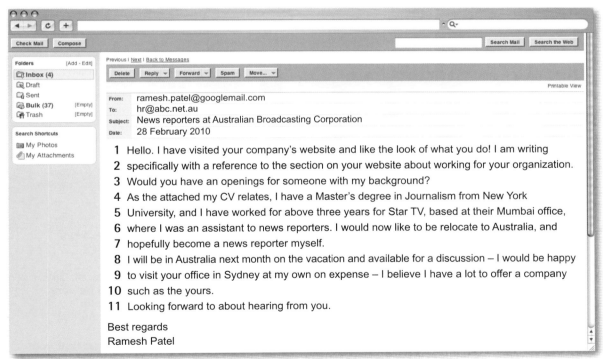

From: ramesh.patel@googlemail.com
To: hr@abc.net.au
Subject: News reporters at Australian Broadcasting Corporation
Date: 28 February 2010

1 Hello. I have visited your company's website and like the look of what you do! I am writing
2 specifically with a reference to the section on your website about working for your organization.
3 Would you have an openings for someone with my background?
4 As the attached my CV relates, I have a Master's degree in Journalism from New York
5 University, and I have worked for above three years for Star TV, based at their Mumbai office,
6 where I was an assistant to news reporters. I would now like to be relocate to Australia, and
7 hopefully become a news reporter myself.
8 I will be in Australia next month on the vacation and available for a discussion – I would be happy
9 to visit your office in Sydney at my own on expense – I believe I have a lot to offer a company
10 such as the yours.
11 Looking forward to about hearing from you.

Best regards
Ramesh Patel

Over to you

You have read about an organization that you find interesting and would like to work for. Write the beginning of an email (about 100 words) to the organization (name it) saying why you would be a suitable candidate.

64 Business writing 2

Invitation

Riku Henderson receives this email from Singapore Renewables (see Unit 63):

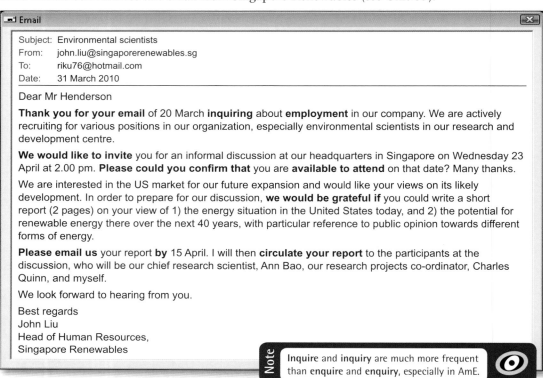

Email

Subject: Environmental scientists
From: john.liu@singaporerenewables.sg
To: riku76@hotmail.com
Date: 31 March 2010

Dear Mr Henderson

Thank you for your email of 20 March **inquiring** about **employment** in our company. We are actively recruiting for various positions in our organization, especially environmental scientists in our research and development centre.

We would like to invite you for an informal discussion at our headquarters in Singapore on Wednesday 23 April at 2.00 pm. **Please could you confirm that** you are **available to attend** on that date? Many thanks.

We are interested in the US market for our future expansion and would like your views on its likely development. In order to prepare for our discussion, **we would be grateful if** you could write a short report (2 pages) on your view of 1) the energy situation in the United States today, and 2) the potential for renewable energy there over the next 40 years, with particular reference to public opinion towards different forms of energy.

Please email us your report **by** 15 April. I will then **circulate your report** to the participants at the discussion, who will be our chief research scientist, Ann Bao, our research projects co-ordinator, Charles Quinn, and myself.

We look forward to hearing from you.

Best regards
John Liu
Head of Human Resources,
Singapore Renewables

Note: **Inquire** and **inquiry** are much more frequent than **enquire** and **enquiry**, especially in AmE.

B

Acknowledgement

Here are two possible replies from Riku Henderson. The first email is written in a more formal style than the second. Both styles are acceptable when writing emails.

From: riku76@hotmail.com
Subject: Environmental scientists
Date: 2 April 2010
To: john.liu@singaporerenewables.sg

Dear Mr Liu

Thank you for your email of 31 March. **This is to confirm that I would be delighted** to come to your headquarters for a discussion on Wednesday 23 April at 2.00 pm.

I would be happy to write the report **that you specify**. **I have noted** what you mentioned about length and content. I will **send it to you** by 15 April **as requested**.

Best wishes

Riku Henderson

From: riku76@hotmail.com
Subject: Environmental scientists
Date: 2 April 2010
To: john.liu@singaporerenewables.sg

Dear Mr Liu

Thanks for your mail of 31 March. **This is to let you know that I'd be very pleased** to come to your HQ for a discussion on Wednesday 23 April at 2.00 pm.

I'd be glad to write the report **that you describe**. I've noted what you mentioned about length and content. I'll **let you have it** by 15 April **as you've asked**.

Best wishes

Riku Henderson

Note: It's not possible to say or write 'very delighted' in this context

64.1 Look at A opposite. Choose the correct alternatives to complete this email.

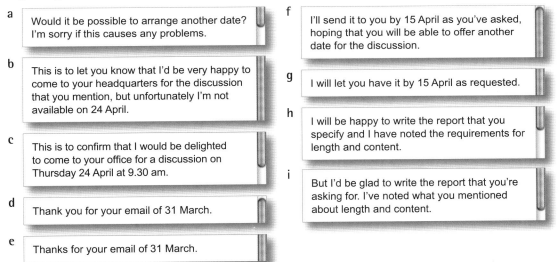

Thank you for your email of 13 May **(1)** .... about positions in our company. We are actively **(2)** .... for various **(3)** .... in our organization, particularly finance specialists.

We **(4)** .... to invite you for an interview at our headquarters in Singapore on Monday 5 June at 2.00 pm. Please could you confirm that you would be able to **(5)** .... on that date?

Before the interview, we would be **(6)** .... if you could prepare a presentation on what you see as the economic situation in the world today, illustrated by PowerPoint slides.

Please email us your slides by 2 June. I will then copy them onto the computer that you will be using for your presentation, **(7)** .... them also to the other people who will be present.

1	a ask	b asking	c asked	d asks
2	a employing	b joining	c recruiting	d proposing
3	a posting	b positions	c vacant	d situations
4	a would want	b would like	c may	d might
5	a present	b partake	c assist	d attend
6	a thankful	b please	c grateful	d oblige
7	a circulating	b dispatching	c purveying	d shipping

64.2 Look at B opposite. Below, email replies from two other candidates have been mixed up. Put each email into the correct order. (The beginning of the first – more formal – email is d, and the beginning of the second – more informal – one is e.)

a Would it be possible to arrange another date? I'm sorry if this causes any problems.

f I'll send it to you by 15 April as you've asked, hoping that you will be able to offer another date for the discussion.

b This is to let you know that I'd be very happy to come to your headquarters for the discussion that you mention, but unfortunately I'm not available on 24 April.

g I will let you have it by 15 April as requested.

c This is to confirm that I would be delighted to come to your office for a discussion on Thursday 24 April at 9.30 am.

h I will be happy to write the report that you specify and I have noted the requirements for length and content.

d Thank you for your email of 31 March.

i But I'd be glad to write the report that you're asking for. I've noted what you mentioned about length and content.

e Thanks for your email of 31 March.

Over to you

Write the beginning of the reply (100 words) from the organization that you wrote to in the Over to you section of Unit 63, inviting you for an informal discussion.

65 Business writing 3

A Outlines

Riku Henderson (see Units 63 and 64) makes notes for the outline of his presentation:

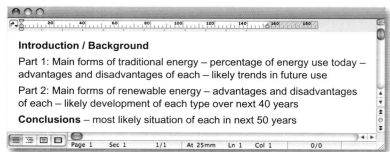

Introduction / Background

Part 1: Main forms of traditional energy – percentage of energy use today – advantages and disadvantages of each – likely trends in future use

Part 2: Main forms of renewable energy – advantages and disadvantages of each – likely development of each type over next 40 years

Conclusions – most likely situation of each in next 50 years

B Openings and introductions

- **The purpose of this report is to** …
- **In the first part, I'll outline / explain / illustrate / analyze / break down** …
- **I'll give a breakdown / description / overview** …
- In the **second part, I'll move on to look at / examine** …
- In the **final part, I'll (try to) draw some conclusions about** … **/ make some predictions about** …

C Describing visuals

- **As you can see from** the pie chart / graph / diagram / table …
- **The** pie chart / graph / diagram / table **shows that** …

nuclear energy gas oil coal	now currently at present	accounts for represents makes up constitutes	x per cent of current energy use.

- **By far the largest** source of energy **is** …
- **Next / In second place come(s)** …
- **Thirdly, there is** …
- **In fourth position is** …
- **Not far behind / Quite a long way behind is** …

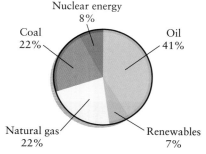

Nuclear energy 8%
Coal 22%
Oil 41%
Natural gas 22%
Renewables 7%

65.1 Complete the table with words from A and B opposite.

Noun	Verb
	describe
analysis	
outline	
explanation	
examination	
look	
breakdown	
	predict
	conclude

65.2 Now write a possible introduction to Riku's report, using appropriate forms of expressions from the table in 65.1 above and underlining them, beginning in this way:

The purpose of this report is to <u>examine</u> the current energy situation in the United States today and the potential for renewable energy there over the next 50 years. In the first part, I'll <u>outline</u> the place of different sources of energy in the US economy. I'll give a ...

65.3 Write part 1 of Riku's report using expressions from C opposite, the information in the pie chart and the notes next to it. Begin like this:

As you can see from the pie chart, by far the largest source of energy is oil, which accounts for 41 per cent of energy use in the US. This is problematic as much of the oil comes from politically unstable countries. ...

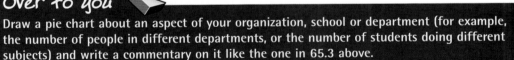

Over to you

Draw a pie chart about an aspect of your organization, school or department (for example, the number of people in different departments, or the number of students doing different subjects) and write a commentary on it like the one in 65.3 above.

66 Business writing 4

A Linking ideas

Here are some expressions you can use to add one idea to another.

Energy from biomass comes mainly in the form of ethanol, which is made from corn (maize). Critics say that maize should only be used as a food source.	**Moreover,**	they say that large areas of rainforest have been cleared to make way for maize production around the world.
Geothermal energy, using heat from underground springs, only makes a very small contribution to energy use.	**In addition,**	geothermal plants are expensive to build and maintain.
Tidal power requires installing equipment offshore that is very expensive.	**What's more,**	the equipment breaks down frequently due to the violent seas.

Here are some expressions you can use to compare and contrast one idea with another, or introduce another idea which might seem surprising.

The US is well-placed to produce more solar energy.	**However,**	solar panels are concentrated in the south and southwest.
Wind energy is very clean and efficient.	**Nevertheless,**	there is strong opposition from people who object to seeing more wind turbines.
Hydroelectric schemes especially in the western US, such as the Hoover dam, provide 41 per cent of renewable energy.	**On the other hand,**	future development of this form of energy is unlikely, as most of the potential schemes have already been realized.

B Forecasts

Look at these ways of expressing future trends.

By 2050, **on current trends:**

1 renewable energy **is going to** provide about 30 per cent of the country's needs, as opposed to 7 per cent today.
2 the amount of energy consumed in the US overall **will** have decreased by 20 per cent – the economy will be bigger, of course, but energy will be used more efficiently.
3 solar energy **should** probably represent 20 per cent of renewable energy.
4 oil, gas and coal **might** each represent about 20 per cent of total energy use, **unless** something unexpected happens.
5 the environmental argument that nuclear energy does not contribute to global warming **may** win out.

66.1 Match the two parts of these sentences containing expressions from A opposite.

1 I can assure you that there are no plans to sell the newspaper division.

2 A switch of truck suppliers involves the important costs of changing spare part inventories.

3 IBM studies have indicated that seven per cent of employees believe that technological advancements have improved their ability to balance work and personal life.

4 Boldness is an essential moral characteristic in a leader, for it generates combat power beyond the physical means at hand.

5 Older managers were suspicious of the big expansion and later even opposed to internationalization efforts.

6 These new hotels create employment for local people.

a However, 62 per cent of employees also have growing concerns about technology's impact on the length of the workday.

b What's more, there are no immediate plans to sell individual newspapers.

c Moreover, a good leader understands that good leadership is about who you are, not so much about what you do or can do.

d Nevertheless, the new chairman and new managers were able to persuade the board members and the Koç directors.

e On the other hand, the animals that you see here will be driven away from their homes.

f In addition, a client may sometimes incur important risks, especially those of not being fully satisfied with a new supplier.

66.2 Look at B opposite. Use the same structures (1–5) to make predictions for the future containing these ideas.

By 2050:

1 electric cars / account for more than half the cars on the road

2 climate change / not have had the effects predicted today

3 population growth / level off

4 nuclear energy / represent 30 per cent of energy production / unless / another big nuclear accident before then

5 attitudes to personal consumption / change enormously

66.3 Now make alternative forecasts to the ones above in 66.2. (You can use different verbs for each one this time.) The first one has been done as an example.

1 Electric cars will *account for less than a third of all cars on the road.*

Over to you

Make some forecasts about trends in your own profession or industry, or one you would like to work in.

Key

1.1
1 rewarding, stimulating
2 client contact
3 get on well with
4 hands-on
5 No two days are the same
6 Originality, creativity

1.2
1 working on my own
2 putting ideas into practice
3 admin, paperwork
4 teamwork
5 snowed under
6 sense of achievement
7 red tape, bureaucracy

1.3
1 Stress
2 Commuting
3 Hours worked
4 Telecommuting

Over to you (sample answer)
I'm the personal assistant to the chief executive of a retail organization. I'm not able to telecommute – the nature of my job means that I have to be in the office all the time. I get four weeks' holiday a year, which is good. If I have family problems, for example if one of my children is ill, my boss gives me time off. My work is pleasant and not stressful at all. I work 40 hours a week. I live ten miles from my office, so there's only a short commute by train.

2.1
2 use our initiative
3 Morale, motivated
4 responsibility
5 job satisfaction

2.2 (sample answers)
1 McGregor's thinking has influenced participative styles of management and the continued practice of staff performance appraisal.
2 Managers' beliefs can be seen from the things that they say and do.
3 These lead to managers having particular policies towards employees and to relate to them in particular ways.
4 No – he did not think that either Theory X or Y should be taken as a 'model'.

5 Abraham Maslow; he thought that motivation was key in people's needs.
6 He thought that workers were dissatisfied because of the way that jobs were badly designed, the way that managers behaved, and the lack of opportunities for people to be satisfied with their jobs.

Over to you (sample answer)
I would recommend developing initiative in the following way. Car production workers should be able to submit ideas for improvement in the production process. If an idea leads to increased efficiency, the worker concerned should receive a bonus.

3.1
1 salary
2 supervision
3 peer relationships
4 policy
5 working conditions
6 security

3.2
1 the work itself
2 recognition
3 responsibility
4 achievement
5 advancement
6 personal growth

3.3

Verb	Noun	Adjective
empower	empowerment	empowered
consult	consultation	consulted
–	hierarchy	hierarchical
delegate	delegation	delegated

Over to you (sample answer)
I sell packaging equipment to food manufacturers. I have a great sense of achievement when I reach my sales objective for the year. If we do a good job, we get recognition in the form of a generous bonus and positive feedback from our sales manager. The work itself is fascinating – I have a technical background, and the technical progress in packaging machinery has been amazing since I started out. There are good opportunities for advancement – I hope to become sales team leader next year. And in terms of personal growth, the company I work for is great – we are encouraged to go on training courses in areas that are unrelated to our work. I'm learning to play the classical guitar at the moment.

4.1
1 competitive edge   4 outsourced
2 cost-effective   5 contractors
3 offshore

4.2 (sample answers)
1 Mergers and acquisitions.
2 $75 per hour. This allowed the company to be competitive.
3 India, because lawyers there had access to the same research tools as those in the US, they were highly motivated and intelligent, and they were willing to do the kind of work that people in the US look down on.
4 Two.
5 Document review, and maintenance of the database used to store details of contractors.

4.3
1 lifelong learning, current trends
2 career move
3 activities
4 consultancy services
5 freelancers
6 in-house

Over to you (sample answers)
I write technical documentation for manufacturers of domestic appliances – dishwashers, washing machines, and so on. I could do this work as a freelancer, but I prefer being a salaried employee – I like coming into work every day, and it's easier to keep up with what's going on. I hear about technical developments with the new models, for example, and also office gossip!

Advantages of being a freelancer:
- You can organize your work the way that you want to.
- You don't have to get to the office by a particular time every day.
- You can take holidays when it suits you rather than your employer.

Disadvantages:
- It's possible to feel isolated and unmotivated.
- You always have to be thinking about finding the next project.
- It's possible to waste a lot of time if you don't discipline yourself.

5.1
1 job sharing
2 part-time work
3 temporary work

5.2
1 make people redundant
2 consultation
3 trade unions
4 hire and fire
5 inflexibility
6 Unemployment
7 give them three months' notice
8 social charges
9 sick pay
10 flexible
11 job creation

5.3
1 true   5 true
2 true   6 false
3 false   7 true
4 true

Over to you (sample answers)
- Spain is probably more like France. The labour market is quite inflexible, with similar obstacles to hiring and firing people as there.
- One advantage of flexible working for employers is that they can get rid of workers when they no longer need them, and hire them again when they do need them. One disadvantage is that employees feel less loyalty to the organization, and therefore less motivated.

6.1
1 b
2 a
3 e
4 c
5 d

6.2
1 lack of management support
2 role ambiguity
3 home–work imbalance
4 heavy workloads
5 office politics
6 effort–reward imbalance

6.3   1 d   2 a   3 b   4 c

Over to you (sample answers)
- Currency dealer, teacher and policeman are three stressful jobs.
- As a production manager, the main causes of stress in my job are unexpected increases in demand, which mean increasing production, and this is difficult to do quickly. I combat stress by doing a lot of sport, especially running and swimming.

7.1
1 uncountable		4 uncountable	
2 countable		5 countable	
3 uncountable			

7.2   1 h   2 b   3 d   4 g   5 a
       6 c   7 e   8 f

Over to you (sample answer)
There is employee assessment every six months, with managers talking to their employees individually to tell them how they are doing. There is no assessment of managers by employees, no 360-degree assessment.

8.1
1 super-talent	5 Talent management
2 core competents	6 core competents
3 talent manager	7 talent pool
4 talent pool	8 ABC approach

8.2   creatives: 2, 3, 6
       suits: 1, 4, 5

8.3
1 mentees, mentees
2 mentoring/coaching
3 reverse mentoring, mentoring
4 coach, coachee
5 mentoring/mentorship, mentor

Over to you (sample answer)
I work for a small electronics company (30 employees). There is a formal system of mentoring, where each new recruit is assigned one of the senior managers, who has regular sessions with them and gives them advice about the firm's values and culture.

9.1   (sample answers)
1 She manages a team of nurses.
2 Daily and monthly.
3 There tend to be fewer daily meetings.
4 They encourage positive emotion and energy, and sharing out tasks for the day, and help nurses to think about the unit's work as a whole. Knowing who may need help allows the work of the unit to be shared out among team members. Meetings also keep people engaged in learning and develop commitment.
5 They help limit mistakes.
6 The monthly meetings encourage nurses to think about the performance of their own and other teams.

9.2
1 true		5 true	
2 true		6 false	
3 false		7 true	
4 true		8 false	

9.3   1 e   2 a   3 c   4 b   5 d

Over to you (sample answers)
- I've worked in a number of teams on big engineering projects.
- Yes, we work well as a team – perhaps because someone performs each role.
- I'm a Completer. I like to ensure that project deadlines are met, any mistakes corrected, and nothing forgotten or omitted.

10.1
1 hard		4 soft	
2 soft		5 hard	
3 soft		6 hard	

10.2   1 e   2 d   3 c   4 e   5 c
        6 b   7 a   8 b   9 d   10 a

10.3
1 self-awareness	5 integrity
2 conscientiousness	6 decisiveness
3 sensitivity	7 motivation
4 influence	

Over to you (sample answer)
I'm a corporate trainer. I'd like to think that I have soft skills – the ability to work with all sorts of people tactfully and in a non–authoritarian way. Training these days requires these sorts of skills rather than more authoritarian methods.

11.1 age, ageist, ageism
race, racist, racism
sex, sexist, sexism
stereotype, stereotypical, stereotyping
diversity, diverse, –
discrimination, discriminatory, –
equality, equal, –
ethnicity, ethnic, –

11.2 1 stereotypical
2 Discriminatory (or Racist)
3 ethnicity (or race)
4 racism (or discrimination)
5 ageist
6 sexism
7 equality
8 diversity

11.3 1 d   2 a   3 e   4 c   5 b

Over to you (sample answer)
Traditionally, my company, a newspaper
publisher, has recruited graduates from the
country's top two universities. However, it
could increase diversity and inclusion by
employing journalists from non-university
backgrounds, for example those who have
worked on regional papers for a few years.
It could also increase diversity by
employing more people from ethnic
minorities.

12.1 1 Total Quality Management, TQM
2 consistency, employee involvement
3 faults, defects
4 zero defects
5 reworking

12.2 1 (customer) delight
2 conformity/conformance to specification
3 elimination of variation
4 (customer) expectations

12.3 1 c   2 h   3 e   4 f   5 b
6 d   7 a   8 g

Over to you (sample answer)
In my organization, a train operating
company, the criteria for quality include:
- punctuality – fewer than five per cent of
  trains should arrive more than ten
  minutes late
- features – seats are comfortable, all with
  waiter service
- aesthetics – the trains are good to look
  at, inside and out
- perceived quality is high – trains give a
  feeling of luxury
- value for money – fares are very
  reasonable

13.1 apply; application; applied
certify; certificate, certification; certified
standardize; standard(s), standardization;
standardized

13.2 1 application
2 certification, certified
3 standardized

13.3 1 f   2 a   3 b   4 g   5 c
6 d   7 e

Over to you (sample answer)
Since we adopted ISO 9000, the company
has been affected in the following ways: top
managers – not just middle managers –
have been involved in quality issues; we pay
much more attention to regulatory
requirements on product safety; we have
put in place measurable objectives so that
we can measure quality; we have improved
resource management; we are much better
at monitoring customer satisfaction, with
regular surveys. We also measure the
effectiveness of our staff training, and we
look at all possible ways to work on
continual improvement of our products.

14.1 1 b   2 a   3 d   4 c   5 b
6 d   7 c   8 a

14.2 1 people management
2 policy & strategy
3 resources
4 people satisfaction
5 customer satisfaction
6 impact on society

Over to you (sample answer)

The leadership of my business school is in the hands of the director. With her colleagues, she makes decisions on people management, recruiting the best teachers in their respective areas. The policy and strategy of the school are both directed to becoming the leading business school in the country by recruiting the best staff and students. Resources include a state-of-the-art campus just outside the capital city. Processes include lectures, tutorials and written work. These are the enablers.

Results include people satisfaction: lecturers are very happy with their jobs and rarely move to other institutions. The 'customers' – the students – give very high evaluations in their course questionnaires. The impact on society is harder to judge, but society surely benefits from having well-qualified managers running companies. And the business results of the school are very good; it has a special status and does not talk about profits, but it certainly makes money.

15.1
1 performance, benchmark
2 reverse engineering
3 benchmarking, best practices
4 competitive benchmarking
5 Functional benchmarking

15.2 (sample answers)
1 If you can measure how many defects you have in a process, you can systematically figure out how to eliminate them and get as close to zero defects as possible.
2 A chance for non-conformance, i.e. not conforming to the quality criteria.
3 flawless
4 Failing to deliver what the customer wants.
5 consistent
6 predictable

Over to you (sample answer)

As the second biggest clothing retailer, we are always looking at the biggest company and what it does. Of course, there are some industrial secrets that it will not reveal, but it's always interesting to go into their shops and see how they do things – the clothes they sell, how they display them, the decor of their stores, and so on.

16.1
1 strategy   3 resource allocation
2 resources, planning   4 mission statement

16.2
1 b   2 d   3 e   4 c   5 f   6 a

16.3
1 dominated the market
2 attack the market
3 invade
4 established a foothold/toehold
5 still dominated
6 withdraw from

Over to you (sample answer)

Eli Lilly's mission statement is 'to create and deliver innovative pharmaceutical-based healthcare solutions that enable people to live longer, healthier and more active lives'.

17.1
1 stifling, encouraging   4 inhibit
2 intensified   5 sharpening
3 harm

17.2
1 b   2 d   3 a   4 c

17.3
1 threat   4 position
2 advantage/edge   5 pressure
3 prices   6 strategy

Over to you (sample answer)

I work for Waterstones bookshops. Our fiercest competitor is the online retailer Amazon. We hope that customers will keep coming to our stores to browse and buy books, rather than ordering them online. But we also know that we have to make our stores as attractive as possible, with coffee shops and sofas where people can read and relax before making their purchases.

18.1
1 industry competitors   4 buyers
2 entrant   5 suppliers
3 substitutes

18.2

Strengths	Weaknesses
• situated in one of the UK's most attractive cities • the English language	• need to improve our facilities
Opportunities	**Threats**
• potentially more and more students from abroad	• economic slowdown next year • excellent universities in the US

18.3
1 focus
2 cost leadership
3 differentiation

Over to you (sample answer)
I work for a supermarket chain. We are criticized for having too much power over our suppliers, for example farmers, but we think they get fair prices for what they sell. Competition between the supermarket chains is intense, and there is always the danger of more low-cost entrants to the industry. We don't think there's a danger from substitutes as people will always have to eat! The bargaining power of customers is high – they can always go to our lower-cost competitors, so we have to make sure that we offer an attractive alternative in terms of range of goods, attractive stores, and so on.

19.1

Across	Down
5 barriers	1 portfolio theory
8 entry	2 concentrated
9 chaebol	3 merge
11 divestment	4 core
13 integration	6 acquisitive
15 high	7 fragmented
17 conglomerate	10 attractive
	12 vertical
	14 share
	16 low

19.2
1 strategic acquisitions
2 acquisitions/takeovers
3 subsidiaries
4 unwieldy conglomerate
5 profitability
6 entrants

Over to you (sample answer)
Daimler merged with Chrysler so that Daimler would have better access to the US car market and Chrysler to the European market. They planned to develop models together, reduce costs, etc. But the cultural differences between the two companies were too great and the merger fell apart.

20.1
| 1 d | 2 c | 3 f | 4 a |
| 5 b | 6 f | 7 b | 8 e |

20.2
| 1 trendsetter | 3 pioneers |
| 2 innovator | 4 follower |

20.3
1 dropped out
2 shakeout and consolidation
3 emerging industry
4 dominate
5 mature
6 established

Over to you (sample answers)
• Yes, many organizations are bureaucratic and slow to come up with new ideas.
• I work for Procter and Gamble, and one way that we have of getting new ideas is to encourage contributions and input from people not actually working for the company, via the company's website. The company then rewards the best suggestions and contributions.

21.1
1 (social and economic) environment
2 futurologists/futurists
3 the Delphi method, panel, a consensus
4 forecasts
5 futurology
6 scenario planning
7 mini-Delphi / Estimate–Talk–Estimate / ETE
8 evolve

21.2 | 1 e | 2 a | 3 b | 4 d | 5 c |

Over to you (sample answers)
- I work for a tour operator and the biggest risk is that, through no fault of our own, we go bankrupt. This can leave thousands of customers abroad and unable to get home. This would be very unfortunate, for our customers and for us, so we do everything we can to avoid bankruptcy!
- We almost went bankrupt once a few years ago when we had financial controls that were less strict than today's, but we learnt our lesson and now the business is run much better, with close attention to costs and financial results.

22.1
1 pricing	4 place
2 product	5 promotion
3 promotion	6 promotion

22.2
a physical evidence
b people
c process

1 intangible	5 service
2 contact	6 process
3 motivated	7 helpful
4 attitude	

Over to you (sample answers)
- I was attracted to my new LG high-definition screen (*product*) by their TV advertising (*promotion*). The product was available in department stores and electrical goods stores, but I preferred to buy it on online (*place*). I paid slightly less than I would have done in traditional retail outlets (*pricing*).
- I took my car to be serviced yesterday. When I went into the service centre, it took five minutes for someone to come to greet me (*people*). I left the car, but they didn't phone me to tell me what was going on. So when I went to pick it up, I found they had done all sorts of work, some of which wasn't necessary (*process*). But they did show me a component that had broken and that had really needed replacing (*physical evidence*).

23.1
1 convenience	3 customer cost
2 communication	4 customer solution

23.2 1 b   2 a   3 d   4 e   5 c

23.3 (sample answers)
1 Banking, IT services, mass grocery (food supermarkets), financial services and mail order.
2 'Deliberatives' who rationally choose their current provider again because it offers the best deal; 'emotives' who have special feelings for the brand; and 'inertials' who can't be bothered to switch.
3 People who spend less on a brand have a greater financial impact than people who actually defect and stop buying it.
4 Customers who purchase steadily from a company over time are not necessarily cheaper to serve, they are not less sensitive to different price levels, or particularly effective at bringing in new business. Long-standing customers are not cheaper to manage than short-term customers because one-off transactions are cheaper.

Over to you (sample answer)
As a supermarket customer, I'm an inertial. I just keep going to the nearest one because the others are too far away. Trying another supermarket would mean taking the car, rather than walking, and I don't want to do this.

24.1
1 mystery shopper
2 market intelligence
3 primary data, secondary data
4 market research firm
5 latest trends

24.2 1 c   2 d   3 e   4 b   5 a

24.3 1 b   2 a   3 b   4 a   5 a

Over to you (sample answer)
I work in the marketing department of a car company. We organize regular market research to see what people think of our models and those of our competitors. The latest findings are that people are looking more and more for environmentally friendly cars.

25.1
1 segmentation, segments
2 social class, demographic segmentation
3 behavioural segmentation
4 target groups

25.2 1 e 2 d 3 a 4 c 5 f 6 b

25.3
1 traffic   4 conversion
2 visitors   5 convert
3 interact

Over to you (sample answer)
I recently bought a ticket on a low-cost airline to go clubbing in Mallorca this summer. For this flight, I'm in the leisure travel segment, rather than a business traveller. Demographically, I'm in the 25–34 segment, and in terms of VALS, I guess I'm an experiencer, spending a lot of money on music, clothes and clubbing, and the tickets to get to places where I can meet other people like me!

26.1
1 true   4 true
2 false   5 false
3 true   6 false

26.2 1 d 2 a 3 b 4 c 5 e

Over to you (sample answer)
I work at Boeing. We hold a lot of information about our customers, the airlines. We have a lot of data about their requirements on different routes and in many other areas. They also let us have some of the results that they have gathered from their own market research, which we also hold on our database. And of course, the technical people here hold a lot of information from the airlines relating to the operation of our planes by our customers.

27.1 1 c 2 a 3 e 4 f 5 b 6 d

27.2
1 positioned   4 differentiate
2 positioning   5 differentiation
3 positioning   6 differentiate

27.3 The real outcome is given in each case, followed by a possible explanation.
1 Successful: The idea of 'gentleness' carried across smoothly to the new products.

2 Unsuccessful: Bic is too closely associated with pens and razors.
3 Unsuccessful: Coke was 'the real thing', so New Coke could not logically also be the real thing.
4 Successful: all in the same category and closely associated
5 Successful: both in the same category and closely associated
6 Unsuccessful: soup and spaghetti sauce not close enough together

Over to you (sample answer)
I work for Unilever and our food brands include Lipton, Flora, Becel, Blue Band, Hellmann's, Knorr, Bertolli, Calve, Magnum and Cornetto. There's no flagship brand as such, as we are strong in so many different product categories. We prefer to develop completely new brands rather than brand extensions of different brands.

28.1
a joint venture, joint venture
b indirect export, agents
c licensing agreement, licensing agreement, under licence, joint venture
d export manager, agent, direct export, export manager

Order:
1 b 2 d 3 c 4 a

28.2 1 b 2 b 3 a

Over to you (sample answer)
Rolls Royce is one of the UK's biggest exporters. It makes aircraft engines for civilian and military aircraft, plus turbines for applications such as power generation. It has its main base in Derby, and also has other plants, including one in Bristol. It has about 37,000 employees, 40 per cent outside the UK.

29.1 1 c 2 a 3 b 4 g 5 d
         6 e 7 f

29.2
1 suppliers
2 process
3 warehouse
4 just-in-time
5 integrated
6 captive plants
7 suppliers

29.3

Verb	Noun(s)
retail	retail, retailing
warehouse	warehouse, warehousing
transport	transport, transportation
distribute	distribution
outsource	outsourcing

Over to you (sample answer)
Dell manufactures computers in Lodz, Poland, but many of its suppliers are elsewhere. Many of the components come from China, for example. Components arrive in Gdansk by container ship and are then taken to the plant by truck.

30.1
1 supply chain management
2 logistician
3 logistics
4 work-in-progress (BrE), work-in-process (AmE), inventory-in-process (AmE)
5 finished goods
6 stock(s) (BrE), inventory (AmE)
7 stock(s) (BrE), inventory (AmE)

30.2 1 e   2 d   3 a   4 c   5 b

30.3
1 refurbishment   4 disposal
2 waste   5 dismantle
3 remanufacturing   6 recycle

Over to you (sample answer)
I work for an airline and our biggest logistical nightmare is when our planes are delayed by congestion at airports, especially Heathrow. The outward flight arrives late, which means that the return flight takes off late, causing passengers to become very angry.

31.1
1 Core competences/competencies
2 Subcontractors, in-house, expertise, non-core
3 Transaction cost analysis, outsourcing them / subcontracting them / farming them out
4 our competitive edge
5 Our corporate culture

31.2 1 b   2 e   3 d   4 c   5 a

31.3
1 False: The CEO has to think about the human dimension too.
2 True
3 False: The article mentions three areas: training, helping employees find other jobs and financial compensation.
4 False: They will be worried about their own future in the organization.
5 True
6 False: The article mentions two areas: investment in new infrastructure, and increased spending on research and development.

Over to you (sample answer)
Here in India, we have benefited greatly from outsourcing. Many of our graduates work in call centres for UK banks. But outsourcing is increasing in other areas which require higher levels of expertise, for example software development.

32.1
1 Internet   5 download
2 bandwidth   6 video-on-demand
3 video-conferencing 7 wireless
4 webcams

32.2
1 3G   4 GPS
2 wireless   5 the browser
3 from the Optimum site

32.3 c

Over to you (sample answers)
• Yes, mobile devices are suitable for accessing the Internet now – the screens are bigger and the download speeds are faster.
• I use my mobile to download football-action replays. I don't use it for internet shopping (for that I use my computer when I'm at home), but I do look at the weather forecast occasionally to see if it's going to rain.

33.1
1 interoperability
2 external social networking sites, posted, profile
3 video-sharing sites, uploaded
4 internal social networking site, online community, vetted
5 wiki, collaboration
6 messaging, networking sites, communication

33.2

Adjective	Noun
attractive	attractiveness
interactive	interactivity
user-friendly	user-friendliness
sticky	stickiness

33.3
1 unique users
2 traffic
3 page views
4 sticky
5 user-friendly
6 generating, revenue
7 rankings
8 website management company

Over to you (sample answer)
I think it's acceptable for recruiters to check social networking sites in this way. What people say about themselves there is probably more reliable than what they put in their CVs. Companies need to know everything about the people they are recruiting!

34.1 1 b   2 d   3 c   4 a

34.2 1 e   2 d   3 a   4 b   5 f   6 c

34.3
1 collaborating
2 proprietary
3 prosumers
4 networks
5 collaborative sites
6 collaborate

Over to you (sample answer)
At my university, there is an intranet that allows us to get information about different courses and members of staff, to look at our lecturers' PowerPoint presentations, and to check availability of the sports facilities, among many other things.

35.1
1 scams
2 security
3 infiltrated
4 identity theft
5 infected
6 malware

35.2
1 identity theft
2 password
3 phishing
4 cybercrime, cybercriminals
5 encryption
6 security details
7 spyware

35.3
1 law enforcement agencies
2 Big Brother
3 privacy, confidentiality
4 civil liberties
5 electronic trail
6 snoop

Over to you (sample answer)
I don't feel nervous about using internet banking. One way of minimizing the risk is to change the password often and not write it down anywhere. And I never put the account details into emails that I might send to people, for example when I write to someone about transferring money to my account.

36.1 1 d   2 b   3 e   4 a   5 c

36.2 1 b   2 c   3 d   4 a

36.3
1 Supplier relationships
2 Key buyers
3 a private e-marketplace
4 reverse auctions

Over to you (sample answer)
My washing machine broke down recently, and I ordered a new part for it over the Internet. The whole experience was very good. It was easy to identify the part that I needed, the credit card payment process was painless, and the part was delivered the next day.

37.1

Verb	Noun
copyright	copyright
download	download
encrypt	encryption
infringe	infringement
pirate	piracy
protect	protection

37.2
1 copyright protection
2 encryption
3 infringement
4 download
5 piracy

37.3
1 downloading, copyrighted, file sharing
2 intellectual property, peer-to-peer
3 revenue, pirates
4 encrypting, digital watermarks

Over to you (sample answer)
I think it's acceptable, because groups these days have lots of other ways of making money from concerts, and so on. Music companies have to find new ways of generating revenues – the idea of selling songs through download sites is just a hangover from the days of selling records.

38.1
1 financed, financiers
2 financing
3 finances

38.2

Across	Down
3 profit and loss	1 finance officer
6 interest	2 undervalued
8 dividends	3 prelims
10 cashflow	4 financial
12 full	5 bondholder
14 balance sheet	7 account
15 interim results	9 CFO
	11 lenders
	13 loan

Over to you (sample answers)
- Companies make their reports look attractive because they want to communicate in a way that seems friendly, open, etc. Annual reports are intended for investors and potential investors including shareholders; they are also directed at financial journalists reporting on the company, and of course the company's employees themselves.
- The report can be seen as a marketing tool intended to impress each of these audiences.

39.1
accruals principle
exceptional items
general expenses
interest payable
operating profit
profit and loss account
reporting period
retained earnings

39.2
1 reporting period
2 operating profit
3 retained earnings
4 exceptional items
5 accruals principle
6 interest payable
7 profit and loss account
8 general expenses

39.3

1 false	6 false
2 true	7 true
3 false	8 false
4 false	9 false
5 true	

Over to you (sample answer)
General Motors recently made a loss of $39 billion in the third quarter of its financial year, the second-worst loss in US corporate history.

40.1

a Cash	g 188
b Securities	h Land
c 12	i 62
d Debtors	j Goodwill
e 15	k 30
f Buildings	

40.2

1 false	4 false
2 true	5 true
3 false	6 true

Over to you (sample answer)
Carphone Warehouse is a retailer of mobile phones in the UK. It has a chain of outlets in strategic locations in most UK cities, but most of the sites are rented, and the rented sites do not appear on its balance sheet. It has knowledgeable staff, but employees don't appear either. It has stocks of mobile phones to sell, which do appear, and money in its bank accounts, which also appears on its balance sheet.

41.1
a Overdraft
b 4
c Interest payable
d Tax payable
e 10
f 40
g Bonds repayable in seven years
h Shareholders' equity
i 200
j Retained earnings
k 21

41.2
1 true	4 false
2 true	5 false
3 true	6 false

Over to you (sample answer)
When a company goes out of business, it usually has liabilities in the form of money owed to suppliers, lenders, the tax authorities, and in some cases employees' unpaid salaries.

42.1
a 6	f 0.5
b (1)	g (1.5)
c (8)	h 1.25
d 5	i 1
e (7.5)	j 5.6

Over to you (sample answer)
Credit terms in Germany and Sweden are quite short – 30 days is normal, with interest payable after that time. But in southern Europe – Spain and Italy, for example – they can be up to 120 or even 150 days.

43.1
1 amortization and depreciation
2 net income
3 EBITDA
4 cashflow
5 EBITDA

43.2
1 Knowledge workers, physical assets, return on assets (ROA)
2 sweating its assets / operating at full capacity
3 return on equity (ROE)
4 return on assets (ROA)
5 shareholders' equity

43.3 1 f   2 a   3 b   4 e   5 d   6 c

Over to you (sample answer)
The university that I go to is really sweating its assets. All the lecture rooms are full all the time, there are usually long queues in the restaurants and there are normally people waiting to use the computers in the library. I don't think they could increase the number of students without making further investments.

44.1
Across	Down
2 shareholder value	1 returns
6 outstanding	3 on investment
7 PE ratio	4 dividend payout
8 retained earnings	5 growth
10 distributed	8 ROI
12 maximize	9 decision
13 acquisitions	11 income
14 EPS	
15 strategic	

44.2
1 maximize shareholder value
2 divestment
3 strategic decision
4 returns on investment (ROI)
5 acquisition

Over to you (sample answers)
• This is not always easy to do because managers may have high commitment to the industry that they know and in which many will have spent their entire careers. They may even have an emotional attachment to it.
• In smaller firms, and in some cultures, managers may not want to be forced to fire loyal employees.
• And the knowledge that managers have of their industry may not be usable or applicable in the new activity that they want to get into.

45.1
1 overstated
2 understated
3 cooked the books
4 understated
5 fraud
6 irregularities
7 audits
8 regulators

45.2
1 no
2 $2 billion
3 assets
4 Because PriceWaterhouseCoopers were the auditors.
5 yes

45.3
1 SEC   4 IAS
2 FRC   5 GAAP
3 IOSCO

Over to you (sample answer)
There was recently a case in the UK of a charity whose chief accountant was taking money to finance his luxurious lifestyle. He ended up in prison.

46.1
1 f   2 d   3 a   4 c   5 h
6 b   7 g   8 i   9 e

46.2
1 recovery   4 trough
2 prosperity   5 contraction
3 peak   6 expansion

46.3
1 boomed
2 overheating
3 soft landing
4 economic stability
5 recession
6 boom and bust

Over to you (sample answer)
Here in Spain right now, the business cycle is bottoming out, with signs that things will improve next year, when the economy will pick up. But for the moment, unemployment is very high, house prices are falling by 15 per cent per year, inflation is rising and the currency is falling in value.

47.1
1 f   2 g   3 e   4 b   5 a
6 c   7 d

47.2
1 a regulator
2 a ratings agency
3 the real economy
4 light-touch regulation
5 deleverage
6 default
7 toxic assets
8 full-blown economic crisis

47.3

Noun	Verb
crash	crash
default	default
deflation	deflate
deleveraging	deleverage
regulation, regulator	regulate
rescue	rescue
stimulus	stimulate

Over to you (sample answer)
In France, the credit crunch did not affect us too badly. There was a slowdown – economic growth declined for a while, but there was no actual recession. Declining demand for our products from Europe and the US was partly replaced by demand from Asia.

48.1
1 e   2 c   3 f   4 b   5 a   6 d

48.2
1 board
2 integrity, probity
3 professional misconduct
4 transparent
5 accountable

48.3
1 b   2 a   3 a   4 a   5 c

Over to you (sample answer)
I'm writing about your company's continued pollution of our local river. This has been going on for some years now, with obvious effects on wildlife: there are dead fish floating on the surface, for example. Your company says that it wants to be seen as a good corporate citizen, but your apparent disregard for the environment makes it hard to believe that you are sincere in this. What actions will you be taking to improve the situation?

49.1
1 stakeholder theory
2 social reporting, public relations exercise
3 social performance
4 stakeholders
5 social audits

49.2
1 justice/welfare   4 programs
2 issues   5 responsibility
3 welfare

49.3   1 b   2 a   3 d   4 c

Over to you (sample answer)
In the tea plantations of southern India, employers have from the beginning invested in the social welfare of their employees by building worker accommodation, schools, etc. and ensuring that working conditions are good.

50.1

Noun	Verb	Adjective
carcinogen	–	carcinogenic
discharge	discharge	–
disposal	dispose (of)	–
environment	–	environmental
pollution pollutant	pollute	polluting
recycling	recycle	recycled recyclable

50.2   1 pollutants
2 recycled
3 disposal
4 discharged
5 carcinogenic

50.3   1 logging
2 deforestation
3 Overfishing
4 renewable
5 greenwash

Over to you (sample answer)
In my area, they have started regular collections of paper and glass for recycling. More could be done to reduce pollution, for example by charging drivers to enter the city centre in their cars.

51.1   1 global warming
2 greenhouse
3 storms
4 emissions
5 emissions
6 Infrastructure
7 infrastructure

51.2   1 my carbon footprint
2 Carbon levels
3 climate treaties
4 Carbon capture / Carbon sequestration
5 The Kyoto protocol
6 carbon offsets
7 carbon credits

51.3   1 capture
2 offset
3 absorbed
4 emit, capping
5 traded

Over to you (sample answer)
I've tried to reduce my carbon footprint by taking the train to work, rather than driving. I fly less – it's now realistic to go by train from the UK to a lot of places on the Continent.

52.1   1 stewardship
2 governance bodies, supervisory, management, supervisory board
3 board, non-execs

52.2

Verb	Noun
remunerate	remuneration
compensate	compensation
reward	reward
incentivize	incentive
pay out	payout
pay off	payoff
bail out	bailout

52.3   1 bailouts
2 compensation, remuneration
3 incentives
4 payoffs, payouts

Over to you (sample answer)
I work for a German company that has a supervisory board, of whom a third are not shareholders, and an executive board responsible for the day-to-day running of the company.

53.1   1 transparency
2 ethical investment fund
3 accountability
4 institutional investors
5 good corporate governance
6 activist shareholders

53.2 ethics, ethical, ethically
transparency, transparent, transparently
accountability, acountable, –
environment, –, environmental
sustainability, sustainable, sustainably

53.3
1 transparent
2 accountable
3 sustainably
4 ethically
5 transparency
6 sustainable

53.4 1 e   2 c   3 a   4 d   5 b
Over to you (sample answer)
Companies have responsibilities other than
just making a profit. They should be good
corporate citizens, encouraging good
relations not just with shareholders, but
also with employees, suppliers, customers,
and so on.

54.1 Across
2 Third World
4 standards
7 rural
9 industrialized
10 South
14 economic output
16 West
18 middle

Down
1 Gross National
3 distribution
5 product
6 prosperity
8 GNP
11 tigers
12 less
13 North
15 income
17 GNI

54.2
1 shipping costs
2 telecommunications costs
3 trade liberalization / free trade
4 free movement of capital
5 protectionism
6 interdependence

Over to you (sample answer)
Some say that material development gives a
false idea about the state of a country. They
look at other factors such as levels of
happiness, satisfaction, etc.

55.1
1 foreign direct investment, capital flows
2 Capital controls
3 devaluation
4 liberalization
5 instability

55.2
1 Poverty reduction
2 unsustainable
3 infrastructure projects
4 stimulation of growth
5 Heavily Indebted Poor Countries (HIPs)
6 the Millennium Development Goals
7 the International Monetary Fund (IMF)
and the World Bank

55.3 1 b   2 c   3 d   4 a   5 f   6 e

Over to you (sample answer)
Many argue that the debt burden of some
developing countries is so great that the
debt burden must be forgiven. These
countries are spending so much on debt
repayments that they cannot afford to pay
for education and health services.

56.1
1 trade barriers, free trade
2 tariffs
3 opening up
4 protectionism
5 dumping, quotas

56.2
1 false   4 true
2 true   5 true
3 true

Over to you (sample answer)
Yes, I buy Fairtrade products because they
help small farmers around the world to
make a decent living.

57.1

	Brazil	Russia
GDP	$1,845bn	$2,089bn
GDP growth 2005–7	3.7%	6.9%
Foreign currency reserves	$179bn	$464bn
Main sources of wealth	agricultural products, but also natural resources and manufacturing	hydrocarbons, especially oil and gas
Average age of population: getting older or younger?	younger	older

	India	China
GDP	$3,094bn	$7,245bn
GDP growth 2005–7	7.9%	10.4%
Foreign currency reserves	$266bn	$1,528bn
Main sources of wealth	offshoring of services, manufacturing	manufacturing
Average age of population: getting older or younger?	younger	older

57.2

1 Basic goods
2 trade surplus
3 GDP
4 middle class
5 Foreign currency reserves
6 wealth level

57.3 (sample answers)

1 Because of its dependence on selling oil and gas, whose prices and hence profitability can vary enormously.
2 China and India produce manufactured goods and services, whereas Russia and Brazil export raw materials and natural resources.
3 Because you have to consider the productive, working population in relation to the non-working section of the population. If the latter is increasing, the country is less productive.
4 Least developed country (1), developing countries (6), newly industrialized countries or NICs (3) and developed country (1).
5 Plentiful raw materials.

Over to you (sample answer)
Spain is a dynamic country with a young population. Its economic base goes beyond tourism to much else besides. Manufacturing and creative industries such as fashion and cinema are two other sources of its wealth, and will continue to contribute to its prosperity in years to come.

58.1

1 aid agencies	5 humanitarian	
2 famine, epidemic	6 seed money	
3 crop failure	7 disasters	
4 relief		

58.2

1 development projects
2 seed money
3 pressure groups
4 tied aid
5 intermediate technology
6 economic development
7 infrastructure

Over to you (sample answer)
No. A country needs long-term economic development that goes beyond humanitarian aid provided to relieve immediate difficulties.

59.1

1 environmental damage, nuclear energy
2 renewable energy
3 sustainability, triple bottom line
4 sustainability, environmental damage, depletion of natural resources
5 environmental damage, depletion of natural resources
6 environmental damage

59.2 vines: on outside of locker building – insulation
paint: 22,000 sq metres – absorbs nitrous oxide and processes oxygen
roof grass: reduces heat in visitor building by 3°C
solar lights and panels: on streets and buildings – panels produce 800 kw each
roadside flowers: absorb noxious emissions
waste heat: 50 per cent recycled in plant
landfill and incinerated waste: eliminated

Over to you (sample answer)
The world's population will eventually stop growing, thanks to rising living standards. But will enough of the world's economies adapt to the sort of sustainable practices described in the article in time? I'm cautiously optimistic about this.

60.1 2 a distance
3 f hospitality
4 e punctuality
5 d task-orientation
6 b glass ceiling
7 e planning
8 c gestures
9 e working year, leisure time

60.2 (sample answers)
1 It decided to merge its Belgian and Dutch operations.
2 You would think that these neighbouring countries have similar cultures and there would be no cultural difficulties.
3 The Belgians perceived their Dutch colleagues as often pompous and rude and not taking enough account of the need to do things in Belgium the Belgian way. The Dutch found the Belgians bureaucratic, over-deferential to the hierarchy before making decisions, and disorganized.
4 Individuals in teams with an acerbic personal style.
5 No, they may be down to individual personalities and there are difficult people in all cultures.
6 When people realized this, they were free to challenge unacceptable behaviour.

Over to you (sample answer)
Here at the advertising agency where I work, people like to think of themselves as creative and independent, so they would criticize colleagues who depend too much on procedures in particular situations. We are proud of our multitasking – we like to be seen to be doing several things at once. We spend a lot of time at the coffee machine, but chatting like this with colleagues is congenial and a good way of coming up with new ideas!

61.1 1 b, c, e   2 a, d, f

61.2

Noun	Adjective
aggression	aggressive
confrontation	confrontational
diplomacy	diplomatic
focus	focused
harmony	harmonious
vagueness	vague

61.3 1 diplomatic   4 vague
2 harmonious   5 confrontational
3 focused   6 aggressive

61.4 1 g   2 f   3 d   4 a   5 c
6 b   7 h   8 e

Over to you (sample answer)
In the Czech Republic, people are usually pretty punctual. We like to plan meetings well in advance and it can be quite difficult to set up a meeting at short notice. We like to arrive with the feeling that we are well-prepared and with all the facts and figures at our disposal. Czechs tend not to show too much emotion within a business meeting and there is limited body language and facial expressions, but this doesn't mean that we're not interested.

62.1 1 b   2 h   3 e   4 a   5 d
6 f   7 c   8 g

62.2
1 Avoid difficult/controversial/sensitive subjects, e.g. politics and religion.
2 Treat business cards with respect.
3 Communicate appropriately, at the right time, etc.
4 Proximity, eye contact, etc.
5 Be careful with humour.
6 Deference / Forms of address.

62.3
1 appropriate
2 inappropriate
3 inappropriate
4 appropriate

Over to you (sample answer)
In South Korea:
- Keep eye contact for half the time. Don't stare at the person you are talking to.
- Stand about a metre and a half away. Don't get too close.
- Don't try to be 'interesting' by talking about difficult subjects like politics.
- Treat more senior people with respect – don't use first names.
- Make sure that your business card is up-to-date. Don't make hand-written changes to it.
- Don't try to make people reveal confidential commercial information.

63.1

Ramesh Patel

Career goals
Work as a TV reporter in an English-speaking country

Skills
Good team worker
Good communicator: ability to explain complicated ideas clearly
Calm under stress, even in front of camera

Qualifications
2001–2002: Master's degree in Journalism, New York University. Dissertation: "A comparative study of broadcast TV in three English-speaking countries: India, US, Australia"
1998–2001: Bachelor's degree in Media Studies, New York University

Experience
2002–now Assistant to TV reporters, Star TV, Mumbai

Languages
Bilingual English and Hindi

Interests
Bollywood cinema, rock music

Personal
US nationality, born Brooklyn, 19 May, 1980

63.2
1 ✓
2 a
3 an
4 my
5 above
6 be
7 ✓
8 the
9 on
10 the
11 about

Over to you (sample answer)

> To the Financial Services Authority, London
>
> Hello. Your organization has been in the news a lot recently, and I'm writing to ask if you have openings for someone with my background. I have a Master's degree in Computer Science and was recently made redundant from my job as an IT specialist in the share trading department at UBS, where I worked for 15 years. I have detailed knowledge of how trading systems work, and I think I would be an ideal candidate to work in the department at FSA that deals with illegal trading practices. …

64.1
1 b   2 c   3 b   4 b   5 d
6 c   7 a

64.2
Email 1: d, c, h, g
Email 2: e, b, a, i, f

Over to you (sample answer)

> Dear Ms Karamanlis
> Thank you for your enquiry about employment at the Financial Services Authority. The FSA is actively recruiting people for the area that you mention – irregular share trading practices. We would like you to attend our Canary Wharf offices for an informal discussion on Tuesday 22 January at 3.30 pm. We would like you to prepare a short PowerPoint presentation (10 minutes) on your work at USB – there is no need for you to send the slides beforehand. Pls could you confirm that you will be able to attend? Many thanks. …

65.1

Noun	Verb
description	describe
analysis	analyze
outline	outline
explanation	explain
examination	examine
look	look
breakdown	break down
prediction	predict
conclusion	conclude

65.2 (sample answer)

I'll give a <u>description</u> of each energy source and a <u>breakdown</u> of the contribution of each source to the overall energy consumption of the US. In the second part, I'll move on to a more detailed <u>analysis</u> of the contribution of each type of renewable energy, and try to <u>explain</u> the situation of each one.

I'll <u>conclude</u> by having a <u>look</u> at the likely evolution of renewable energy over the next 50 years, and make some (risky!) <u>predictions</u> about the future contribution of the different types of renewables, in relation to the probable situation then of traditional energy sources.

65.3 (sample answer)

Next come natural gas and coal with 22 per cent each. Again, much of the gas comes from abroad, but the coal is mined in the US. Emissions that cause global warming are of course coal's biggest problem. In fourth position is nuclear energy with 8 per cent, with all its problems of disposal of radioactive waste. But not far behind nuclear is renewable energy, with 7 per cent.

Over to you (sample answer)

As you can see from the pie chart, at my university, the most popular subject in the languages department is English – just over 30 per cent of the students here study it as their main subject. Next comes Mandarin, with 25 per cent. In third place is Arabic, with 15 per cent. Fourth is Spanish, with 10 per cent and fifth equal are French, Italian and Portuguese, with just under 7 per cent each.

66.1   1 b   2 f   3 a   4 c   5 d   6 e

66.2 By 2050:

1 Electric cars are going to account for more than half the cars on the road.
2 Climate change will not have had the effects predicted today.
3 Population growth should have levelled off.
4 Nuclear energy might represent 30 per cent of energy production, unless there is another big nuclear accident before then.
5 Attitudes to personal consumption may have changed enormously.

66.3 (sample answers)

2 Climate change might have had bigger effects than those predicted today.
3 Population growth may not have levelled off.
4 Nuclear energy will not represent as much as 30 per cent of energy production – more like 10 per cent.
5 Attitudes to personal consumption will stay the same.

Over to you (sample answer)

Accountancy will probably see some big changes over the next 30 years. Computers will probably have a much bigger role, analyzing figures and spotting trends. This will make accountants more productive. However, the human element will still be very important. The relationship with clients might become more difficult, as, following the credit crunch and cases of fraud in 2009, governments may put more pressure on accounting firms to spot signs of problems before they become serious.

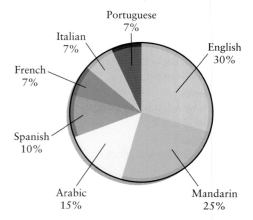

Index

*The numbers in the index are **Unit** numbers, not page numbers.*

abandon /ə'bændən/ 25
ABC approach /ˌeɪbiː'siː ə'prəʊtʃ/ 8
above board /ə'bʌv bɔːd/ 48
absorb /əb'zɔːb/ 51
account for /ə'kaʊnt fə/ 65
accountability /əˌkaʊntə'bɪləti/ 48, 52, 53
accountable /ə'kaʊntəbəl/ 48
accounting irregularities /ə'kaʊntɪŋ ɪˌregjə'lærətiz/ 45
accruals method /ə'kruːəlz ˌmeθəd/ 39, 42
accruals principle /ə'kruːəlz ˌprɪnsəpəl/ 39, 42
acerbic /ə'sɜːbɪk/ 60
achievement /ə'tʃiːvmənt/ 3
acquisition /ˌækwɪ'zɪʃən/ 19, 44
acquisitive /ə'kwɪzɪtɪv/ 19
act with integrity /ækt wɪð ɪn'tegrəti/ 48
act with probity /ækt wɪð 'prəʊbəti/ 48
action /'ækʃən/ 14
activist shareholders /ˌæktɪvɪst 'ʃeəˌhəʊldəz/ 53
activities /æk'tɪvətiz/ 25
actualizer /'æktʃələaɪzə/ 25
adapt /ə'dæpt/ 28
adaptable /ə'dæptəbəl/ 62
added-value /ˌædɪd'væljuː/ 18
admin /'ædmɪn/ 1
advanced economy /ədˌvɑːntst ɪ'kɒnəmi/ 54
advancement /əd'vɑːntsmənt/ 3
advertising /'ædvətaɪzɪŋ/ 22
aesthetics /iːs'θetɪks/ 12
affirmative action /ə'fɜːmətɪv 'ækʃən/ 11
after-sales service /ˌɑːftəseɪlz 'sɜːvɪs/ 22
ageing population /'eɪdʒɪŋ ˌpɒpjə'leɪʃən/ 57
ageism /'eɪdʒɪzəm/ 11
ageist attitude /ˌeɪdʒɪst 'ætɪtjuːd/ 11
agent /'eɪdʒənt/ 28
aggressive /ə'gresɪv/ 61
agricultural products /ˌægrɪ'kʌltʃərəl 'prɒdʌkts/ 57
aid agency /eɪd 'eɪdʒəntsi/ 58
alternative energy source /ɔːlˌtɜːnətɪv 'enədʒi ˌsɔːs/ 50
amortization /əˌmɔːtaɪ'zeɪʃən/ 40
amortize /ə'mɔːtaɪz/ 40
analogies /ə'nælədʒiz/ 34
analyse the data /'ænəlaɪz ðə 'deɪtə/ 24
annual report /ˌænjuəl rɪ'pɔːt/ 38

anticipate /æn'tɪsɪpeɪt/ 21
anti-virus program /ˌænti'vaɪrəs ˌprəʊgræm/ 35
appeal to /ə'piːl tə/ 25
applications /ˌæplɪ'keɪʃənz/ 21, 32
apply for certification /əˌplaɪ fə ˌsɜːtɪfɪ'keɪʃən/ 13
appoint /ə'pɔɪnt/ 28
apps /æps/ 32
Asian tiger /ˌeɪʒən 'taɪgə/ 54
assembly line /ə'sembli laɪn/ 29
assembly plant /ə'sembli plɑːnt/ 29
assets /'æsets/ 16, 37, 41, 43
associate /ə'səʊʃiət/ 27
at the top of the market /æt ðə tɒp əv ðə 'mɑːkɪt/ 47
attack a market /əˌtæk ə 'mɑːkɪt/ 16
attitude /'ætɪtjuːd/ 22
attractive /ə'træktɪv/ 19, 20
attractiveness /ə'træktɪvnəs/ 33
audit /'ɔːdɪt/ 45
auditor /'ɔːdɪtə/ 45
auditor rotation /ˌɔːdɪtə rə'teɪʃən/ 45
authoritarian /ˌɔːθɒrɪ'teəriən/ 2
automated warehouse /ˌɔːtəmeɪtɪd 'weəhaʊs/ 29
autonomy /ɔː'tɒnəmi/ 6, 61

B2B (business-to-business) /ˌbiːtuː'biː/ 36
B2C (business-to-consumer) /ˌbiːtuː'siː/ 36
back office outsourcing /bæk ˌɒfɪs 'aʊtsɔːsɪŋ/ 31
background /'bækgraʊnd/ 11, 63
bad debts /bæd dets/ 40
bail (sb) out /'beɪl aʊt/ 52
balance sheet /'bæləns ʃiːt/ 38, 40, 41
bandwidth /'bændwɪtθ/ 32
banking crisis /'bæŋkɪŋ ˌkraɪsɪs/ 47
basic goods /'beɪsɪk gʊdz/ 57
be chained to a desk /bi 'tʃeɪnd tə ə ˌdesk/ 1
be snowed under (with sthg) /bi snəʊd 'ʌndə/ 1
behavioural data /bɪˌheɪvjərəl 'deɪtə/ 24
behavioural segmentation /bɪˌheɪvjərəl ˌsegmen'teɪʃən/ 25
believer /bɪ'liːvə/ 25
benchmark (sb) against /'bentʃmɑːk əˌgenst/ 15
benchmarking /'bentʃmɑːkɪŋ/ 15
benchmarking exercise /'bentʃmɑːkɪŋ 'eksəsaɪz/ 15
best practice /best 'præktɪs/ 15
Big Brother /bɪg 'brʌðə/ 35

billing /'bɪlɪŋ/ 31
blocs /blɒks/ 56
blog /blɒg/ 33
blogger /'blɒgə/ 33
blogosphere /'blɒgəsfɪə/ 33
board member /'bɔːd ˌmembə/ 52
board of directors /bɔːd əv dɪ'rektəz/ 52
boast /bəʊst/ 60
body /'bɒdi/ 45
body language /'bɒdi ˌlæŋgwɪdʒ/ 60
bond /bɒnd/ 38
bond market /'bɒnd ˌmɑːkɪt/ 38
bondholder /'bɒndhəʊldə/ 38
bonus /'bəʊnəs/ 52
book value /'bʊk ˌvæljuː/ 40
boom and bust cycle /buːm ən 'bʌst ˌsaɪkəl/ 46
booming /'buːmɪŋ/ 46
borrow /'bɒrəʊ/ 38
borrowing /'bɒrəʊɪŋ/ 46
bottom out /'bɒtəm aʊt/ 46
boundary /'baʊndri/ 6
BPO (business process outsourcing) /ˌbiːpiː'əʊ/ 31
brand /brænd/ 27, 40
brand awareness /brænd ə'weənəs/ 27
brand differentiation /brænd ˌdɪfərenʃi'eɪʃən/ 27
brand dilution /brænd daɪ'luːʃən/ 27
brand equity /brænd 'ekwɪti/ 27
brand extension /brænd ɪk'stenʃən/ 27
brand identity /brænd aɪ'dentəti/ 27
brand image /brænd 'ɪmɪdʒ/ 27
brand loyalty /brænd 'lɔɪəlti/ 27
brand positioning /brænd pə'zɪʃənɪŋ/ 27
brand recognition /brænd rekəg'nɪʃən/ 27
brand stretching /brænd 'stretʃɪŋ/ 27
branding /'brændɪŋ/ 27
breakdown /'breɪkdaʊn/ 6, 12
bribe /braɪb/ 48
BRIC countries /'brɪk ˌkʌntriz/ 54
BRIC economies /'brɪk ɪˌkɒnəmiz/ 57
bricks-and-mortar outlet /'brɪksæn'mɔːtə ˌaʊtlet/ 36
bring a product to market /brɪŋ ə ˌprɒdʌkt tə 'mɑːkɪt/ 20
broadband access /'brɔːdbænd ˌækses/ 32
browse the Internet /'braʊz ðə ˌɪntənet/ 32
bubble /'bʌbəl/ 33, 47

bubble bursts /'bʌbəl bɜːsts/ 33, 47

budget deficit /ˌbʌdʒɪt 'defɪsɪt/ 46

budget surplus /ˌbʌdʒɪt 'sɜːpləs/ 46

build a competitive advantage /bɪld ə kəm'petɪtɪv əd'vɑːntɪdʒ/ 18

bureaucracy /bjʊə'rɒkrəsi/ 1

bureaucratic /ˌbjʊərə'krætɪk/ 20

burn-out /'bɜːnaʊt/ 6

business continuity plan /'bɪznɪs kɒntɪˌnjuːəti plæn/ 21

business cycle /'bɪznɪs saɪkəl/ 46

business functions /'bɪznɪs fʌŋkʃənz/ 31

business model /'bɪznɪs mɒdəl/ 7, 37

business process outsourcing (BPO) /bɪznɪs prəʊses 'aʊtsɔːsɪŋ/ 31

business results /'bɪznɪs rɪˌzʌlts/ 14

business-to-business (B2B) /ˌbɪznɪstə'bɪznɪs/ 36

business-to-consumer (B2C) /ˌbɪznɪstəkən'sjuːmə/ 36

buy in /baɪ ɪn/ 29

buyer /'baɪə/ 18

buying habits /'baɪɪŋ 'hæbɪts/ 26

candidate /'kændɪdət/ 7

cap /kæp/ 51

capabilities /ˌkeɪpə'bɪlətiz/ 7, 31

capacity /kə'pæsəti/ 43

capital controls /'kæpɪtəl kən'trəʊlz/ 55

capital flows /'kæpɪtəl fləʊs/ 55

captive plant /'kæptɪv plɑːnt/ 29

capture /'kæptʃə/ 51

carbon capture /'kɑːbən ˌkæptʃə/ 51

carbon credits /'kɑːbən ˌkredɪts/ 51

carbon dioxide /'kɑːbən daɪˌɒksaɪd/ 51

carbon footprint /ˌkɑːbən 'fʊtprɪnt/ 51, 59

carbon levels /'kɑːbən ˌlevəlz/ 51

carbon offsets /'kɑːbən ˌɒf'sets/ 51

carbon sequestration /ˌkɑːbən ˌsiːkwes'treɪʃən/ 51

carbon trading /ˌkɑːbən 'treɪdɪŋ/ 51

carbon-neutral /ˌkɑːbən 'njuːtrəl/ 51

carcinogenic /ˌkɑːsɪnə'dʒenɪk/ 50

career ladder /kə'rɪə 'lædə/ 3

career move /kə'rɪə muːv/ 4

carry an item /'kæri ən aɪtəm/ 40

cash /kæʃ/ 40

cash inflow /kæʃ 'ɪnfləʊ/ 42

cash outflow /kæʃ 'aʊtfləʊ/ 42

cashflow /'kæʃfləʊ/ 43

cashflow problem /'kæʃfləʊ prɒbləm/ 42

cashflow statement /'kæʃfləʊ steɪtmənt/ 38, 42

central bank /'sentrəl bæŋk/ 46

CEO (chief executive officer) /ˌsiːiː'əʊ/ 52

CFO (chief finance officer) /ˌsiːef'əʊ/ 38

chaebol /'tʃeɪbəl/ 19

chairman /'tʃeəmən/ 52

chairwoman /'tʃeəˌwʊmən/ 52

challenging /'tʃælɪndʒɪŋ/ 63

charge /tʃɑːdʒ/ 40

chat room /tʃæt ruːm/ 24, 33, 34

chief executive officer (CEO) /tʃiːf ɪg'zekjətɪv ɒfɪsə/ 52

chief finance officer (CFO) /tʃiːf 'faɪnæns ɒfɪsə/ 38

child labour /tʃaɪld 'leɪbə/ 49

churn /tʃɜːn/ 23

civil liberties /'sɪvəl 'lɪbətiz/ 35

clicks-and-mortar outlet /klɪksən'mɔːtə ˌaʊtlet/ 36

client contact /klaɪənt 'kɒntækt/ 1

climate change /'klaɪmət tʃeɪndʒ/ 48, 49, 50, 51, 59

climate treaty /'klaɪmət triːti/ 51

cluster /'klʌstə/ 29

coach /kəʊtʃ/ 8

coachee /kəʊ'tʃiː/ 8

coaching /'kəʊtʃɪŋ/ 7, 8

code /kəʊd/ 35

code of conduct /kəʊd əv 'kɒndʌkt/ 48

code of ethics /kəʊd əv 'eθɪks/ 48

COGS (cost of goods sold) /kɒgz/ 39

collaborate on /kə'læbəreɪt ɒn/ 34

collaboration /kəˌlæbə'reɪʃən/ 33, 34

collaborative site /kə'læbərətɪv saɪt/ 34

collect the data /'kɒlekt ðə 'deɪtə/ 24

collective intelligence /kəˌlektɪv ɪn'telɪdʒəns/ 34

combination /ˌkɒmbɪ'neɪʃən/ 34

come up with /kʌm ʌp wɪð/ 1

commitment /kə'mɪtmənt/ 7, 9, 14, 16

commodity /kə'mɒdəti/ 56

common purpose /ˌkɒmən 'pɜːpəs/ 9

communication /kəˌmjuːnɪ'keɪʃən/ 22, 23, 33

commute /kə'mjuːt/ 1

commuting /kə'mjuːtɪŋ/ 6

company intranet /'kʌmpəni 'ɪntrənet/ 34

compensation for contribution /ˌkɒmpən'seɪʃən fə ˌkɒntrɪ'bjuːʃən/ 7

competing /kəm'piːtɪŋ/ 17

competing bids /kəmpiːtɪŋ 'bɪdz/ 17

competing offerings /kəmpiːtɪŋ 'ɒfərɪŋz/ 17

competing products /kəmpiːtɪŋ 'prɒdʌkts/ 17

competing suppliers /kəmpiːtɪŋ sə'plaɪəz/ 17

competing technologies /kəmpiːtɪŋ tek'nɒlədʒiz/ 17

competitive /kəm'petɪtɪv/ 17

competitive advantage /kəmˌpetɪtɪv əd'vɑːntɪdʒ/ 17, 18

competitive benchmarking /kəmˌpetɪtɪv 'bentʃmɑːkɪŋ/ 15

competitive edge /kəmˌpetɪtɪv 'edʒ/ 4, 17, 31

competitive forces /kəmˌpetɪtɪv 'fɔːsɪz/ 18

competitive position /kəmˌpetɪtɪv pə'zɪʃən/ 17

competitive pressure /kəmˌpetɪtɪv 'preʃə/ 17

competitive price /kəmˌpetɪtɪv 'praɪs/ 17

competitive product /kəmˌpetɪtɪv 'prɒdʌkt/ 17

competitive strategy /kəmˌpetɪtɪv 'strætədʒi/ 17, 18

competitive threat /kəmˌpetɪtɪv 'θret/ 17

competitor /kəm'petɪtə/ 17

completer /kəm'pliːtə/ 9

components /kəm'pəʊnənts/ 12, 29, 30

computer chip /kəm'pjuːtə tʃɪp/ 32

computing costs /kəm'pjuːtɪŋ kɒsts/ 54

computing power /kəm'pjuːtɪŋ paʊə/ 32

concentrate on /'kɒnsəntreɪt ɒn/ 19

concentrated /'kɒnsəntreɪtɪd/ 19

confidentiality /ˌkɒnfɪdenʃi'æləti/ 25, 26, 35

confirm /kən'fɜːm/ 64

conflict of interests /ˌkɒnflɪkt əv 'ɪntrəsts/ 45

conformance to specification /kənˌfɔːməns tə ˌspesɪfɪ'keɪʃən/ 12

conformity to specification /kən'fɔːməti tə ˌspesɪfɪ'keɪʃən/ 12

confrontational /ˌkɒnfrʌn'teɪʃənəl/ 61

congenial /kən'dʒiːniəl/ 60

conscientiousness /ˌkɒntʃi'entʃəsnəs/ 10

consistency /kən'sɪstəntsi/ 12

consortium e-marketplace /kənsɔːtiəm iːˈmaːkɪtpleɪs/ 36

constitute /ˈkɒnstɪtjuːt/ 65

constrainer /kənˈstreɪnə/ 10

consult /kənˈsʌlt/ 3

consultancy service /kənˈsʌltənsi sɜːvɪs/ 4

consultation /ˌkɒnsəlˈteɪʃən/ 2, 5

consumer behaviour /kənˌsjuːmə bɪˈheɪvjə/ 26

consumer borrowing /kənˌsjuːmə ˈbɒrəʊɪŋ/ 46

consumer profile /kənˌsjuːmə ˈprəʊfaɪl/ 26

consumer spending /kənˌsjuːmə ˈspendɪŋ/ 46

contact /ˈkɒntækt/ 60

containerization /kənˌteɪnəraɪˈzeɪʃən/ 54

content /ˈkɒntent/ 34, 37, 50

content provider /ˈkɒntent prəʊˈvaɪdə/ 37

contingency plan /kənˈtɪndʒəntsi plæn/ 21

continual improvement /kənˌtɪnjuəl ɪmˈpruːvmənt/ 13

contract (v)/kənˈtrækt/ 46

contraction /kənˈtrækʃən/ 46

contractor /kənˈtræktə/ 4

convenience /kənˈviːniəns/ 23

converge /kənˈvɜːdʒ/ 21

conversion /kənˈvɜːʃən/ 25

convertibility /kənˌvɜːtəˈbɪləti/ 55

convertible /kənˈvɜːtəbəl/ 55

cook the books /ˈkʊk ðə bʊks/ 45

cooperation /kəʊˌɒpəˈreɪʃən/ 10

co-operative /kəʊˈɒpərətɪv/ 56

coordinator /kəʊˈɔːdɪneɪtə/ 9

copy-protected /ˌkɒpiprəˈtektɪd/ 37

copyright /ˈkɒpiˌraɪt/ 37

copyright protection /ˈkɒpiraɪt prəˌtekʃən/ 37

copyright theft /ˈkɒpiraɪt ˌθeft/ 37

core activities /kɔːr ækˈtɪvətiz/ 4

core business /kɔː ˈbɪznɪs/ 19

core competences /kɔː ˈkɒmpɪtənsəz/ 31

core competencies /kɔː ˈkɒmpɪtənsiz/ 31

core competents /kɔː ˈkɒmpɪtənts/ 8

corporate board /ˈkɔːpərət bɔːd/ 52

corporate citizen /kɔːpərət ˈsɪtɪzən/ 48

corporate collapse /ˈkɔːpərət kəˈlæps/ 45

corporate culture /ˈkɔːpərət ˈkʌltʃə/ 31

corporate governance /kɔːpərət ˈgʌvənəns/ 52, 53

corporate intranet /kɔːpərət ˈɪntrənet/ 34

corporate social responsibility (CSR) /kɔːpərət səʊʃəl rɪˌspɒnsəˈbɪləti/ 48, 50

corporate sustainability /ˈkɔːpərət səˌsteɪnəˈbɪləti/ 53

corporation tax /ˌkɔːpərˈeɪʃən tæks/ 39

corruption /kəˈrʌpʃən/ 48

cost leadership /kɒst ˈliːdəʃɪp/ 18

cost of goods sold (COGS) /kɒst əv gʊdz ˈsəʊld/ 39

cost savings /kɒst ˈseɪvɪŋz/ 31

cost-effective /ˌkɒstɪˈfektɪv/ 4

crash /kræʃ/ 47

create brands /kriˈeɪt brændz/ 27

creative (adj) /kriˈeɪtɪv/ 20

creative (n) /kriˈeɪtɪv/ 8

creativity /ˌkriːeɪˈtɪvəti/ 1

creator /kriˈeɪtə/ 37

credit crunch /ˈkredɪt krʌntʃ/ 47, 54

credit period /ˈkredɪt pɪəriəd/ 42

credit terms /ˈkredɪt tɜːmz/ 42

creditor /ˈkredɪtə/ 41

crisis /ˈkraɪsɪs/ 21

crisis management plan /kraɪsɪs ˈmænɪdʒmənt plæn/ 21

criteria /kraɪˈtɪəriə/ 7, 13

CRM (customer relationship management) /ˌsiːaːrˈem/ 26

CRM software package /siːaːrem ˈsɒftweə pækɪdʒ/ 26

CRM solutions /siːaːrem səˈluːʃənz/ 26

crop failure /ˈkrɒp feɪljə/ 58

cross-border capital flows /krɒsbɔːdə ˈkæpɪtəl fləʊz/ 55

crowd intelligence /kraʊd ɪnˈtelɪdʒəns/ 34

crowdsourcing /ˈkraʊdsɔːsɪŋ/ 34

CSR (corporate social responsibility) /ˌsiːesˈaː/ 48, 50

cultural differences /ˈkʌltʃərəl ˈdɪfərəntsɪz/ 10, 60

culture /ˈkʌltʃə/ 7

culture intervention /ˈkʌltʃə ˌɪntəˈvenʃən/ 7

currency /ˈkʌrənsi/ 46

current assets /kʌrənt ˈæsets/ 40

current liabilities /kʌrənt laɪəˈbɪlətiz/ 41

current trends /ˈkʌrənt trendz/ 4

currently /ˈkʌrəntli/ 65

customer allegiance /kʌstəmər əˈliːdʒəns/ 23

customer and product /ˈkʌstəmər ən ˈprɒdʌkt/ 53

customer approval /ˈkʌstəmər əˈpruːvəl/ 12

customer base /ˈkʌstəmə ˌbeɪs/ 23

customer cost /ˈkʌstəmə ˌkɒst/ 23

customer defection /ˈkʌstəmə dɪˌfekʃən/ 23

customer delight /ˈkʌstəmə dɪˌlaɪt/ 12, 23

customer dissatisfaction /ˈkʌstəmə dɪssætɪsˌfækʃən/ 23

customer expectations /ˈkʌstəmər ekspekˌteɪʃənz/ 12

customer experience /ˈkʌstəmər ɪkˌspɪəriəns/ 22

customer focus /ˈkʌstəmə ˌfəʊkəs/ 23

customer loyalty /ˈkʌstəmə ɪlɔɪəlti/ 23

customer orientation /ˈkʌstəmər ɔːrienˌteɪʃən/ 23

customer relationship management (CRM) /ˈkʌstəmə rɪˌleɪʃənʃɪp mænɪdʒmənt/ 26

customer retention /ˈkʌstəmə rɪˌtenʃən/ 23

customer satisfaction /ˈkʌstəmə sætɪsˌfækʃən/ 13, 14, 23

customer solution /ˈkʌstəmə səˌluːʃən/ 23

customer-facing services /ˌkʌstəməfeɪsɪŋ ˈsɜːvɪsɪz/ 31

cut-throat competition /kʌtθrəʊt ˌkɒmpəˈtɪʃən/ 17

cybercrime /ˈsaɪbəkraɪm/ 35

cybercriminal /ˈsaɪbəkrɪmɪnəl/ 35

damage the core brand /ˈdæmɪdʒ ðə kɔː brænd/ 27

data analysis /ˈdeɪtə əˌnæləsɪs/ 26

data management /ˈdeɪtə ˌmænɪdʒmənt/ 26

data mining /ˈdeɪtə ˌmaɪnɪŋ/ 26

data protection /ˈdeɪtə prəˌtekʃən/ 26

data warehouse /ˈdeɪtə ˌweəhaʊs/ 26

data warehousing /ˈdeɪtə ˌweəhaʊzɪŋ/ 26

database /ˈdeɪtəbeɪs/ 26

dealings /ˈdiːlɪŋz/ 48

debt burden /det ˈbɜːdən/ 55

debt forgiveness /det fəˈgɪvnəs/ 55

debt load /ˈdet ləʊd/ 55

debt reduction programme /det rɪˌdʌkʃən ˈprəʊgræm/ 55

debt relief /ˈdet rɪliːf/ 55

debt rescheduling /det ˌriːˈʃedjuːlɪŋ/ 55

debt restructuring /det ˌriːˈstrʌktʃərɪŋ/ 55

debt service /ˈdet sɜːvɪs/ 55

debtor /ˈdetə/ 40

decision-making process /dɪˈsɪʒənmeɪkɪŋ prəʊses/ 2

decisiveness /dɪˈsaɪsɪvnəs/ 10

decline /dɪˈklaɪn/ 46

declining birth rate /dɪklaɪnɪŋ ˈbɜːθ reɪt/ 57

default /dɪˈfɔːlt/ 47
default on /dɪˈfɔːlt ɒn/ 47
defect (n) /ˈdiːfekt/ 12
defect (v) /diːˈfekt/ 23
defects per million /ˌdiːfekts pɜː ˈmɪljən/ 15
defend a market /dɪfend ə ˈmɑːkɪt/ 16
deference /ˈdefərəns/ 60, 62
deferential /ˌdefəˈrenʃəl/ 60
define the problem /dɪˈfaɪn ðə ˈprɒbləm/ 24
define the research objectives /dɪˈfaɪn ðə rɪˈsɜːtʃ əbˈdʒektɪvz/ 24
deflation /dɪˈfleɪʃən/ 47
deforestation /diːˌfɒrɪˈsteɪʃən/ 50
delegate /ˈdelɪgeɪt/ 3
delegation /ˌdelɪˈgeɪʃən/ 3
deleverage /diːˈliːvərɪdʒ/ 43, 47
Delphi method /ˈdelfi meθəd/ 21
demand /dɪˈmɑːnd/ 47, 57
demographic /ˌdeməˈgræfɪk/ 25
demographic changes /ˌdeməˈgræfɪk ˈtʃeɪndʒɪz/ 11
demographic segmentation /ˌdeməˈgræfɪk ˌsegmenˈteɪʃən/ 25
demographics /ˌdeməʊˈgræfɪks/ 57
denial of service attack /dɪnaɪəl əv ˈsɜːvɪs ətæk/ 35
depletion of natural resources /dɪˈpliːʃən əv ˈnætʃərəl rɪˈzɔːsɪz/ 59
depreciate /dɪˈpriːʃieɪt/ 40
depreciation /dɪˌpriːʃiˈeɪʃən/ 39, 40, 42
depression /dɪˈpreʃən/ 46
de-stress /diːˈstres/ 6
detailed proposal /ˌdiːteɪld prəˈpəʊzəl/ 61
devaluation /ˌdiːvæljuˈeɪʃən/ 55
develop the research plan /dɪˈveləp ðə rɪˈsɜːtʃ plæn/ 24
developed country /dɪˌveləpt ˈkʌntri/ 57
developing country /dɪˌveləpɪŋ ˈkʌntri/ 54, 57
development aid /dɪˈveləpmənt eɪd/ 58
development process /dɪˈveləpmənt ˌprəʊses/ 20
development project /dɪˈveləpmənt ˌprɒdʒekt/ 58
differentiate /ˌdɪfəˈrenʃieɪt/ 25
differentiation /ˌdɪfərenʃiˈeɪʃən/ 18, 27
digital rights management (DRM) /dɪdʒɪtəl raɪts ˈmænɪdʒmənt/ 37
digital watermark /dɪdʒɪtəl ˈwɔːtəmɑːk/ 37
digitalized /ˈdɪdʒɪtəlaɪzd/ 37
digitized /ˈdɪdʒɪtaɪzd/ 37

dignity at work policy /ˈdɪgnəti ət ˈwɜːk pɒləsi/ 11
digressions /daɪˈgreʃənz/ 61
diplomacy /dɪˈpləʊməsi/ 61
direct approach /dɪrekt əˈprəʊtʃ/ 61
direct export /dɪrekt ˈekspɔːt/ 28
direct investment /dɪrekt ɪnˈvestmənt/ 28
directive /dɪˈrektɪv/ 30
disband /dɪsˈbænd/ 8
discharge /ˈdɪstʃɑːdʒ/ 50
disciplinary procedure /ˌdɪsəˈplɪnəri prəʊsiːdʒə/ 2
discipline /ˈdɪsəplɪn/ 2
discriminate against /dɪˈskrɪmɪneɪt əˈgenst/ 11
discriminatory /dɪˈskrɪmɪnətəri/ 11
dismantle /dɪˈsmæntəl/ 30, 56
disorganized /dɪˈsɔːgənaɪzd/ 60
disposable income /dɪspəʊzəbəl ˈɪŋkʌm/ 46
disposal /dɪˈspəʊzəl/ 19, 30
dispose of /dɪˈspəʊz əv/ 19, 50
dispose of waste /dɪspəʊz əv ˈweɪst/ 50
dispute resolution /dɪspjuːt ˌrezəˈluːʃən/ 10
dissatisfaction /dɪsˌsætɪsˈfækʃən/ 3
dissertation /ˌdɪsəˈteɪʃən/ 63
distance /ˈdɪstəns/ 60
distribute /ˌdɪstrɪˈbjuːt/ 44
distribution /ˌdɪstrɪˈbjuːʃən/ 29
distribution channel /ˌdɪstrɪˈbjuːʃən tʃænəl/ 22
diverse workforce /daɪvɜːs ˈwɜːkfɔːs/ 11
diversity /daɪˈvɜːsəti/ 11
diversity initiative /daɪˈvɜːsəti ɪˌnɪʃətɪv/ 11
diversity management /daɪˈvɜːsəti ˌmænɪdʒmənt/ 11
diversity programme /daɪˈvɜːsəti ˌprəʊgræm/ 11
diversity statement /daɪˈvɜːsəti ˌsteɪtmənt/ 11
diversity strategy /daɪˈvɜːsəti ˌstrætədʒi/ 11
diversity training /daɪˈvɜːsəti ˌtreɪnɪŋ/ 11
divest /daɪˈvest/ 19
divestment /daɪˈvestmənt/ 19, 44
dividend /ˈdɪvɪdend/ 38, 39, 41
dividend payout /ˌdɪvɪdend ˈpeɪaʊt/ 44
dividend per share /dɪvɪdend pɜː ˈʃeə/ 39, 44
DJSI Stoxx /ˌdiːdʒeɪesˈaɪ stɒks/ 53
DJSI World /ˌdiːdʒeɪesˈaɪ wɜːld/ 53
Doha round /ˈdəʊhɑː raʊnd/ 56
dominate /ˈdɒmɪneɪt/ 20

dominate a market /dɒmɪneɪt ə ˈmɑːkɪt/ 16
donor country /dəʊnə ˈkʌntri/ 58
dotcom bubble /dɒtkɒm ˈbʌbəl/ 33
Dow Jones Sustainability indexes /daʊ dʒəʊnz səˌsteɪnəˈbɪləti ɪndeksɪz/ 53
download /daʊnˈləʊd/ 32, 37
downshift /ˈdaʊnʃɪft/ 6
draw conclusions /drɔː kənˈkluːʒənz/ 24
driver /ˈdraɪvə/ 10
DRM (digital rights management) /ˌdiːɑːrˈem/ 37
drop out /ˈdrɒp aʊt/ 20
drought /draʊt/ 51
dual nationality /ˈdjuːəl ˌnæʃənˈæləti/ 63
dump /dʌmp/ 56

earnings /ˈɜːnɪŋz/ 39, 43, 44
earnings per share (EPS) /ɜːnɪŋz pɜː ˈʃeə/ 39, 44
earthquake /ˈɜːθkweɪk/ 58
EBITDA (earnings before interest, tax, depreciation and amortization) /ˌiːbɪtˈdə/ 43
eco-friendly /ˈiːkəʊˌfrendli/ 50
e-commerce /ˈiːˌkɒmɜːs/ 36
e-commerce application /iːˈkɒmɜːs æplɪˌkeɪʃən/ 36
e-commerce platform /iːˈkɒmɜːs ˌplætfɔːm/ 36
e-commerce portal /iːˈkɒmɜːs ˌpɔːtəl/ 36
e-commerce site /iːˈkɒmɜːs ˌsaɪt/ 36
e-commerce software /iːˈkɒmɜːs ˌsɒfweə/ 36
e-commerce solution /iːˈkɒmɜːs səˌluːʃən/ 36
economic bubble /ˌiːkənɒmɪk ˈbʌbəl/ 47
economic cycle /ˌiːkəˈnɒmɪk ˈsaɪkəl/ 46
economic development /ˌiːkənɒmɪk dɪˈveləpmənt/ 57, 58
economic foundations /ˌiːkənɒmɪk faʊnˈdeɪʃənz/ 57
economic growth /ˌiːkənɒmɪk ˈgrəʊθ/ 5, 46
economic output /ˌiːkəˈnɒmɪk ˈaʊtpʊt/ 54
economic stability /iːkəˌnɒmɪk stəˈbɪləti/ 46, 57
economic value /ˌiːkəˈnɒmɪk ˈvæljuː/ 59
edit /ˈedɪt/ 33
education /ˌedʒʊˈkeɪʃən/ 11, 57
EEA (European Economic Area) /ˌiːiːˈeɪ/ 56

efficient /ɪ'fɪʃənt/ 22

effluent /'efluənt/ 50

effort–reward imbalance /efət rɪ'wɔːd ɪmbæləns/ 6

EFQM Excellence Model /iːefkjuːem 'eksələns mɒdəl/ 14

e-fulfilment /iːfʊl'fɪlmənt/ 36

EI (emotional intelligence) /iː'aɪ/ 10

electronic reader /ˌelek'trɒnɪk 'riːdə/ 25

electronic trail /elek,trɒnɪk 'treɪl/ 35

electronic watermark /elek,trɒnɪk 'wɔːtəmaːk/ 37

elimination of variation /ɪlɪmɪneɪʃən əv veəri'eɪʃən/ 12

e-marketplace /iːmaːkɪtpleɪs/ 36

emergency relief /ɪmɜːdʒənsi rɪ'liːf/ 58

emerging economy /ɪmɜːdʒɪŋ ɪ'kɒnəmi/ 57

emerging industry /ɪmɜːdʒɪŋ 'ɪndəstri/ 20

emissions /ɪ'mɪʃənz/ 51

emit /ɪ'mɪt/ 51

emotional /ɪ'məʊʃənəl/ 10

emotional competencies /ɪˌməʊʃənəl 'kɒmpɪtənsiz/ 10

emotional intelligence (EI) /ɪˌməʊʃənəl ɪn'telɪdʒəns/ 10

emotional quotient (EQ) /ɪˌməʊʃənəl 'kwəʊʃənt/ 10

empathy /'empəθi/ 10

employability /ɪmˌplɔɪə'bɪlɪti/ 4

employable /ɪm'plɔɪəbəl/ 4

employee /ɪm'plɔɪiː/ 2, 5

employee involvement /ɪmplɔɪiː ɪn'vɒlvmənt/ 12

employment and community /ɪm'plɔɪmənt ən kə'mjuːnəti/ 48

empower /ɪm'paʊə/ 3

empowerment /ɪm'paʊəmənt/ 2, 3

enabler /ɪ'neɪblə/ 10, 14

encourage competition /ɪnˌkʌrɪdʒ kɒmpə'tɪʃən/ 17

encrypt /ɪn'krɪpt/ 35

encryption /ɪn'krɪpʃən/ 35, 37

endanger /ɪn'deɪndʒə/ 48

engagement /ɪn'geɪdʒmənt/ 9

enhance brands /ɪn'haːns brændz/ 27

enquire /ɪn'kwaɪə/ 64

enquiry /ɪn'kwaɪəri/ 64

enrich a database /ɪn'rɪtʃ ə 'deɪtəbeɪs/ 26

entrant /'entrənt/ 19

environment /ɪn'vaɪrənmənt/ 18, 48

environmental impact /ɪnvaɪrən,mentəl 'ɪmpækt/ 59

environmental issues /ɪnvaɪrən,mentəl 'ɪʃuːz/ 50

environmental management /ɪnvaɪrən,mentəl 'mænɪdʒmənt/ 13

environmental pollution /ɪnvaɪrən,mentəl pə'luːʃən/ 48, 50

environmental protection /ɪnvaɪrən,mentəl prə'tekʃən/ 48

environmental regulation /ɪnvaɪrən,mentəl regjə'leɪʃən/ 50

environmental value /ɪnvaɪrən,mentəl 'væljuː/ 59

environmentally sustainable /ɪnvaɪrən,mentəli sə'steɪnəbəl/ 13

epidemic /ˌepɪ'demɪk/ 58

e-procurement /iːprə'kjʊəmənt/ 36

EPS (earnings per share) /ˌiːpiː'es/ 39, 44

EQ (emotional quotient) /iː'kjuː/ 10

equal basis /ˌiːkwəl 'beɪsɪs/ 61

equal opportunities /ˌiːkwəl ɒpə'tjuːnətiz/ 11

equal opportunities policy /ˌiːkwəl ɒpə'tjuːnətiz ˌpɒləsi/ 11

equality /ɪ'kwɒləti/ 11

establish /ɪ'stæblɪʃ/ 20

establish a foothold in a market /ɪˌstæblɪʃ ə 'fʊthəʊld ɪn ə ˌmaːkɪt/ 16

establish a toehold in a market /ɪˌstæblɪʃ ə 'təʊhəʊld ɪn ə ˌmaːkɪt/ 16

Estimate–Talk–Estimate /'estɪmət tɔːk 'estɪmət/ 21

ethical behaviour /ˌeθɪkəl bɪ'heɪvjə/ 48

ethical dilemma /ˌeθɪkəl daɪ'lemə/ 48

ethical investment fund /ˌeθɪkəl ɪn'vestmənt fʌnd/ 53

ethical issue /ˌeθɪkəl 'ɪʃuː/ 48

ethical lapse /ˌeθɪkəl 'læps/ 48

ethical stance /ˌeθɪkəl 'staːns/ 48

ethical standard /ˌeθɪkəl 'stændəd/ 48

ethically managed company /ˌeθɪkəli ˌmænɪdʒd 'kʌmpəni/ 53

ethics /'eθɪks/ 48

ethnic minority /ˌeθnɪk maɪ'nɒrəti/ 11

ethnicity /eθ'nɪsəti/ 11

European Economic Area (EEA) /jʊərə,piːən iːkə'nɒmɪk 'eəriə/ 56

evaluate outcomes /ɪˌvæljueɪt 'aʊtkʌmz/ 14

evolve /ɪ'vɒlv/ 21

exceed expectations /ɪk'siːd ˌekspek'teɪʃənz/ 12, 23

exceptional items /ɪk,sepʃənəl 'aɪtəmz/ 39

exchange rate /ɪks'tʃeɪndʒ reɪt/ 46

exclusive agent /ɪks,kluːsɪv 'eɪdʒənt/ 28

executive compensation /ɪg,zekjətɪv ˌkɒmpən'seɪʃən/ 52

executive director /ɪg,zekjətɪv daɪ'rektə/ 52

executive education /ɪg,zekjətɪv edʒʊ'keɪʃən/ 7

executive pay /ɪg,zekjətɪv 'peɪ/ 52

executive remuneration /ɪg,zekjətɪv rɪ,mjuːnə'reɪʃən/ 52

expansion /ɪk'spænʃən/ 46

expectation gap /ˌekspek'teɪʃən gæp/ 45

expectations /ˌekspek'teɪʃənz/ 23

experiencer /ɪkspɪərɪənsə/ 25

experimental research /ɪksperɪ,mentəl rɪ'sɜːtʃ/ 24

expertise /ˌekspɜː'tiːz/ 31

export /ɪk'spɔːt/ 50

export manager /'ekspɔːt ˌmænɪdʒə/ 28

external factor /ɪk,stɜːnəl 'fæktə/ 18

external social networking site /ɪk'stɜːnəl 'səʊʃəl 'netwɜːkɪŋ saɪt/ 33

externalization /ɪk,stɜːnəlaɪ'zeɪʃən/ 34

fab plant /'fæb plaːnt/ 29

factory /'fæktəri/ 29

fair trade /feə 'treɪd/ 56

fairtrade mark /feə'treɪd maːk/ 56

fall below expectations /'fɔːl bɪ,ləʊ ˌekspek'teɪʃənz/ 23

false accounting /fɔːls ə'kaʊntɪŋ/ 45

family-owned businesses /'fæməliəʊnd 'bɪznɪsɪz/ 19

famine /'fæmɪn/ 58

farm out /faːm 'aʊt/ 31

FASB (Financial Accounting Standards Board) /ˌefeɪes'biː/ 45

fat cat /'fæt kæt/ 52

fault /fɔːlt/ 12

FDI (foreign direct investment) /ˌefdiː'aɪ/ 55

features (n) /'fiːtʃəz/ 12

feedback /'fiːdbæk/ 7

ferocious competition /fə,rəʊʃəs kɒmpə'tɪʃən/ 17

fierce competition /fɪəs ˌkɒmpə'tɪʃən/ 17

file sharing /faɪl 'ʃeərɪŋ/ 37

finance /'faɪnæns/ 38

finance department /'faɪnæns dɪ,paːtmənt/ 38

finances /ˈfaɪnænsɪz/ 38
financial /faɪˈnænʃəl/ 38, 53
Financial Accounting Standards Board (FASB) /faɪˌnænʃəl əˌkaʊntɪŋ ˈstændədz bɔːd/ 45
financial bubble /faɪˌnænʃəl ˈbʌbəl/ 47
financial market /faɪˌnænʃəl ˈmɑːkɪt/ 46
financial performance /faɪˌnænʃəl pəˈfɔːməns/ 38
financial reporting /faɪˌnænʃəl rɪˈpɔːtɪŋ/ 38
Financial Reporting Council (FRC) /faɪˌnænʃəl rɪˈpɔːtɪŋ ˌkaʊnsəl/ 45
financial results /faɪˈnænʃəl rɪˈzʌlts/ 38
financial statement /faɪˌnænʃəl ˈsteɪtmənt/ 38
financial year /faɪˌnænʃəl ˈjɪə/ 38
financier /faɪˈnænsiə/ 38
financing /ˈfaɪnænsɪŋ/ 38
finished goods /ˌfɪnɪʃt ˈgʊdz/ 30, 40
firewall /ˈfaɪəwɔːl/ 35
first mover advantage /fɜːst ˌmuːvər ədˈvɑːntɪdʒ/ 20
fit for purpose /ˌfɪt fə ˈpɜːpəs/ 13
fit intervention /fɪt ˌɪntəˈvenʃən/ 7
fixed assets /fɪkst ˈæsets/ 40
flagship brand /ˈflægʃɪp brænd/ 27
flexibility /ˌfleksɪˈbɪləti/ 1
flexible job market /ˌfleksɪbəl ˈdʒɒb ˌmɑːkɪt/ 5
flexible working /ˌfleksɪbəl ˈwɜːkɪŋ/ 5
flood /flʌd/ 51, 58
fluent /ˈfluːənt/ 63
focus (n) /ˈfəʊkəs/ 18
focus group /ˈfəʊkəs gruːp/ 20, 24
follower /ˈfɒləʊə/ 20
forecast /ˈfɔːkɑːst/ 21
foreign currency reserves /ˌfɒrɪn ˈkʌrənsi rɪˌzɜːvz/ 57
foreign direct investment (FDI) /ˌfɒrɪn dɪˌrekt ɪnˈvestmənt/ 55
foreign exchange crisis /ˌfɒrɪn ɪksˈtʃeɪndʒ ˌkraɪsɪs/ 55
forming /ˈfɔːmɪŋ/ 9
formulate strategy /ˌfɔːmjəleɪt ˈstrætədʒi/ 16
forum /ˈfɔːrəm/ 33, 34
forward flow /fɔːwəd ˈfləʊ/ 30
fossil fuel /ˈfɒsəl fjuːəl/ 51
foster creativity /ˌfɒstə kriːeɪˈtɪvəti/ 20
foster innovation /ˌfɒstə ˌɪnəˈveɪʃən/ 20
four Cs /fɔː ˈsiːz/ 23
four Ps /fɔː ˈpiːz/ 22
fragmented /frægˈmentɪd/ 19
framework /ˈfreɪmwɜːk/ 14

fraud /frɔːd/ 45
FRC (Financial Reporting Council) /ˌefɑːˈsiː/ 45
free movement of capital /friː ˈmuːvmənt əv ˈkæpɪtəl/ 54
free trade /friː ˈtreɪd/ 54, 56
free trade areas /friː treɪd ˈeəriəz/ 56
freelance /ˈfriːlɑːns/ 4
freelancer /ˈfriːlɑːnsə/ 4
from cradle to grave /frəm ˈkreɪdəl tə greɪv/ 30
front office outsourcing /frʌnt ˌɒfɪs ˈaʊtsɔːsɪŋ/ 31
FTSE4Good /ˈfʊtsifəˈgʊd/ 53
full contribution /fʊl ˌkɒntrɪˈbjuːʃən/ 61
full report and accounts /fʊl rɪˈpɔːt ənd əˈkaʊnts/ 38
full-blown economic crisis /ˌfʊlˈbləʊn ˌiːkəˈnɒmɪk ˌkraɪsɪs/ 47
functional benchmarking /ˌfʌŋʃənəl ˈbentʃmɑːkɪŋ/ 15
functions /ˈfʌŋkʃənz/ 30
futurist /ˈfjuːtʃərɪst/ 21
futurologist /ˌfjuːtʃəˈrɒlədʒɪst/ 21
futurology /ˌfjuːtʃəˈrɒlədʒi/ 21

GAAP (Generally Accepted Accounting Principles) /ˌdʒiːeɪeɪˈpiː/ 45
GAFTA (Greater Arab Free Trade Area) /ˈgæftə/ 56
galloping inflation /ˈgæləpɪŋ ɪnˈfleɪʃən/ 47
GDP (gross domestic product) /ˌdʒiːdiːˈpiː/ 54
GDP growth /dʒiːdiːˌpi ˈgrəʊθ/ 57
GDP per capita /dʒiːdiːˌpi pɜː ˈkæpɪtə/ 54, 57
gearing /ˈgɪərɪŋ/ 43
gender stereotyping /ˈdʒendə ˈsteriəʊtaɪpɪŋ/ 11
general expenses /ˌdʒenərəl ɪkˈspentsɪz/ 39
Generally Accepted Accounting Principles (GAAP) /ˌdʒenərəli əkˌseptɪd əˈkaʊntɪŋ ˌprɪnsəpəlz/ 45
generate /ˈdʒenəreɪt/ 42
generate cash /ˌdʒenəreɪt ˈkæʃ/ 43
generate cashflow /ˌdʒenəreɪt ˈkæʃfləʊ/ 43
generate revenue /ˌdʒenəreɪt ˈrevənjuː/ 33, 37
generic brand /dʒəˌnerɪk ˈbrænd/ 27
generic standards /dʒəˌnerɪk ˈstændədz/ 13
generous /ˈdʒenərəs/ 58
gesture /ˈdʒestʃə/ 60

get off the point /get ɒf ðə ˈpɔɪnt/ 61
get on well with /get ɒn ˈwel wɪð/ 1
give notice /gɪv ˈnəʊtɪs/ 5
glass ceiling /glɑːs ˈsiːlɪŋ/ 11, 60
global brand /ˈgləʊbəl brænd/ 28
global economy /ˌgləʊbəl ɪˈkɒnəmi/ 54
global ecosystem /ˌgləʊbəl ˈiːkəʊˌsɪstəm/ 59
global offerings /ˌgləʊbəl ˈɒfərɪŋz/ 28
Global Positioning System (GPS) /ˌgləʊbəl pəˈzɪʃənɪŋ ˌsɪstəm/ 32
global temperatures /ˌgləʊbəl ˈtemprətʃəz/ 51
global warming /ˌgləʊbəl ˈwɔːmɪŋ/ 50, 51
globalization /ˌgləʊbəlaɪˈzeɪʃən/ 54
globalize /ˈgləʊbəlaɪz/ 31
glocalization /ˌgləʊkəlaɪˈzeɪʃən/ 28
glut /glʌt/ 56
GNI (gross national income) /ˌdʒiːenˈaɪ/ 54
GNP (gross national product) /ˌdʒiːenˈpiː/ 54
good corporate governance /ˌgʊd ˌkɔːpərət ˈgʌvənəns/ 52, 53
good practice /gʊd ˈpræktɪs/ 14
goodwill /gʊdˈwɪl/ 40
governance and stakeholder /ˈgʌvənəns ən ˈsteɪkˌhəʊldə/ 53
governance body /ˈgʌvənəns ˌbɒdi/ 52
government spending /ˌgʌvənmənt ˈspendɪŋ/ 46
GPS (Global Positioning System) /ˌdʒiːpiːˈes/ 32
Greater Arab Free Trade Area (GAFTA) /ˌgreɪtə ærəb friː treɪd ˈeəriə/ 56
green issues /ˈgriːn ˌɪʃuːz/ 50
greenhouse effect /ˈgriːnhaʊs ɪˌfekt/ 51
greenhouse gases /ˌgriːnhaʊs ˈgæsɪz/ 51
greenwash /ˈgriːnwɒʃ/ 50
gross domestic product (GDP) /ˌgrəʊs dəˌmestɪk ˈprɒdʌkt/ 54
gross national income (GNI) /ˌgrəʊs ˌnæʃənəl ˈɪŋkʌm/ 54
gross national product (GNP) /ˌgrəʊs ˌnæʃənəl ˈprɒdʌkt/ 54
ground rules /graʊnd ruːlz/ 61
growers /ˈgrəʊəz/ 56
growth shares /ˈgrəʊθ ʃeəz/ 44

hacker /ˈhækə/ 35
hand over /hænd ˈəʊvə/ 62
handheld /ˈhændheld/ 32
handling /ˈhændlɪŋ/ 29
hands-on /ˌhænzˈɒn/ 1

hands-on experience /ˈhænz,ɒn ɪkˈspɪərɪəns/ 34
hard skills /hɑːd ˈskɪlz/ 10
harm competition /ˈhɑːm kɒmpəˈtɪʃən/ 17
harmony /ˈhɑːməni/ 61
health and safety record /helθ ən ˈseɪfti ,rekɔːd/ 49
heavily indebted /,hevɪli ɪnˈdetɪd/ 43
Heavily Indebted Poor Countries (HIPCs) /,hevɪli ɪn,detɪd ˈpɔː ,kʌntriz/ 55
heavily leveraged /,hevɪli ˈliːvərɪdʒd/ 43
heavy workload /,hevi ˈwɜːkləʊd/ 6
helpful /ˈhelpfəl/ 22
hierarchical /,haɪəˈrɑːkɪkəl/ 3
hierarchy /ˈhaɪərɑːki/ 3
high entry barriers /haɪ ,entri ˈbæriəz/ 19
high flier /haɪ ˈflaɪə/ 8
higher-priced goods /,haɪəpraɪst ˈɡʊdz/ 57
highly geared /,haɪli ˈɡɪəd/ 43
highly informed /,haɪli ɪnˈfɔːmd/ 22
highly leveraged /ˈhaɪli ˈliːvərɪdʒd/ 43
highly motivated /,haɪli ˈməʊtɪveɪtɪd/ 22
high-risk /,haɪˈrɪsk/ 47
hijack /ˈhaɪdʒæk/ 35
HIPCs (heavily indebted poor countries) /,eitʃaɪpiːˈsiːs/ 55
hire and fire /haɪər ən ˈfaɪə/ 5
hit it off with /hɪt ɪt ˈɒf wɪð/ 1
hits /hɪts/ 33
hold on a database /həʊld ɒn ə ˈdeɪtəbeɪs/ 26
home–work balance /həʊm wɜːk ˈbæləns/ 6
home–work imbalance /həʊm wɜːk ,ɪmˈbæləns/ 6
homeworker /ˈhəʊm,wɜːkə/ 6
homogenous /həˈmɒdʒənəs/ 28
hospitality /,hɒspɪˈtæləti/ 60
hotspot /ˈhɒtspɒt/ 32
house prices /ˈhaʊs praɪsɪz/ 46
household waste /,haʊshəʊld ˈweɪst/ 50
housing bubble /ˈhaʊzɪŋ ,bʌbəl/ 47
housing market /ˈhaʊzɪŋ ,mɑːkɪt/ 46
however /haʊˈevə/ 66
human /ˈhjuːmən/ 53
human resources /,hjuːmən rɪˈzɔːsɪz/ 13
humanitarian aid /hjuː,mænɪteərɪən ˈeɪd/ 58
hydrocarbons /,haɪdrəʊˈkɑːbənz/ 57

hygiene factors /ˈhaɪdʒiːn ˈfæktəz/ 3

IAS (International Accounting Standards) /,aɪeɪˈes/ 45
identity theft /aɪˈdentəti θeft/ 35
idle /ˈaɪdəl/ 29
illegal downloading /ɪ,liːɡəl daʊnˈləʊdɪŋ/ 37
image /ˈɪmɪdʒ/ 21
IMF (International Monetary Fund) /,aɪemˈef/ 55
impact on society /,ɪmpækt ɒn səˈsaɪəti/ 14
implementation /,ɪmplɪmenˈteɪʃən/ 16
implementer /ˈɪmplɪ,mentə/ 9
impose /ɪmˈpəʊz/ 2
improviser /ˈɪmprəvaɪzə/ 60
impulse /ˈɪmpʌls/ 10
in contact with /ɪn ˈkɒntækt wɪð/ 22
in employment /ɪn ɪmˈplɔɪmənt/ 46
incentive /ɪnˈsentɪv/ 52
incineration /ɪn,sɪnərˈeɪʃən/ 59
incinerator /ɪnˈsɪnəreɪtə/ 59
inclusion /ɪnˈkluːʒən/ 11
income distribution /,ɪŋkʌm dɪstrɪˈbjuːʃən/ 54
income leverage /ˈɪŋkʌm ,liːvərɪdʒ/ 43
income per head /,ɪŋkʌm pə ˈhed/ 57
income shares /ˈɪŋkʌm ʃeəz/ 44
income statement /ˈɪŋkʌm ,steɪtmənt/ 39
indebted /ɪnˈdetɪd/ 43
independence /,ɪndɪˈpendəns/ 6
independent board member /ɪndɪ,pendənt ˈbɔːd ,membə/ 52
index /ˈɪndeks/ 53
indirect export /ɪndɪ,rekt ˈekspɔːt/ 28
individual (n) /,ɪndɪˈvɪdʒuəl/ 9
induction /ɪnˈdʌkʃən/ 7
industrial revolution /ɪn,dʌstrɪəl revəˈluːʃən/ 51
industrial waste /ɪn,dʌstrɪəl ˈweɪst/ 50
industrialization /ɪn,dʌstrɪəlaɪˈzeɪʃən/ 54
industrialized country /ɪn,dʌstrɪəlaɪzd ˈkʌntri/ 54
industry /ˈɪndəstri/ 18
industry competitor /,ɪndəstri kəmˈpetɪtə/ 18
infect /ɪnˈfekt/ 35
infiltrate /ˈɪnfɪltreɪt/ 35
inflation /ɪnˈfleɪʃən/ 46
inflexibility /ɪn,fleksəˈbɪləti/ 5
inflows /ˈɪnfləʊz/ 55
influence /ˈɪnfluəns/ 10

information /,ɪnfəˈmeɪʃən/ 45
information overload /ɪnfə,meɪʃən ˈəʊvələʊd/ 34
information sharing /ɪnfəˈmeɪʃən ,ʃeərɪŋ/ 33
information technology (IT) outsourcing /,ɪnfəˈmeɪʃən tekˈnɒlədʒi ˈaʊtsɔːsɪŋ/ 31
infrastructure /ˈɪnfrə,strʌktʃə/ 36, 51, 58
infrastructure project /ˈɪnfrəstrʌktʃə ,prɒdʒekt/ 55
infringe copyright /ɪnˈfrɪndʒ ˈkɒpiraɪt/ 37
inhibit competition /ɪnˈhɪbɪt kɒmpəˈtɪʃən/ 17
in-house /,ɪnˈhaʊs/ 4, 19, 31, 63
initiative /ɪˈnɪʃətɪv/ 10
innovation /,ɪnəˈveɪʃən/ 34
innovator /ˈɪnəveɪtə/ 20
input /ˈɪnpʊt/ 13
inquire /ɪnˈkwaɪə/ 64
inquiry /ɪnˈkwaɪəri/ 64
instability /,ɪnstəˈbɪləti/ 55
install /ɪnˈstɔːl/ 35
instant messaging /,ɪnstənt ˈmesɪdʒɪŋ/ 33
institutional investor /ɪnstɪ,tjuːʃənəl ɪnˈvestə/ 53
intangible /ɪnˈtændʒəbəl/ 22
intangible assets /ɪn,tændʒəbəl ˈæsets/ 40
integrate into /ˈɪntɪɡreɪt ,ɪntə/ 29
integrity /ɪnˈteɡrəti/ 10, 48
intellectual capital /ɪntə,lektjuəl ˈkæpɪtəl/ 34
intellectual property /ɪntə,lektjuəl ˈprɒpəti/ 37
intellectually stimulating /,ɪntəˈlektjuəli stɪmjəleɪtɪŋ/ 63
intelligence quotient (IQ) /ɪnˈtelɪdʒəns ,kwəʊʃənt/ 10
intense competition /ɪn,tens kɒmpəˈtɪʃən/ 17
intensify /ɪnˈtensɪfaɪ/ 17
interact /ˈɪntərækt/ 25
interactive /,ɪntərˈæktɪv/ 33
interdependence /,ɪntədɪˈpendəns/ 54
interest /ˈɪntrəst/ 25, 38
interest cover /ˈɪntrəst ,kʌvə/ 43
interest payable /,ɪntrəst ˈpeɪəbəl/ 39
interest payment /ˈɪntrəst ,peɪmənt/ 41
interest rate /ˈɪntrəst ,reɪt/ 46, 47
interim results /,ɪntərɪm rɪˈzʌlts/ 38
interims /ˈɪntərɪmz/ 38
intermediate technology /ɪntə,miːdiət tekˈnɒlədʒi/ 58
internal benchmarking /ɪn,tɜːnəl ˈbentʃmɑːkɪŋ/ 15

internal factor /ɪn,tɜːnəl 'fæktə/ 18

internal social networking site /ɪn,tɜːnəl ,səʊʃəl 'netwɜːkɪŋ saɪt/ 33

internalization /ɪn,tɜːnəlaɪ'zeɪʃən/ 34

International Accounting Standards (IAS) /ɪntə,næʃənəl ə'kaʊntɪŋ ,stændədz/ 45

International Monetary Fund (IMF) /ɪntə,næʃənəl 'mʌnɪtəri fʌnd/ 55

International Organization for Standardization /,ɪntə'næʃənəl ,ɔːɡənaɪ'zeɪʃən fə ,stændədaɪ'zeɪʃən/ 13

International Organization of Securities Commissions (IOSCO) /,ɪntə'næʃənəl ,ɔːɡənaɪ'zeɪʃən əv sɪ'kjʊərətiz kə'mɪʃənz/ 45

International Standards /ɪntə,næʃənəl 'stændədz/ 13

internet ratings agency /,ɪntənet 'reɪtɪŋz ,eɪdʒəntsi/ 33

internet security /,ɪntənet sɪ'kjʊərəti/ 33, 35

internet TV /,ɪntənet tiː'viː/ 32

internet usage /'ɪntənet ,juːsɪdʒ/ 25

interoperability /ɪntər,ɒpərə'bɪlɪti/ 33

invade a market /ɪn,veɪd ə 'mɑːkɪt/ 16

inventory /'ɪnvəntri/ 30

investment fund /ɪn'vestmənt fʌnd/ 53

investment ratio /ɪn'vestmənt ,reɪʃiəʊ/ 43

Investors in People /ɪn,vestəz ɪn 'piːpəl/ 14

Investors in People Standard /ɪn,vestəz ɪn 'piːpəl ,stændəd/ 14

invoicing /'ɪnvɔɪsɪŋ/ 31

involved /ɪn'vɒlvd/ 23

involvement /ɪn'vɒlvmənt/ 23

IOSCO (International Organization of Securities Commissions) /,aɪɒsk'əʊ/ 45

IQ (intelligence quotient) /aɪ'kjuː/ 10

irreversible environmental damage /ɪrɪ,vɜːsəbəl ɪnvaɪrən,mentəl 'dæmɪdʒ/ 59

isolated /'aɪsəleɪtɪd/ 6

issue /'ɪʃuː/ 38

IT (information technology) outsourcing /aɪ'tiː 'aʊtsɔːsɪŋ/ 31

iterative /'ɪtərətɪv/ 21

job creation /dʒɒb kri'eɪʃən/ 5

job flexibility /,dʒɒb fleksɪ'bɪləti/ 5

job for life /dʒɒb fə 'laɪf/ 4

job insecurity /dʒɒb ,ɪnsɪ'kjʊərəti/ 5

job protection /,dʒɒb prə'tekʃən/ 5

job rotation /,dʒɒb rə'teɪʃən/ 7

job satisfaction /,dʒɒb sætɪs'fækʃən/ 1, 2

job sharing /'dʒɒb ,ʃeərɪŋ/ 5

jobs market /'dʒɒbz ,mɑːkɪt/ 46

joint venture /,dʒɔɪnt 'ventʃə/ 28

just-in-time /dʒʌstɪntaɪm/ 29

kaizen /'kaɪzen/ 13

key buyer /kiː 'baɪə/ 36

key indicator /kiː 'ɪndɪkeɪtə/ 46

key people /kiː 'piːpəl/ 8

key player /kiː 'pleɪə/ 17, 19

killer app /,kɪlər 'æp/ 33

knowledge base /'nɒlɪdʒ beɪs/ 34

knowledge creation /,nɒlɪdʒ kri'eɪʃən/ 34

knowledge process outsourcing (KPO) /,nɒlɪdʒ ,prəʊses 'aʊtsɔːsɪŋ/ 31

knowledge worker /'nɒlɪdʒ ,wɜːkə/ 31, 43

kowtow /kaʊ'taʊ/ 60

KPO (knowledge process outsourcing) /,keɪpiː'əʊ/ 31

Kyoto protocol /,kjəʊtəʊ 'prəʊtəkɒl/ 51

labour costs /'leɪbə kɒsts/ 39

labour exploitation /,leɪbər eksplɔɪ'teɪʃən/ 49

labour standards /,leɪbə 'stændədz/ 49

lack of focus /læk əv 'fəʊkəs/ 61

lack of management support /læk əv ,mænɪdʒməntsə'pɔːt/ 6

latest trend /,leɪtɪst 'trend/ 24

law enforcement agency /lɔː ɪn'fɔːsmənt ,eɪdʒənsi/ 35

LDC (less-developed country) /,eldiː'siː/ 54

leadership /'liːdəʃɪp/ 14, 52

learn by doing /,lɜːn baɪ 'duːɪŋ/ 34

learning organization /'lɜːnɪŋ ,ɔːɡənaɪ,zeɪʃən/ 34

least developed country /liːst dɪ,veləpt 'kʌntri/ 57

leisure time /'leʒə taɪm/ 60

lender /'lendə/ 38

lending /'lendɪŋ/ 38

less-developed country (LDC) /lesdɪ,veləpt 'kʌntri/ 54

let (sb) go /,let 'ɡəʊ/ 5

leverage /'liːvərɪdʒ/ 43

liabilities /,laɪə'bɪlətiz/ 41

liberalization /,lɪbərəlaɪ'zeɪʃən/ 55

license (v) /'laɪsəns/ 28, 37

licensing agreement /'laɪsənsɪŋ ə,ɡriːmənt/ 28

licensing arrangement /'laɪsənsɪŋ ə,reɪndʒmənt/ 28

licensing deal /'laɪsənsɪŋ diːl/ 28

licensing pact /'laɪsənsɪŋ pækt/ 28

lifelong learning /,laɪflɒŋ 'lɜːnɪŋ/ 4

lifestyle /'laɪfstaɪl/ 25

light-touch regulation /laɪt,tʌtʃ reɡjə'leɪʃən/ 47

living standards /'lɪvɪŋ ,stændədz/ 54, 59

loaded /'ləʊdɪd/ 32

loan /ləʊn/ 38, 47

logging /'lɒɡɪŋ/ 50

logistic /lə'dʒɪstɪk/ 30

logistical /lə'dʒɪstɪkəl/ 30

logistical challenge /lə,dʒɪstɪkəl 'tʃælɪndʒ/ 30

logistical difficulty /lə,dʒɪstɪkəl 'dɪfɪkəlti/ 30

logistical hurdle /lə,dʒɪstɪkəl 'hɜːdəl/ 30

logistical nightmare /lə,dʒɪstɪkəl 'naɪtmeə/ 30

logistical obstacle /lə,dʒɪstɪkəl 'ɒbstəkəl/ 30

logistical problem /lə,dʒɪstɪkəl 'prɒbləm/ 30

logistician /lɒdʒɪs'tɪʃən/ 30

logistics /lə'dʒɪstɪks/ 29, 30

logistics outsourcing /lə,dʒɪstɪks 'aʊtsɔːsɪŋ/ 31

long hours /lɒŋ 'aʊəz/ 1

long-term bank bonds /lɒŋ,tɜːm 'bæŋk bɒndz/ 41

long-term bank loans /lɒŋ,tɜːm 'bæŋk ləʊnz/ 41

long-term interests /lɒŋ,tɜːm 'ɪntrəsts/ 59

long-term liabilities /lɒŋ,tɜːm laɪə'bɪlətiz/ 41

look and feel /lʊk ən fiːl/ 12

loss /lɒs/ 39

lost customer analysis /lɒst ,kʌstəmə ə'næləsɪs/ 23

low entry barriers /ləʊ 'entri ,bæriəz/ 19

loyalty card /'lɔɪəlti kɑːd/ 19, 23, 25, 26

maintain a competitive advantage /meɪn'teɪn ə kəm'petɪtɪv əd'vɑːntɪdʒ/ 18

maintain brands /meɪn'teɪn brændz/ 27

make forecasts /,meɪk 'fɔːkɑːsts/ 21

make or buy decision /meɪk ɔː baɪ dɪ'sɪʒən/ 19

make (sb) redundant /meɪk rɪ'dʌndənt/ 4, 5

make up /meɪk ˈʌp/ 65
maker /ˈmeɪkə/ 25
malicious software /məˌlɪʃəs ˈsɒfweə/ 35
mall intercept /mɔːl ˈɪntəsept/ 24
malware /ˈmælweə/ 35
management board /ˈmænɪdʒmənt bɔːd/ 52
management level /ˈmænɪdʒmənt ˌlevəl/ 3
management support /ˌmænɪdʒmənt səˈpɔːt/ 6
manufacture /ˌmænjəˈfæktʃə/ 28
manufacturing capacity /mænjəˈfæktʃərɪŋ kəˌpæsəti/ 29
manufacturing jobs /mænjəˈfæktʃərɪŋ ˌdʒɒbz/ 29
manufacturing operations /mænjəˈfæktʃərɪŋ ɒpəˌreɪʃənz/ 29
manufacturing plant /mænjəˈfæktʃərɪŋ ˌplɑːnt/ 29
manufacturing process /mænjəˈfæktʃərɪŋ ˌprəʊses/ 29
manufacturing productivity /mænjəˈfæktʃərɪŋ prɒdʌkˌtɪvəti/ 29
manufacturing sector /mænjəˈfæktʃərɪŋ ˌsektə/ 29
manufacturing-based economy /mænjəˌfæktʃərɪŋbeɪst ɪˈkɒnəmi/ 57
mapping /ˈmæpɪŋ/ 32
market /ˈmɑːkɪt/ 24
market intelligence /ˌmɑːkɪt ɪnˈtelɪdʒəns/ 24
market research /ˌmɑːkɪt rɪˈsɜːtʃ/ 24
market research firm /ˌmɑːkɪt rɪˈsɜːtʃ fɜːm/ 24
market share /ˈmɑːkɪt ʃeə/ 19
market value /ˈmɑːkɪt ˈvæljuː/ 40
marketing /ˈmɑːkɪtɪŋ/ 31
marketing mix /ˈmɑːkɪtɪŋ mɪks/ 22, 24
marketing plan /ˈmɑːkɪtɪŋ plæn/ 24
marketing research /ˈmɑːkɪtɪŋ rɪˌsɜːtʃ/ 24
marketing research firm /ˈmɑːkɪtɪŋ rɪˈsɜːtʃ fɜːm/ 24
mass collaboration /ˌmæs kəlæbəˈreɪʃən/ 34
mass customization /ˌmæs kʌstəmaɪˈzeɪʃən/ 26
materials /məˈtɪəriəlz/ 13
maternity leave /məˈtɜːnəti liːv/ 5
mature /məˈtjʊə/ 20
maximize shareholder value /ˌmæksɪmaɪz ˌʃeəhəʊldə ˈvæljuː/ 44
measurable objective /ˌmeʒərəbəl əbˈdʒektɪv/ 13

meet expectations /miːt ˌekspekˈteɪʃənz/ 23
mentee /menˈtiː/ 8
mentor /ˈmentɔː/ 8
mentoring /ˈmentərɪŋ/ 8
mentorship /ˈmentəʃɪp/ 8
Mercosur /ˈmɜːkəʊsuːə/ 56
merge /mɜːdʒ/ 19
mergers and acquisitions /ˈmɜːdʒəz ənd ˌækwɪˈzɪʃənz/ 19
metadata /ˈmetədeɪtə/ 34
middle class /ˌmɪdəl ˈklɑːs/ 57
middle-income country /ˌmɪdəlˌɪŋkʌm ˈkʌntri/ 54
middlemen /ˈmɪdəlmen/ 56
Millennium Development Goals /mɪˌleniəm dɪˈveləpmənt gəʊlz/ 55
mini-Delphi /ˌmɪniˈdelfi/ 21
minimal supervision /ˌmɪnɪməl suːpəˈvɪʒən/ 63
minor player /ˌmaɪnə ˈpleɪə/ 17
misleading information /mɪsˈliːdɪŋ ˌɪnfəˈmeɪʃən/ 45
mission statement /ˌmɪʃən ˈsteɪtmənt/ 16
mission-critical /ˌmɪʃənˈkrɪtɪkəl/ 8
mobile device /ˈməʊbaɪl dɪˌvaɪs/ 32
mobility /məˈbɪləti/ 7
model /ˈmɒdəl/ 14
moderator /ˈmɒdəreɪtə/ 24
modest /ˈmɒdɪst/ 60
monitor–evaluator /ˌmɒnɪtər ɪˈvæljuːeɪtə/ 9
monopoly /məˈnɒpəli/ 17
Moore's law /ˈmɔːz lɔː/ 32
morale /məˈrɑːl/ 2
moreover /mɔːrˈəʊvə/ 66
mortgage /ˈmɔːgɪdʒ/ 46, 47
mortgage bubble /ˈmɔːgɪdʒ ˌbʌbəl/ 47
motivation /ˌməʊtɪˈveɪʃən/ 2, 10
motivator factor /ˈməʊtɪveɪtə ˌfæktə/ 3
mourning /ˈmɔːnɪŋ/ 9
multitasker /ˈmʌltiˈtɑːskə/ 60, 63
mystery shopper /ˌmɪstəri ˈʃɒpə/ 24

N-11 (Next Eleven) /enɪˈlevən/ 57
NAFTA (North American Free Trade Area) /ˈnæftə/ 56
nationalization of assets /næʃənəlaɪˌzeɪʃən əv ˈæsets/ 21
native speaker /ˈneɪtɪv ˈspiːkə/ 63
natural disaster /ˌnætʃərəl dɪˈzɑːstə/ 58
natural resources /ˈnætʃərəl rɪˈzɔːsɪz/ 57
navigate /ˈnævɪgeɪt/ 32
nervous breakdown /ˌnɜːvəs ˈbreɪkdaʊn/ 6

net cash position /net ˈkæʃ pəˌzɪʃən/ 42
net cashflow from financing activities /ˌnet ˈkæʃfləʊ frɒm ˈfaɪnænsɪŋ ækˈtɪvətiz/ 42
net cashflow from investment activities /ˌnet kæʃˈfləʊ frɒm ɪnˈvestmənt ækˌtɪvətiz/ 42
net cashflow from operations /ˌnet kæʃˈfləʊ frɒm ɒpərˈeɪʃənz/ 42
net income /net ˈɪŋkʌm/ 43
netbook /ˈnetbʊk/ 32
network /ˈnetwɜːk/ 34
networking /ˈnetwɜːkɪŋ/ 62
nevertheless /ˌnevəðəˈles/ 66
new product development /njuː ˈprɒdʌkt dɪˌveləpmənt/ 20
new technology /njuː tekˈnɒlədʒi/ 59
newly industrialized country (NIC) /ˌnjuːli ɪnˌdʌstriəlaɪzd ˈkʌntri/ 54, 57
Next Eleven (N-11) /nekst ɪˈlevən/ 57
NGO (non-government organization) /ˌendʒiːˈəʊ/ 58
NIC (newly industrialized country) /ˌenaɪˈsiː/ 54, 57
niche /niːʃ/ 18
NINJA mortgage /ˌnɪndʒə ˈmɔːgɪdʒ/ 47
No two days are the same. /nəʊ tuː deɪz ɑː ðə seɪm/ 1
non-authoritarian /ˌnɒnɔːˌθɒrɪˈteəriən/ 10
non-core /ˌnɒnˈkɔː/ 31
non-core business /nɒnkɔː ˈbɪznɪs/ 19
non-dictatorial /ˌnɒndɪktəˈtɔːriəl/ 10
non-exec /ˌnɒnɪgˈzek/ 52
non-executive director /nɒnɪgˌzekjətɪv dɪˈrektə/ 52
non-government organization (NGO) /nɒnˌgʌvənmənt ɔːgənaɪˈzeɪʃən/ 58
non-native /nɒnˈneɪtɪv/ 60
non-polluting energy source /nɒnpəˌluːtɪŋ ˈenədʒi sɔːs/ 59
norming /ˈnɔːmɪŋ/ 9
North /nɔːθ/ 54
North American Free Trade Area (NAFTA) /ˌnɔːθ əˈmerɪkən friː treɪd ˈeəriə/ 56
nuclear energy /ˌnjuːkliər ˈenədʒi/ 59

objective /əbˈdʒektɪv/ 16
observational approach /ˌɒbzəˈveɪʃənəl əˌprəʊtʃ/ 24
obsolete /ˈɒbsəliːt/ 12, 40
occupation /ˌɒkjəˈpeɪʃən/ 25

ODA (official development assistance) /ˌəʊdiːˈeɪ/ 58

off the point /ɒf ðə ˈpɔɪnt/ 61

offer /ˈɒfə/ 22

offering /ˈɒfərɪŋ/ 22

office politics /ˈɒfɪs ˈpɒlətɪks/ 6

official development assistance (ODA) /əˌfɪʃəl dɪˈveləpmənt əˌsɪstəns/ 58

offset /ˌɒfˈset/ 51

offshore /ˌɒfˈʃɔː/ 31

offshore companies /ˌɒfˈʃɔː ˈkʌmpəniz/ 4

offshore outsourcing /ɒfˌʃɔːr ˈaʊtsɔːsɪŋ/ 31

offshoring /ˌɒfˈʃɔːrɪŋ/ 4, 31, 57

omit the dividend /əˈmɪt ðə ˈdɪvɪdend/ 39

one-to-one marketing /wʌntəˌwʌn ˈmɑːkɪtɪŋ/ 26

online community /ɒnˌlaɪn kəˈmjuːnəti/ 33

online focus group /ɒnˌlaɪn ˈfəʊkəs gruːp/ 24

online music store /ɒnˌlaɪn ˈmjuːzɪk stɔː/ 37

open up a market /ˌəʊpən ʌp ə ˈmɑːkɪt/ 56

open-door policy /əʊpənˌdɔː ˈpɒləsi/ 61

opening /ˈəʊpnɪŋ/ 63

openness of trade and investment policies /ˈəʊpənnəs əv ˈtreɪd ənd ɪnˈvestmənt ˌpɒləsiz/ 57

operate at full capacity /ˌɒpəreɪt ət fʊl kəˈpæsəti/ 29, 43

operate below capacity /ˈɒpəreɪt bɪˌləʊ kəˈpæsəti/ 29

operating performance /ˈɒpəreɪtɪŋ pəˌfɔːməns/ 43

operating profit /ˈɒpəreɪtɪŋ ˌprɒfɪt/ 39

operational /ˌɒpərˈeɪʃənəl/ 24

opinion /əˈpɪnjən/ 25

opportunities /ˌɒpəˈtjuːnətiz/ 18

originality /əˌrɪdʒənˈæləti/ 1

out of work /aʊt əv ˈwɜːk/ 46

outflows /ˈaʊtfləʊz/ 55

outlet /ˈaʊtlet/ 22

outsource /ˈaʊtsɔːs/ 4, 29, 31

outsourcing /ˈaʊtsɔːsɪŋ/ 31

overdraft /ˈəʊvədrɑːft/ 41

overfarming /ˌəʊvəˈfɑːmɪŋ/ 50

overfishing /ˌəʊvəˈfɪʃɪŋ/ 50

overheating /ˌəʊvəˈhiːtɪŋ/ 46

overlap /ˈəʊvəlæp/ 6

over-leveraged /ˌəʊvəˈliːvərɪdʒd/ 43

overload /ˈəʊvələʊd/ 35

overproduction /ˌəʊvəprəˈdʌkʃən/ 56

oversight /ˈəʊvəsaɪt/ 45

overstate /ˌəʊvəˈsteɪt/ 45

overvalued /ˌəʊvəˈvæljuːd/ 38

overworked /ˌəʊvəˈwɜːkt/ 6

owners' equity /ˌəʊnəz ˈekwɪti/ 41

P&L (profit and loss) account /ˌpiːənˈel əˌkaʊnt/ 38, 39

P2P (peer-to-peer) site /ˌpiːtəˈpiː ˈsaɪt/ 37

page views /peɪdʒ vjuːz/ 33

panel of experts /ˌpænəl əv ˈekspɜːts/ 21

paperwork /ˈpeɪpəwɜːk/ 1

parental leave /pəˌrentəl ˈliːv/ 5

participative /pɑːˈtɪsɪpətɪv/ 2

part-time worker /pɑːtˌtaɪm ˈwɜːkə/ 5

pass the dividend /pɑːs ðə ˈdɪvɪdend/ 39

password /ˈpɑːswɜːd/ 35

payoff /ˈpeɪɒf/ 52

payout /ˈpeɪaʊt/ 52

payroll /ˈpeɪrəʊl/ 31

PDA (personal digital assistant) /ˌpiːdiːˈeɪ/ 32

PE ratio (price–earnings ratio) /piːˈiː ˌreɪʃiəʊ/ 44

peak /piːk/ 46

peer relationship /pɪə rɪˈleɪʃənʃɪp/ 3

peer-to-peer (P2P) site /pɪətəˈpɪə saɪt/ 37

people /ˈpiːpəl/ 22

people management /ˈpiːpəl ˌmænɪdʒmənt/ 14

people satisfaction /ˈpiːpəl sætɪsˌfækʃən/ 14

perceived quality /pəˌsiːvd ˈkwɒləti/ 12

performance /pəˈfɔːməns/ 12, 15

performance assessment /pəˈfɔːməns əˌsesmənt/ 7, 8

performance improvement interventions /pəˈfɔːməns ɪmˈpruːvmənt ˌɪntəˈvenʃənz/ 7

performing /pəˈfɔːmɪŋ/ 9

perk /pɜːk/ 1

personal digital assistant (PDA) /ˌpɜːsənəl dɪdʒɪtəl əˈsɪstənt/ 32

personal growth /ˈpɜːsənəl ˈgrəʊθ/ 3

phishing /ˈfɪʃɪŋ/ 35

physical assets /ˌfɪzɪkəl ˈæsets/ 40, 43

physical evidence /ˌfɪzɪkəl ˈevɪdəns/ 22

pick up /pɪk ˈʌp/ 46

pioneer /ˌpaɪəˈnɪə/ 20

piracy /ˈpaɪrəsi/ 37

pirate /ˈpaɪrət/ 37

place /pleɪs/ 22

planning /ˈplænɪŋ/ 14, 16, 60

plant /plɑːnt/ 9

platform /ˈplætfɔːm/ 33

play politics /ˌpleɪ ˈpɒlətɪks/ 6

points (n) /pɔɪnts/ 26

policy /ˈpɒləsi/ 3, 14

policy & strategy /ˈpɒləsi ən ˈstrætədʒi/ 14

political maturity /pəˌlɪtɪkəl məˈtjʊərəti/ 57

pollutant /pəˈluːtənt/ 50

pollute /pəˈluːt/ 50

pollution /pəˈluːʃən/ 48

pompous /ˈpɒmpəs/ 60

portfolio /ˌpɔːtˈfəʊliəʊ/ 4

portfolio theory /pɔːtˈfəʊliəʊ ˌθɪəri/ 19

portfolio worker /pɔːtˈfəʊliəʊ ˌwɜːkə/ 4

position /pəˈzɪʃən/ 25, 27

position brands /pəˌzɪʃən ˈbrændz/ 27

position itself /pəˌzɪʃən ɪtˈself/ 27

position products /pəˌzɪʃən ˈprɒdʌkts/ 27

positioning map /pəˈzɪʃənɪŋ mæp/ 27

positive discrimination /ˌpɒzətɪv dɪskrɪmɪˈneɪʃən/ 11

positive feedback /ˌpɒzətɪv ˈfiːdbæk/ 3

post /pəʊst/ 33

potential entrant /pəˌtenʃəl ˈentrənt/ 18

poverty reduction /ˈpɒvəti rɪˌdʌkʃən/ 55, 58

predict /prɪˈdɪkt/ 21

prediction /prɪˈdɪkʃən/ 21

preliminary results /prɪˌlɪmɪnəri rɪˈzʌlts/ 38

prelims /ˈpriːlɪmz/ 38

present the findings /prɪˈzent ðə ˈfaɪndɪŋz/ 24

pressure group /ˈpreʃə ˌgruːp/ 58

pre-tax profit /ˌpriːtæks ˈprɒfɪt/ 39

price comparison site /praɪs kəmˈpærɪsən saɪt/ 36

price–earnings ratio (PE ratio) /praɪs ˈɜːnɪŋz ˌreɪʃiəʊ/ 44

pricing /ˈpraɪsɪŋ/ 22

primary data /ˌpraɪməri ˈdeɪtə/ 24

principal /ˈprɪnsəpəl/ 38

print money /ˌprɪnt ˈmʌni/ 47

prioritize /praɪˈɒrɪtaɪz/ 63

privacy /ˈprɪvəsi/ 25, 26, 35

private e-marketplace /ˌpraɪvɪt iːˈmɑːkɪtpleɪs/ 36

proactive /ˌprəʊˈæktɪv/ 60

probity /ˈprəʊbəti/ 48

process /ˈprəʊses/ 14, 22

procurement /prəˈkjʊəmənt/ 29

producers /prəˈdjuːsəz/ 56

product /ˈprɒdʌkt/ 22

product positioning /ˌprɒdʌkt pəˈzɪʃənɪŋ/ 27

production line /prəˈdʌkʃən laɪn/ 29

professional development /prəˌfeʃənəl dɪˈveləpmənt/ 4

professional misconduct /prəˌfeʃənəl mɪsˈkɒndʌkt/ 48

profile /ˈprəʊfaɪl/ 25, 33

profit /ˈprɒfɪt/ 38, 39, 43

profit after tax /ˌprɒfɪt ɑːftə ˈtæks/ 39

profit and loss (P&L) account /ˌprɒfɪt ən ˈlɒs əˌkaʊnt/ 38, 39

profit on ordinary activities before tax /ˌprɒfɪt ɒn ˌɔːdənəri ækˌtɪvətiz bɪˌfɔː ˈtæks/ 39

profitability /ˌprɒfɪtəˈbɪlɪti/ 16, 19, 43

profits /ˈprɒfɪts/ 43

promotion /prəˈməʊʃən/ 22

property bubble /ˈprɒpəti ˌbʌbəl/ 47

property market /ˈprɒpəti ˌmɑːkɪt/ 46

proportion /prəˈpɔːʃən/ 50

proprietary /prəˈpraɪətəri/ 34

prosperity /prɒsˈperəti/ 46, 54

prosumer /prəʊˈsjuːmə/ 34

protect /prəˈtekt/ 37

protect brands /prəˈtekt brændz/ 27

protectionism /prəˈtekʃənɪzəm/ 54, 56, 57

proximity /prɒkˈsɪməti/ 60, 62

psychographics /ˌsaɪkəˈgræfɪks/ 25

public relations disaster /ˌpʌblɪk rɪˌleɪʃənz dɪˈzɑːstə/ 21

public relations exercise /ˌpʌblɪk rɪˈleɪʃənz ˌeksəsaɪz/ 49

punctuality /ˌpʌŋktʃuˈæləti/ 60

purchasing /ˈpɜːtʃəsɪŋ/ 31

pure e-tailing /ˌpjʊə ˈiːteɪlɪŋ/ 36

pure-play /ˌpjʊəˈpleɪ/ 36

put ideas into practice /pʊt aɪˌdɪəz ɪntə ˈpræktɪs/ 1

qualifications /ˌkwɒlɪfɪˈkeɪʃənz/ 45

quality management /ˌkwɒləti ˈmænɪdʒmənt/ 13

quality management system /ˌkwɒləti ˈmænɪdʒmənt ˌsɪstəm/ 13

quality of life /ˌkwɒləti əvˈ laɪf/ 6

quarter /ˈkwɔːtə/ 38

questionnaire /ˌkwestʃəˈneə/ 24

quota /ˈkwəʊtə/ 56

R&D (research and development) /ˌɑːrənˈdiː/ 20

race /reɪs/ 11

racial discrimination /ˈreɪʃəl dɪˌskrɪmɪˈneɪʃən/ 11

racism /ˈreɪsɪzəm/ 11

racist /ˈreɪsɪst/ 11

radioactivity /ˌreɪdiəʊækˈtɪvəti/ 50

radio-frequency identification (RFID) /ˌreɪdiəʊˌfriːkwəntsi aɪdentɪfɪˈkeɪʃən/ 25

ramp up /ræmp ˈʌp/ 29

rankings /ˈræŋkɪŋz/ 33

rapport /ræpˈɔː/ 1

ratings agency /ˈreɪtɪŋz ˌeɪdʒəntsi/ 47

raw materials /rɔː məˈtɪəriəlz/ 29, 30, 40, 57

raw talent /rɔː ˈtælənt/ 7

reach a consensus /riːtʃ ə kənˈsensəs/ 21

reach a trough /ˌriːtʃ ə ˈtrɒf/ 46

reafforestation /ˌriːəˌfɒrɪˈsteɪʃən/ 50

real economy /rɪəl ɪˈkɒnəmi/ 47

real estate /ˈrɪəl ɪˌsteɪt/ 46

real estate bubble /ˈrɪəl ɪˌsteɪt ˌbʌbəl/ 47

rebalance /ˌriːˈbælənts/ 6

recession /rɪˈseʃən/ 46

recipient /rɪˈsɪpiənt/ 58

recognition /ˌrekəgˈnɪʃən/ 3

recover /rɪˈkʌvə/ 46

recovery /rɪˈkʌvəri/ 46

recruit the raw talent /rɪˈkruːt ðə ˌrɔː ˈtælənt/ 7

recyclable /ˌriːˈsaɪkləbəl/ 50

recycle /ˌriːˈsaɪkəl/ 50

recycling /ˌriːˈsaɪklɪŋ/ 30, 59

red tape /red ˈteɪp/ 1

redeem against /rɪˈdiːm əˌgenst/ 26

redundancy payment /rɪˈdʌndənsi ˌpeɪmənt/ 5

refurbished /ˌriːˈfɜːbɪʃt/ 30

refurbishment /ˌriːˈfɜːbɪʃmənt/ 30

regulate /ˈregjəleɪt/ 45

regulator /ˈregjəleɪtə/ 45, 47

regulatory power /ˌregjələtəri ˈpaʊə/ 45

regulatory requirements /ˌregjə,lətəri rɪˈkwaɪəmənts/ 13

relationship-oriented /rɪˈleɪʃənʃɪp ˈɔːrientɪd/ 60

release /rɪˈliːs/ 37

reliability /rɪˌlaɪəˈbɪləti/ 12

relocate /ˌriːləˈkeɪt/ 63

remanufacturing /ˌriːmænjəˈfæktʃərɪŋ/ 30

remuneration /rɪˌmjuːnərˈeɪʃən/ 52

remuneration committee /rɪmjuːnərˈeɪʃən kəˌmɪti/ 52

remuneration consultant /rɪmjuːnərˈeɪʃən kənˌsʌltənt/ 52

remuneration package /rɪmjuːnərˈeɪʃən ˌpækɪdʒ/ 52

renewable energy source /rɪˌnjuːəbəl ˈenədʒi ˌsɔːs/ 59

renewable resources /rɪˌnjuːəbəl rɪˈzɔːsɪz/ 50, 59

renewables /rɪˈnjuːəbəlz/ 50, 59

repackage /ˌriːˈpækɪdʒ/ 47

repair /rɪˈpeə/ 30

repatriate /riːˈpætrieɪt/ 55, 56

repeat business /rɪˈpiːt ˈbɪznɪs/ 23

reporting period /rɪˈpɔːtɪŋ ˌpɪəriəd/ 39, 42

represent /ˌreprɪˈzent/ 28, 65

rescue /ˈreskjuː/ 47

research and development (R&D) /rɪˌsɜːtʃ ən dɪˈveləpmənt/ 20

research objectives /rɪˌsɜːtʃ əbˈdʒektɪvz/ 24

researcher /rɪˈsɜːtʃə/ 24

reserves /rɪˈzɜːvz/ 41

resource /rɪˈzɔːs/ 62

resource allocation /rɪˈzɔːs æləˌkeɪʃən/ 16

resource investigator /rɪˈzɔːs ɪnˌvestɪgeɪtə/ 9

resource management /rɪˈzɔːs ˌmænɪdʒmənt/ 13

resources /rɪˈzɔːsɪz/ 14, 16

respond to changes /rɪˌspɒnd tə ˈtʃeɪndʒɪz/ 21

responsibility /rɪˌspɒnsəˈbɪləti/ 2, 3

results /rɪˈzʌlts/ 14

retail /rɪˈteɪl/ 29

retail sales /ˌriːteɪl ˈseɪlz/ 46

retailing /ˈriːteɪlɪŋ/ 29

retain /rɪˈteɪn/ 39

retained earnings /rɪˌteɪnd ˈɜːnɪŋz/ 39, 41, 44

retired /rɪˈtaɪəd/ 30

return on assets (ROA) /rɪˌtɜːn ɒn ˈæsets/ 43

return on equity (ROE) /rɪˌtɜːn ɒn ˈekwɪti/ 43

return on investment (ROI) /rɪˌtɜːn ɒn ɪnˈvestmənt/ 44

reuse /riːˈjuːz/ 30

reverse auction /rɪˌvɜːs ˈɔːkʃən/ 36

reverse engineering /rɪˌvɜːs endʒɪˈnɪərɪŋ/ 15

reverse flow /rɪˌvɜːs ˈfləʊ/ 30

reverse logistics /rɪˌvɜːs ləˈdʒɪstɪks/ 30

reverse mentoring /rɪˌvɜːs ˈmentɔːrɪŋ/ 8

reward (n) /rɪˈwɔːd/ 7

reward (v) /rɪˈwɔːd/ 52

rewarding /rɪˈwɔːdɪŋ/ 1

reworking /ˌriːˈwɜːkɪŋ/ 12

RFID (radio-frequency identification) /ɑːrˌefaɪˈdiː/ 25

right first time /raɪt fɜːst ˈtaɪm/ 12

rights /raɪts/ 28

rigid labour market /ˌrɪdʒɪd ˈleɪbə ˌmɑːkɪt/ 5

rising sea levels /ˌraɪzɪŋ 'siː ˌlevəlz/ 51

risk management /rɪsk 'mænɪdʒmənt/ 21

risks of overheating /rɪsks əv ˌəʊvə'hiːtɪŋ/ 46

ROA (return on assets) /ˌaːrəʊ'eɪ/ 43

ROE (return on equity) /ˌaːrəʊ'iː/ 43

ROI (return on investment) /ˌaːrəʊ'aɪ/ 44

role /rəʊl/ 11

role ambiguity /ˌrəʊl æmbɪ'gjuːəti/ 6

royalties /'rɔɪəltiz/ 37

rural economy /ˌrʊərəl ɪ'kɒnəmi/ 54

salary /'sæləri/ 3

sales /seɪlz/ 39

sales area /'seɪlz ˌeəriə/ 28

sales process /'seɪlz ˌprəʊses/ 22

sales support /'seɪlz sə'pɔːt/ 22

salvage /'sælvɪdʒ/ 30

sample /'saːmpəl/ 24

satellite navigation /'sætəlaɪt nævɪˌgeɪʃən/ 32

satisfaction /ˌsætɪs'fækʃən/ 2

satisfy customer needs /'sætɪsfaɪ 'kʌstəmə ˌniːdz/ 12

SatNav /'sætnæv/ 32

scam /skæm/ 35

scan /skæn/ 25

scenario planning /sɪ'naːriəʊ ˌplænɪŋ/ 21

screenscraper /'skriːnskreɪpə/ 36

search engine /'sɜːtʃ ˌendʒɪn/ 33

seat on the board /siːt ɒn ðə bɔːd/ 52

SEC (Securities and Exchange Commission) /ˌesiː'siː/ 45

secondary data /ˌsekəndəri 'deɪtə/ 24

securities /sɪ'kjʊərətiz/ 24, 40, 47

Securities and Exchange Commission (SEC) /sɪˌkjʊərətiz ənd ɪks'tʃeɪndʒ kəˌmɪʃən/ 45

security /sɪ'kjʊərəti/ 3

security details /sɪ'kjʊərəti ˌdiːteɪlz/ 35

seed money /'siːd ˌmʌni/ 58

segment /'segmənt/ 25

segmentation /'segmənteɪʃən/ 25

segment-of-one marketing /ˌsegmənt əv 'wʌn ˌmaːkɪtɪŋ/ 26

self-awareness /ˌselfə'weərnəs/ 10

self-confident /ˌself'kɒnfɪdənt/ 10

self-regulation /ˌselfregjə'leɪʃən/ 10

self-starter /ˌself'staːtə/ 63

sell on /sel 'ɒn/ 47

sense of achievement /sens əv ə'tʃiːvmənt/ 1

sensitivity /ˌsensɪ'tɪvəti/ 10

separation of roles /ˌsepər'eɪʃən əv rəʊlz/ 52

service (v) /'sɜːvɪs/ 12

serviceability /ˌsɜːvɪsə'bɪləti/ 12

set up on your own /set ʌp ɒn jɔːr əʊn/ 4

setting /'setɪŋ/ 60

severe recession /sɪ'vɪə rɪ'seʃən/ 46

sex discrimination /ˌseks dɪskrɪmɪ'neɪʃən/ 11

sexism /'seksɪzəm/ 11

sexist attitude /ˌseksɪst 'ætɪtjuːd/ 11

shakeout and consolidation /ˌʃeɪkaʊt ən kənsɒlɪ'deɪʃən/ 20

shaper /'ʃeɪpə/ 9

share /ʃeə/ 38

share option /'ʃeər ˌɒpʃən/ 52

share price /'ʃeə ˌpraɪs/ 38

shareholder /'ʃeəˌhəʊldə/ 38

shareholder value /'ʃeəˌhəʊldə 'væljuː/ 44

shareholders' equity /ˌʃeəˌhəʊldəz 'ekwɪti/ 41, 43

shareholders' funds /ˌʃeəhəʊldəz 'fʌndz/ 41

shares outstanding /'ʃeəz aʊtˌstændɪŋ/ 44

sharpen /'ʃaːpən/ 17

shipping costs /'ʃɪpɪŋ kɒsts/ 54

shop around /'ʃɒp əraʊnd/ 36

short-term profit /ʃɔːtˌtɜːm 'prɒfɪt/ 59

shrink /ʃrɪŋk/ 46

sick pay /'sɪk peɪ/ 5

signs of overheating /ˌsaɪnz əv ˌəʊvə'hiːtɪŋ/ 46

silence /'saɪləns/ 60

silicon chip /'sɪlɪkən tʃɪp/ 29

sincere /sɪn'sɪə/ 60

situation of use /ˌsɪtju'eɪʃən əv juːs/ 25

Six Sigma quality /sɪks ˌsɪgmə 'kwɒləti/ 15

skip the dividend /skɪp ðə 'dɪvɪdend/ 39

skunk works /'skʌŋk ˌwɜːks/ 20

slowdown /'sləʊdaʊn/ 46

slump /slʌmp/ 46

smallholders /'smɔːlhəʊldəz/ 56

snoop into /snuːp 'ɪntuː/ 35

social and economic environment /ˌsəʊʃəl ənd ˌiːkə'nɒmɪk ɪn'vaɪrənmənt/ 21

social audit /ˌsəʊʃəl 'ɔːdɪt/ 49

social changes /ˌsəʊʃəl 'tʃeɪndʒɪz/ 11

social charges /ˌsəʊʃəl 'tʃaːdʒɪz/ 5

social class /ˌsəʊʃəl 'klaːs/ 25

social issues /ˌsəʊʃəl 'ɪʃuːz/ 49

social justice /ˌsəʊʃəl 'dʒʌstɪs/ 49

social networking /ˌsəʊʃəl 'netwɜːkɪŋ/ 33

social performance /ˌsəʊʃəl pə'fɔːməns/ 49

social program /ˌsəʊʃəl 'prəʊgræm/ 49

social reporting /ˌsəʊʃəl rɪ'pɔːtɪŋ/ 49

social responsibility /ˌsəʊʃəl rɪspɒnsə'bɪləti/ 21, 49

social skills /ˌsəʊʃəl 'skɪlz/ 10

social value /ˌsəʊʃəl 'væljuː/ 59

social welfare /ˌsəʊʃəl 'welfeə/ 49

socialization /ˌsəʊʃəlaɪ'zeɪʃən/ 34

socialize /'səʊʃəlaɪz/ 33

socially responsible /ˌsəʊʃəli rɪ'spɒnsəbəl/ 49

socially responsible investment (SRI) /ˌsəʊʃəli rɪˌspɒnsəbəl ɪn'vestmənt/ 53

soft landing /sɒft 'lændɪŋ/ 46

soft skills /sɒft 'skɪlz/ 10

solar power /'səʊlə paʊə/ 50, 59

someone breathe down your neck /'sʌmwʌn briːð daʊn jɔː nek/ 1

South /saʊθ/ 54

spare capacity /speə kə'pæsəti/ 43

specialized forum /'speʃəlaɪzd 'fɔːrəm/ 33

specification /ˌspesɪfɪ'keɪʃən/ 26

speculative bubble /ˌspekjələtɪv 'bʌbəl/ 47

spot the raw talent /spɒt ðə rɔː 'tælənt/ 7

spyware /'spaɪweə/ 35

SRI (socially responsible investment) /ˌesaːr'aɪ/ 53

staffing /'staːfɪŋ/ 7

stagflation /stæg'fleɪʃən/ 47

stakeholder /'steɪkˌhəʊldə/ 14, 48, 49

stakeholder theory /'steɪkˌhəʊldə ˌθɪəri/ 49

standard /'stændəd/ 45

standards institute /'stændədz ˌɪnstɪtjuːt/ 13

statistical technique /stə'tɪstɪkəl tek'niːk/ 24

statutory requirements /ˌstætjətəri rɪ'kwaɪəmənts/ 13

stereotype /'steriətaɪp/ 10

stereotypical /ˌsteriə'tɪpɪkəl/ 11

stewardship /'stjuːədʃɪp/ 52

stickiness /'stɪkɪnəs/ 33

sticky /'stɪki/ 33

stiff competition /ˌstɪf kɒmpə'tɪʃən/ 17

stifle competition /'staɪfəl ˌkɒmpə'tɪʃən/ 17

stimulating /'stɪmjəleɪtɪŋ/ 1

stimulation /ˌstɪmjə'leɪʃən/ 10

stimulation of growth /ˌstɪmjəˌleɪʃən əv 'grəʊθ/ 55

stimulus package /'stɪmjələs ˌpækɪdʒ/ 47

stock market /'stɒk ˌmɑːkɪt/ 38, 46

stock option /'stɒk ˌɒpʃən/ 52

stocks /stɒks/ 30, 40

storage /'stɔːrɪdʒ/ 29, 30

storm /stɔːm/ 51

storming /'stɔːmɪŋ/ 9

strategic acquisition /strəˌtiːdʒɪk ækwɪ'zɪʃən/ 16, 19

strategic decision /strəˌtiːdʒɪk dɪ'sɪʒən/ 16, 44

strategic goal /strəˌtiːdʒɪk 'gəʊl/ 16

strategic marketing plan /strəˌtiːdʒɪk 'mɑːkɪtɪŋ plæn/ 24

strategic move /strəˌtiːdʒɪk 'muːv/ 16

strategic outsourcing /strəˌtiːdʒɪk 'aʊtsɔːsɪŋ/ 31

strategic partnership /strəˌtiːdʒɪk 'pɑːtnəʃɪp/ 16

strategic success /strəˌtiːdʒɪk sək'ses/ 16

strategic vision /strəˌtiːdʒɪk 'vɪʒən/ 16

strategy /'strætədʒi/ 14, 16, 53

stream /striːm/ 32

strengths /streŋkθs/ 18

stress counsellor /stres 'kaʊnsələ/ 6

stress factor /stres 'fæktə/ 6

stress industry /stres 'ɪndəstri/ 6

stress management /stres 'mænɪdʒmənt/ 6

stress symptom /stres 'sɪmtəm/ 6

stressed /strest/ 6

stressed out /ˌstrest 'aʊt/ 6

stressful /'stresfʊl/ 1, 6

stress-related illness /stresrɪˌleɪtɪd 'ɪlnəs/ 6

stringent /'strɪndʒənt/ 50

striver /'straɪvə/ 25

structure /'strʌktʃə/ 20

structured group /'strʌktʃəd gruːp/ 21

struggler /'strʌglə/ 25

stuck in the middle /stʌk ɪn ðə 'mɪdəl/ 18

subcontract (v) /ˌsʌbkən'trækt/ 31

subcontractor /ˌsʌbkən'træktə/ 31

subordinate /sə'bɔːdənət/ 2

sub-prime mortgage /sʌbˌpraɪm 'mɔːgɪdʒ/ 47

subsidiary /səb'sɪdiəri/ 19

substitute /'sʌbstɪtjuːt/ 18

succession planning /sək'seʃən ˌplænɪŋ/ 7

suit /suːt/ 8

super-talents /'suːpəˌtælənts/ 8

supervise /'suːpəvaɪz/ 45

supervision /ˌsuːpə'vɪʒən/ 2, 3

supervisory board /suːpə'vaɪzəri ˌbɔːd/ 52

supplier /sə'plaɪə/ 18, 29

supplier relationship /səˌplaɪə rɪ'leɪʃənʃɪp/ 36

supplier–customer relationship /səˌplaɪə ˌkʌstəmə rɪ'leɪʃənʃɪp/ 13

supply chain /sə'plaɪ ˌtʃeɪn/ 29

supply chain management /səˌplaɪ tʃeɪn 'mænɪdʒmənt/ 29, 30

support /sə'pɔːt/ 61

surf the Internet /'sɜːf ðə ˌɪntənet/ 32

surveillance /sɜː'veɪləns/ 35

survey research /'sɜːveɪ rɪˌsɜːtʃ/ 24

sustainability /səˌsteɪnə'bɪləti/ 50, 53, 59

sustainable /sə'steɪnəbəl/ 50

sustainable development /səˌsteɪnəbəl dɪ'veləpmənt/ 30, 59

sustainable level /səˌsteɪnəbəl 'levəl/ 46

sweat assets /ˌswet 'æsets/ 43

sweatshop labour /ˌswetʃɒp 'leɪbə/ 49

SWOT /swɒt/ 18

SWOT analysis /swɒt ə'næləsɪs/ 18

tacit /'tæsɪt/ 34

tactful /'tæktfəl/ 10

tactical /'tæktɪkəl/ 24

tactless /'tæktləs/ 60

tag /tæg/ 25

takeover /'teɪkˌəʊvə/ 19

talent /'tælənt/ 7

talent manager /'tælənt ˌmænɪdʒə/ 8

talent pool /'tælənt ˌpuːl/ 7, 8

talented /'tæləntɪd/ 7

tangible assets /ˌtændʒəbəl 'æsets/ 40

tap into /tæp 'ɪntuː/ 34

target /'tɑːgɪt/ 26

target group /'tɑːgɪt gruːp/ 25

tariff /'tærɪf/ 54, 56

task-oriented /ˌtɑːsk'ɔːrientɪd/ 60

tax payable /tæks 'peɪəbəl/ 41

TBL (triple bottom line) /ˌtiːbiː'el/ 59

team /tiːm/ 9

team building /'tiːm ˌbɪldɪŋ/ 9

team dynamics /'tiːm daɪˌnæmɪks/ 9

team effectiveness /'tiːm ɪˌfektɪvnəs/ 9

team effort /'tiːm ˌefət/ 9

team leader /'tiːm ˌliːdə/ 9

team learning /'tiːm ˌlɜːnɪŋ/ 9

team management /'tiːm ˌmænɪdʒmənt/ 63

team performance /'tiːm pəˌfɔːməns/ 9

team player /'tiːm ˌpleɪə/ 9

team worker /'tiːm ˌwɜːkə/ 9

teamwork /'tiːmwɜːk/ 1, 9

technical durability /ˌteknɪkəl 'djʊərə'bɪləti/ 12

technical specifications /ˌteknɪkəl spesɪfɪ'keɪʃənz/ 13

technical support /ˌteknɪkəl sə'pɔːt/ 31

technology /tek'nɒlədʒi/ 20

telecommunications costs /ˌtelɪkəˌmjuːnɪ'keɪʃənz kɒsts/ 54

telecommute /ˌtelɪkə'mjuːt/ 1

temp agency /temp 'eɪdʒənsi/ 5

temporary contract /ˌtempəri 'kɒntrækt/ 5

temporary worker /ˌtempəri 'wɜːkə/ 5

test a hypothesis /ˌtest ə haɪ'pɒθəsɪs/ 24

the SECI model /ðə ˌesiːsiː'aɪ mɒdəl/ 34

the work itself /ðə 'wɜːk ɪtself/ 3

theory X /ˌθɪəri 'eks/ 2

theory Y /ˌθɪəri 'waɪ/ 2

Third World /θɜːd 'wɜːld/ 54

threats /θrets/ 18

3G /ˌθriː'dʒiː/ 32

360-degree analysis /θriːˌhʌndrɪdən ˌsɪxtidɪˌgriː ə'næləsɪs/ 7

tidal power /'taɪdəl paʊə/ 50, 59

tied aid /taɪd 'eɪd/ 58

time off /taɪm 'ɒf/ 1

time-waster /taɪm'weɪstə/ 60

tone down /təʊn 'daʊn/ 61

top management /tɒp 'mænɪdʒmənt/ 13

top performers /tɒp pə'fɔːməz/ 8

Total Quality Management (TQM) /ˌtəʊtəl ˌkwɒləti 'mænɪdʒmənt/ 12

toxic assets /ˌtɒksɪk 'æsets/ 47

toxic emissions /ˌtɒksɪk ɪ'mɪʃənz/ 50

TQM (Total Quality Management) /ˌtiːkjuː'em/ 12

track /træk/ 25

trade /treɪd/ 38, 51

trade balance /'treɪd ˌbæləns/ 46

trade barriers /'treɪd ˌbæriəz/ 56

trade disputes /'treɪd dɪˌspjuːts/ 56

trade gap /'treɪd ˌgæp/ 46

trade liberalization /'treɪd lɪbərəlaɪˌzeɪʃən/ 54

trade surplus /'treɪd ˌsɜːpləs/ 46, 57

trade union /'treɪd ˌjuːnjən/ 5, 49

trading hub /'treɪdɪŋ hʌb/ 36

trading platform /'treɪdɪŋ ˌplætfɔːm/ 36

traffic /'træfɪk/ 25, 33

training and development /ˌtreɪnɪŋ ən dɪ'veləpmənt/ 7

training effectiveness /ˌtreɪnɪŋ ɪ'fektɪvnəs/ 13

trait /treɪt/ 10

transaction cost analysis /træn,zækʃən kɒst ə'næləsɪs/ 31

transparency /træn'spærənsi/ 45, 48, 52, 53

transparent /træn'spærənt/ 48

transport /'trɒnspɔːt/ 29

trendsetter /'trend,setə/ 20

triple bottom line (TBL) /,trɪpəl ,bɒtəm 'laɪn/ 59

Trojan horse /,trəʊdʒən 'hɔːs/ 35

trough /trɒf/ 46

true and fair view /truː ən feə 'vjuː/ 45

turnover /'tɜːn,əʊvə/ 39

turn-taking /'tɜːn,teɪkɪŋ/ 60

Two Sigma quality /tuː ,sɪgmə 'kwɒləti/ 15

ultimate bottom line /,ʌltɪmət ,bɒtəm 'laɪn/ 59

uncommunicative /,ʌnkə'mjuːnɪkətɪv/ 60

under (a lot of) pressure /,ʌndə (ə lɒt əv) 'preʃə/ 6

under (a lot of) stress /,ʌndə (ə lɒt əv) 'stres/ 6

under licence /,ʌndə 'laɪsəns/ 28

understate /,ʌndə'steɪt/ 45

undervalued /,ʌndə'væljuːd/ 38

undisciplined /ʌn'dɪsɪplɪnd/ 60

unemployed /,ʌnɪm'plɔɪd/ 46

unemployment /,ʌnɪm'plɔɪmənt/ 5

unemployment benefits /ʌnɪm'plɔɪmənt ,benɪfɪts/ 5

unethically /,ʌn'eθɪkli/ 48

unfair trade practices /ʌn,feə 'treɪd ,præktɪsɪz/ 56

unfinished goods /ʌn'fɪnɪʃt gʊdz/ 40

unique users /juː'niːk 'juːzəz/ 33

United Nations climate change convention /juː,naɪtɪd ,neɪʃənz 'klaɪmət tʃeɪndʒ kən,venʃən/ 51

unnatural /ʌn'nætʃərəl/ 60

unsustainable /,ʌnsə'steɪnəbəl/ 55

unwieldy conglomerate /ʌn,wiːldi kən'glɒmərət/ 19

upgrade /ʌp'greɪd/ 30

upload /ʌp'ləʊd/ 33

use your initiative /juːz jɔːr ɪ'nɪʃətɪv/ 2

user-friendliness /,juːzə'frendlɪnəs/ 33

vacation time /və'keɪʃən taɪm/ 1

vagueness /'veɪgnəs/ 61

valuable outcome /,væljuəbəl 'aʊtkʌm/ 30

value for money /,vælju: fə 'mʌni/ 12

valued /'væljuːd/ 2

values /'væljuːz/ 25

vertical integration /,vɜːtɪkəl ɪntɪ'greɪʃən/ 19, 29

vet /vet/ 33

viable /'vaɪəbəl/ 58

video-conferencing /,vɪdiəʊ'kɒnfərənsɪŋ/ 32

video-on-demand (VOD) /,vɪdiəʊ ɒn dɪ'mɑːnd/ 32

video-sharing site /,vɪdiəʊʃeərɪŋ 'saɪt/ 33

virtual organization /'vɜːtʃuəl ɔːgənaɪ,zeɪʃən/ 8

virtual shopping cart /,vɜːtʃuəl 'ʃɒpɪŋ kɑːt/ 25

virus /'vaɪərəs/ 35

visible /'vɪzəbəl/ 62

vision /'vɪʒən/ 16

visit /'vɪzɪt/ 33

visitor /'vɪzɪtə/ 25

VOD (video-on-demand) /,viːəʊ'diː/ 32

volume industry /'vɒljuːm ,ɪndəstri/ 18

warehouse /'weəhaʊs/ 29

warehousing /'weəhaʊzɪŋ/ 29

waste /weɪst/ 59

waste electrical and electronic equipment (WEEE) /,weɪst ɪ,lektrɪkəl ən ɪlek,trɒnɪk ɪ'kwɪpmənt/ 30

weaknesses /'wiːknəsɪz/ 18

wealth /welθ/ 58

wealth level /'welθ ,levəl/ 57

wear out /weər 'aʊt/ 40

Web 2.0 /'web tuː,pɔɪnt,əʊ/ 33

webcam /'webkæm/ 32

website /'websaɪt/ 25

website management company /'websaɪt ,mænɪdʒmənt ,kʌmpəni/ 33

WEEE (waste electrical and electronic equipment) /wiː/ 30

well-being /'wel,biːɪŋ/ 2

well-trained /wel'treɪnd/ 22

West /west/ 54

Wi-Fi /'waɪfaɪ/ 32

wiki /'wɪki/ 33

win new business /,wɪn njuː 'bɪznɪs/ 48

wind power /'wɪnd paʊə/ 50, 59

wireless LAN (local area network) /waɪələs 'læn/ 32

wireless local area network (LAN) /waɪələs ,ləʊkəl eəriə 'netwɜːk/ 32

withdraw from a market /wɪð,drɔː frəm ə 'mɑːkɪt/ 16

withdraw investment /wɪð'drɔː ɪn'vestmənt/ 55

word-of-mouth /,wɜːdəv'maʊθ/ 23

work from home /wɜːk frəm həʊm/ 1

work on your own /wɜːk ɒn jɔːr əʊn/ 1

work under someone /,wɜːk ʌndə 'sʌmwʌn/ 2

workaholic /,wɜːkə'hɒlɪk/ 6

worker representation /,wɜːkə reprɪzen'teɪʃən/ 49

working conditions /'wɜːkɪŋ ,kən'dɪʃənz/ 3, 49

work-in-progress /wɜːkɪn'prəʊgres/ 30

work-life balance /wɜːk laɪf 'bæləns/ 6

works /wɜːks/ 29

World Bank /wɜːld 'bæŋk/ 55

World Trade Organization (WTO) /'wɜːld treɪd ,ɔːgənaɪ'zeɪʃən/ 56

write down /raɪt 'daʊn/ 40

write off /raɪt 'ɒf/ 40

WTO (World Trade Organization) /,dʌbəlju:ti:'əʊ/ 56

yield /ji:ld/ 44

zero defects /,zɪərəʊ 'di:fekts/ 12, 15

CD-ROM Instructions

What's on the CD-ROM?

- **Interactive practice activities**

  Extra practice and tests based on the key vocabulary from *Business Vocabulary in Use Advanced*. Click on one of the module numbers (1–12) at the top of the screen. Then find the unit you would like to practise choose an activity and click on it to start.

- **Games**

  A choice of games for fun practice of the vocabulary from *Business Vocabulary in Use Advanced*. Click the *Games* button and then select the group of units and game you wish to play. Then click on START to play the game.

- **My activities**

  Create your own lesson. Click on *My Activities* at the top of the screen. Drag activities from the module menus into the *My Activities* panel on the right of the screen. Then click on *Start*.

- **My portfolio**

  Click on *Word List, Phonemes* or *progress* at any time for extra help or information. You can listen to audio recordings and example sentences of the vocabulary from *Business Vocabulary in Use Advanced*, record your own voice as you practise the vocabulary, add your own notes to the *Word List*, and check your progress.

Start the CD-Rom

Windows PC Instructions

- *Business Vocabulary in Use* can be run directly from the CD-ROM and does not require installation. However, you can also install the CD-ROM and run it from the hard disk. The application will run faster if you install it.

Starting the CD-ROM

- Insert the CD-ROM into your CD-ROM drive. If 'Autorun' is enabled, the CD-ROM will start automatically.
- If 'Autorun' is not enabled, to run the application from the disc, open My Computer and double click on your CD-ROM drive (Business Vocabulary in Use Advanced)
- To install the CD-ROM, open My Computer and right click on the CD-ROM drive. Select 'Open' and double click on 'set up'. Follow the instructions on screen.

Mac 0S X Instructions

Run *Business Vocabulary in Use Advanced* from the CD-ROM by double-clicking the 'Business *Vocabulary in Use Advanced*' icon. It is not possible to install this product on a Mac.

System requirements
- Speaker or headphones and microphone (optional)

PC requirements
- Windows® XP, 256 MB of RAM, 800MHz processor or faster
- Windows® Vista, 1GB of RAM, 1GHz processor or faster
- Windows® 7, 1GB of RAM, 1GHz processor or faster
- Approximately 500MB free hard drive space if installing

Mac requirements
- Mac 0S X 10.4 or 10.5, 512MB of RAM, 1GHZ processor or faster

Support
If you experience difficulties with this CD-ROM, please visit: www.cambridge.org/elt/multimedia/help

Terms and conditions

This is a legal agreement between 'You' (which means the individual customer) and Cambridge University Press ('the Licensor') for **Business Vocabulary in Use Advanced.** By placing this CD in the CD-ROM drive of your computer, you agree to the terms of this licence.

1. Licence
(a) You are purchasing only the right to use the CD-ROM and are acquiring no rights, express or implied to it or the software other than those rights granted in this limited licence for not-for-profit educational use only.
(b) Cambridge University Press grants the customer the licence to use one copy of this CD-ROM (i) on a single computer for use by one or more people at different times, or (ii) by a single person on one or more computers (provided the CD-ROM is only used on one computer at one time and is only used by the customer), but not both.
(c) The customer shall not: (i) copy or authorise copying of the CD-ROM, (ii) translate the CD-ROM, (iii) reverse-engineer, disassemble or decompile the CD-ROM, (iv) transfer, sell, assign or otherwise convey any portion of the CD-ROM, or (v) operate the CD-ROM from a network or mainframe system.

2. Copyright
(a) All original content is provided as part of the CD-ROM (including text, images and ancillary material) ('Original Material') and is the copyright of the Licensor, protected by copyright and all other applicable intellectual property laws and international treaties.
(b) You may not copy the CD-ROM except for making one copy of the CD-ROM solely for backup or archival purposes. You may not alter, remove or destroy any copyright notice or other material placed on or with this CD-ROM.

3. Liability
(a) The CD-ROM is supplied 'as-is' with no express guarantee as to its suitability. To the extent permitted by applicable law, the Licensor is not liable for costs of procurement of substitute products, damages or losses of any kind whatsoever resulting from the use of this product, or errors or faults in the CD-ROM, and in every case the Licensor's liability shall be limited to the suggested list price or the amount actually paid by You for the product, whichever is lower.
(b) You accept that the Licensor is not responsible for the persistency, accuracy or availability of any URLs of external or third party internet websites referred to on the CD-ROM and does not guarantee that any content on such websites is, or will remain, accurate, appropriate or available. The Licensor shall not be liable for any content made available from any websites and URLs outside the Software.
(c) Where, through use of the Original Material you infringe the copyright of the Licensor you undertake to indemnify and keep indemnified the Licensor from and against any loss, cost, damage or expense (including without limitation damages paid to a third party and any reasonable legal costs) incurred by the Licensor as a result of such infringement.

4. Termination
Without prejudice to any other rights, the Licensor may terminate this licence if You fail to comply with the terms and conditions of the licence. In such event, You must destroy all copies of the CD-ROM.

5. Governing law
This agreement is governed by the laws of England, without regard to its conflict of laws provision, and each party irrevocably submits to the exclusive jurisdiction of the English courts. The parties disclaim the application of the United Nations Convention on the International Sale of Goods.

Acknowledgements

The author would like to thank Liz Driscoll, as well as Chris Capper, Neil Holloway and the entire team at CUP for their extremely efficient handling of the editorial process.

The authors and publishers acknowledge the following sources of copyright material and are grateful for the permissions granted. While every effort has been made, it has not always been possible to identify the sources of all the materials used, or to trace all copyright holders. If any omissions are brought to our notice, we will be happy to include the appropriate acknowledgements on reprinting.

The publisher has used its best endeavours to ensure that the URLs for external websites referred to in this book are correct and active at the time of going to press. However, the publisher has no responsibility for the websites and can make no guarantee that a site will remain live or that the content is or will remain appropriate.

p. 11, 1.3: Text adapted from 'Most satisfied employees work longer' written by Rob Kelley, taken from http://money.cnn.com/2006/04/10/pf/bestjobs_survey/index.htm; p.17, 4.1: Text adapted from 'Was outsourcing to India the right move?' written by Darren Dahl, taken from http://www.inc.com/magazine/20060101/handson-casestudy.html; p. 25, 8.1: Text adapted from http://www.humanassets.co.uk/downloads/TalentWarArticle-May03-TrainingJournal.pdf, first published in *Training Journal*, May 2003, by Charles Woodruffe; p. 26, 9B: Reproduced by kind permission of Belbin Associates – www.belbin.com; p. 27, 9.1: Extract taken from *Leading with Values Positivity, Virtue and High Performance*, edited by Edward Hess and Kim Cameron, published by Cambridge University Press, 2006; p. 33, 12.1: *The Financial Times* for the text from 'A disciple of Japanese quality management' by Amy Lee, published 28 January, 2008 © The *Financial Times*; p. 34: Extract taken from www.iso.org © ISO; p. 44, 18A & 18C: Reproduced by kind permission of Professor Michael Porter © Michael Porter; p. 49, 20.1: Provided by Lockheed Martin Corporation. Reproduced with permission; p. 44, 23.3: Text adapted from http://www.loyaltyeffect.com/loyaltyrules/Library_Articles_details.asp?ID=8367, 26 July 2002; p. 61, 26.1: Copyright 2004 Michael Meltzer / *The Wise Marketer*; p. 99, 45. 1: *The Telegraph* for the text from 'Inquiry launched in PWC's auditing of Satyam's accounts' by Dean Nelson © Dean Nelson/The Telegraph, 08 Jan 2009; p. 111, 51.1: *The Financial Times* for the text from "Nations must 'act now' on climate change" by Fiona Harvey © Fiona Harvery/The Financial Times, 12 February 2009; p.121, 56.2: *The Guardian* for the text from 'Smallholders farm a route out of poverty' by Harriet Lamb © Harriet Lamb/The Guardian, 23 February 2009; p. 126, 59C: © John Elkington, Founder, SustainAbility; p. 127, 59.2: By Amelia Newcomb. Excerpted with permission from "Japan as ground zero for no-waste lifestyle" from the December 16, 2008 issue of The Christian Science Monitor (www.CSMonitor.com). © 2008 The Christian Science Monitor

The publishers are grateful to the following for permission to reproduce copyright photographs and material:

Key: l = left, c = centre, r = right, t = top, b = bottom

Alamy/©Andrew Holt for p10(c), /©Juice Images for p10(b), /©moodboard for p18, /©Gala Studio for p24(t), /©FogStock for p40, /©Radius Images for p50(t), /©Radius Images for p52(b), /©Vario images gmbH & Co. KG for p64(t), /©Joe Fox WEEE for p68, /©Patrick La Roque for p84, /©Steven May for p120(b), /©Image Source Pink for p124, /©amana images inc for p134, /©Yeugen Timashov for p138; Corbis/©David Woods for p22, /©Randy Faris for p26, /©Radius Images for p28, /©Corbis RF for p36, /©Comstock Select for p42; Getty/©Chris Clinton for p82(t), /©Justin Guariglia for p110; istockphoto/©Jeffrey Smith for p10(t), /©Kristian Sekalic for p12(t), /©quavondo for p12(b), /©Marje Cannon for p16, /©David Newton for p24(b), /©Jacob Wackerhausen for p30, /©FotoIE for p32, /©Enis Izgi for p38, /©Palto for p46, /©Alvin Burrows for p60, /©Emrah Turudu for p64(b), /©Maciej Noskowski for p66, /©iofoto for p70, /©Emrah Turudu for p72, /©Claes Dafgard for p82(b), /©David H Lewis for p88, /©DNY59 for p90, /©Bjorn Meyer for p96, /©Andrew Johnson for p100, /©nullplus for p102, /©Sharon Dominick for p106, /©ideeone for p108, /©Jacob Wackerhausen for p112, /©tiridifilm for p116, /©Dmitry Kutlayev for p120(t); Masterfile/©Blend Images for p48; Panos Pictures/©Mikkel Ostergaard for p118; Photolibrary/©Age fotostock for p20, /©Photos India for p35, /©Image Source for p50(b), /©Glow Images for p64(c), /©Stockbyte for p132(t), /©Comstock for p132(b); Shutterstock/©The Game for p45, /©R T Images for p52(t), /©prism68 for p78(t), /©Antonio Jorge Nunes for p78(b), /©Jack F for p86(l), /©DeshaCAM for p86(r), /©Rafal Olkis for p126.

Picture Research: Hilary Luckcock
Illustrations: Kamae Design and Laura Martinez.
Cover photo: istockphoto/©Chris Schmidt